Voices for Transgender Equality

JOURNALISM AND POLITICAL COMMUNICATION UNBOUND

Series editors: Daniel Kreiss, University of North Carolina at Chapel Hill, and Nikki Usher, University of San Diego

Journalism and Political Communication Unbound seeks to be a high-profile book series that reaches far beyond the academy to an interested public of policymakers, journalists, public intellectuals, and citizens eager to make sense of contemporary politics and media. "Unbound" in the series title has multiple meanings: It refers to the unbinding of borders between the fields of communication, political communication, and journalism, as well as related disciplines such as political science, sociology, and science and technology studies; it highlights the ways traditional frameworks for scholarship have disintegrated in the wake of changing digital technologies and new social, political, economic, and cultural dynamics; and it reflects the unbinding of media in a hybrid world of flows across mediums.

Other books in the series:

Voices for Transgender Equality

Making Change in the Networked Public Sphere

THOMAS J BILLARD

OXFORD

UNIVERSITY PRESS

OXFORD
UNIVERSITY PRESS

Oxford University Press is a department of the University of Oxford. It furthers
the University's objective of excellence in research, scholarship, and education
by publishing worldwide. Oxford is a registered trade mark of Oxford University
Press in the UK and certain other countries.

Published in the United States of America by Oxford University Press
198 Madison Avenue, New York, NY 10016, United States of America.

CIP data is on file at the Library of Congress

ISBN 978–0–19–769543–2 (pbk.)
ISBN 978–0–19–769542–5 (hbk.)

DOI: 10.1093/oso/9780197695425.001.0001

For Abigail, in hopes the world you grow up in is a better one.

Contents

Preface

I began my research on transgender media and politics as an undergraduate student at the George Washington University in Washington, DC. The impetus for doing so was clear: I was pursuing a degree in political communication in the School of Media and Public Affairs and, instead of writing term papers regurgitating framing theory, I wanted to write papers about how to make my life and the lives of my friends and chosen family better. My coursework became an outlet for my activism as I channeled my righteous outrage into scholarly achievement by making the social and political concerns of the transgender community the focus of every course assignment I could. In my course on public opinion, I wrote about the (then) dearth of research on public attitudes toward transgender issues and individuals. In my course on strategic campaign communications, I developed a DC-based media campaign to end violence against trans women based on psychological research on inoculation effects. When it came time to write my undergraduate honors thesis, I wrote about how transgender issues, individuals, and identities were delegitimated in legacy newspapers. (That paper—in a much-revised form—went on to become my first journal article, published in the *International Journal of Communication* in 2016.)

It's important to note that my research and activism blossomed during a time of hopeful progress and productive struggle under the administration of President Barack Obama. At the time, the trans movement was contending with issues of transphobic violence, widespread ignorance of trans identity, regulatory barriers to gender recognition and healthcare access, and representational norms in both journalism and entertainment media that delegitimated transgender identity and justified anti-transgender prejudice. But the trans movement sought recourse for many of those issues from a sympathetic, if not always supportive, administration. Although it entailed much struggle and although the victories won were often temporary patches rather than permanent fixes, the trans movement secured significant progress under Obama. The National Center for Transgender Equality (NCTE), which was responsible for many of the policy victories of the era, tallied over 160 federal policy changes between 2008 and 2016, including easing the process for gender marker changes on US passports and social security records, prohibiting discrimination based on gender identity in healthcare provision under the Affordable Care Act, prohibiting discrimination based on gender identity in federal employment and contracting, prohibiting discrimination based on gender identity in housing, and protecting transgender students' access to public facilities consistent with their gender identity in schools, among many others. And none of that includes the state-level policy changes that were made possible by the victories secured federally or the numerous transgender political appointees named to federal service. In short, the struggle for transgender rights didn't feel hopeless and the battles we were fighting were often *for* change, rather than *against* targeting.

By the time I returned to Washington, DC, in 2017 to conduct the research for this book, things had changed considerably. Donald Trump had been unexpectedly elected to the presidency in November 2016 and his new administration displayed open, active, and relentless hostility to the trans community, which had become hyper-visible in American culture. Within six months of taking office, Trump banned the 15,000 transgender service members in the US armed forces by tweet. His administration then proceeded to roll back nearly every Obama-era protection afforded to trans people and began to take transgender rights to court, where they sought to establish legal precedents for discrimination against trans people. The struggle for trans rights started to feel much more hopeless and the battles we were fighting were suddenly *against* the actions of the Trump administration, rather than *for* positive change.

It is in this context that I conducted my ethnographic fieldwork at NCTE across 2017 and 2018, and this context shaped the dynamics I observed to a significant degree. Most of the incidents I document in this book entailed NCTE's resistance to assaults on transgender rights by the Trump administration or by those empowered by Trump to launch attacks at local levels. Only a few entailed NCTE pushing forward new paths to equality. Nonetheless, the strategic activities that NCTE and its allies relied on in these battles have roots that precede the Trump administration and legacies that outlive it. The approach to activism I describe and theorize in these pages secured the victories of the Obama era, resisted the oppression of the Trump era, and will likely continue to both secure victories and resist oppressions for years to come. But more importantly, and more central to my argument, this approach to activism transformed sociopolitical discourse on transgender issues and identity. It fundamentally changed how trans people are talked about, thought about, and interacted with across American society, from the *New York Times* to the *Wisconsin State Journal* to Facebook comments sections to school board meetings in West Virginia.

The context in which I finished writing this book is dramatically different from the one in which I conducted the research for it. Joe Biden is now president, and his administration is at least as sympathetic to the trans community as the Obama administration was. In his victory speech on November 7, 2020, Biden even named transgender people as part of the coalition that won him the election. And Vice President Kamala Harris, after earlier struggles with the trans community over her work as California's Attorney General, became a staunch advocate for transgender rights in the US Senate. The transgender movement, thanks to activists like those at NCTE, has secured its place in the heart of the Democratic Party. At the same time, the first year of the Biden–Harris administration was a record-breaking year for anti-transgender legislation. Opponents of transgender rights proposed 191 anti-LGBTQ bills in states across the country. Over 150 of those bills specifically and exclusively targeted trans people. By March 15, 2022— only two-and-a-half months into the following year—already more anti-transgender bills had been introduced than in all of 2021 combined. In 2023, as of June 15, legislation targeting trans people has been introduced in forty-nine states and passed in twenty-three, with much of that legislation specifically targeting trans youth. The fate of transgender equality rests on the approach to activism this book discusses. I hope that, in reading it, you come to appreciate what big changes small organizations can make in the networked public sphere and what's at risk if they fail.

Chicago, Illinois
June 2023

Acknowledgments

In his book, *Art Worlds*, the eminent sociologist Howard Becker noted that, despite our tendency to identify the single "artist" to whom responsibility for an artistic work is attributed, producing each work requires the collective labor of countless, often uncredited, people. Academic work is much the same. My name may be on the cover of this book, but that does not mean I achieved this feat alone. Countless people—far more than I can list here—shaped my work in big and small ways. This Acknowledgments section is my humble attempt to credit as many of them as I can.

I begin my thanks with those who supervised the earliest drafts of this book: my dissertation committee members. My first thanks must go to the incredible Larry Gross. Beyond being my PhD advisor for five years in the Annenberg School for Communication and Journalism at the University of Southern California and chair of my dissertation committee, Larry is the reason I became an academic. When I read his work as an undergraduate student with little understanding of what professors even did, I realized I wanted to ask the kinds of questions he asked and write the kinds of scholarship he wrote. To then get to study under him and have his ever-caring guidance through my doctorate and my early years as an assistant professor is more than I could have ever dreamed.

My second thanks must then go to Nina Eliasoph, who was a second advisor to me throughout the PhD in many ways. Her tireless enthusiasm for my work kept me passionate about it even on the days I felt like giving up, and she expanded the boundaries of my theorizing in immeasurable ways. I would not be the scholar I am today without her. The final member of my dissertation committee, Christina Dunbar Hester, pushed me with kindness and encouraging skepticism to reckon with alternative approaches to the craft of research and helped me find new ways of understanding the importance of my own work. Although the book is much revised since Larry, Nina, and Christina first read it as a dissertation, their fingerprints remain all over the final work, and the book is much, much better for it.

The research and writing that went into this book happened across two institutions: the University of Southern California and Northwestern

University. At both institutions, countless mentors, colleagues, and friends supported me and the work that led to this book. At USC, three deserve a special call out. Before their retirement and departure from Annenberg, respectively, Sandra Ball-Rokeach and Sarah Banet-Weiser were key figures in my intellectual development. Sandra taught me that communication could be more than just the study of what media does to people and she fundamentally transformed the questions I ask and the way I try to make my work impactful in the world. For that I cannot thank her enough. Sarah likewise shaped my thinking in driving me to be critical of the perspectives I disagree with, but to be even more critical of those I agree with. She also opened my eyes to the myriad ways my various threads of intellectual interest weave together when I thought they were all separate. Finally, Paul Lichterman was an incredible mentor to me. He taught me everything I know about fieldwork, and he constantly encouraged me to find new ways of theorizing old problems.

A number of other Annenberg faculty and staff were sources of great inspiration and encouragement over the five years of my doctorate—and especially the three years I worked on this project there. Mike Ananny, Manuel Castells, Tom Hollihan, Henry Jenkins, Josh Kun, Lynn Miller, Peter Monge, Sheila Murphy, Patty Riley, Dmitri Williams, and (from political science) Ann Crigler provided valuable guidance to me at various stages of my research development. David Craig, Carmen Lee, Sangita Shresthova, and Alison Trope, despite never teaching me, were incredible mentors, as well as friends. Anne Marie Campian, Jordan Gary, Sarah Holterman, and Christine Lloreda worked tirelessly to ensure I had the money, food, and bureaucratic guidance I needed to survive the PhD and complete my research. Finally, Mark Lloyd and (from the University of Pennsylvania) Victor Pickard, who coordinated the Consortium on Media Policy Studies (COMPASS) program that first brought me to NCTE in the summer of 2017, saw the first seeds of what would become this book. I owe them an immense gratitude both for the opportunity to join the COMPASS program and for their encouragement in the early phases of developing my theoretical argument.

Since joining the faculty at Northwestern, I've had the privilege of working alongside some of the field's brightest minds. Their support, encouragement, and mentorship have been invaluable. In particular, Moya Bailey, Claudio Benzecry, Pablo Boczkowski, AJ Christian, Nosh Contractor, Robin Means Coleman, Jim Schwoch, Michelle Shumate, and Nathan Walter have been steadfast champions for my work and insightful advisors. Dean of the School of Communication E. Patrick Johnson and Chair of the Department of Communication Studies Leslie DeChurch have each invested heavily in my success in ways I could never repay. Thanks also to Jeremy Birnholtz, Larissa Buchholz, Ignacio Cruz, Nick Diakopolous, Dilip Gaonkar, Darren Gergle, Robert Hariman, Ágnes Horvát, Bruce L. Lambert, Erik Nisbet, Jan Radway, Angela Ray, Courtney Scherr, Aaron Shaw, and Ellen Wartella for their warm collegiality.

At Oxford University Press, I owe tremendous thanks to Angela Chnapko, whose belief in the importance of this project saw it over the finish line and into print. Series editors Daniel Kreiss and Nikki Usher saw value in my work early on and I cannot thank them enough for wanting to showcase my work alongside that of so many scholars I respect and admire.

I owe, of course, a million thanks to everyone who was at NCTE during my fieldwork. It was an honor and privilege to fight alongside you, as well as to learn so much from you. Thanks to Mara Keisling, Lisa Mottet, Eric Dyson, Jay Wu, Jason Arrol, Dave Noble, Laurel Powell, Gillian Branstetter, Charlie Girard, Raffi Freedman-Gurspan, Rebecca Kling, Debi Jackson, DeShanna Neal, Hope Giselle, Sandy James, Harper Jean Tobin, Mateo De La Torre, Arli Christian, Luc Athayde-Rizzaro, Ma'ayan Anafi, Andrea Zekis, Jami Westerhold, Daniel Shad, Alex Roberts, K'ai Smith, Patrick Paschall, Meg Yamato, Lo Dow, Tucker Duval, Dylan Yellowlees, Teagan Rabuano, Rony Castellanos, Jen Jenkins, Taylor Payne, Phoebe Thaler, and Jholerina Timbo. Thanks also to the members of NCTE's Voices for Trans Equality and Families for Trans Equality programs who spoke with me: Ray Gibson, Rachel Gonzales, Jo Ivester, Benjamin Kennedy, Chloé LaCasse, Leslie McMurray, Paula Sophia Schonauer, Nicola van Kuilenburg, and Sarah Watson.

Along the way, numerous colleagues, friends, and interlocutors have read portions of this book and provided invaluable feedback. Thanks to the members of Nina Eliasoph's Politics, Organizations, Ethnography, and Theory (POET) reading group at USC, including Valentina Cantori, Yael Findler, Sima Ghaddar, Shang Liu, Oded Marom, Michael Siciliano, Claudia Strauss, and Benjamin Weiss. Thanks also to the members of the Annenberg Paper Exchange (APEX), which Rachel Moran organized with me at USC, including Ming Curran, Donna Kim, Tyler Quick, and Paul Sparks; participants in the Media + Politics workshop at the School of Media and Public Affairs at my undergraduate alma mater, the George Washington University, including organizers Ethan Porter and Will Youmans, as well as Babak Bahador, Kim Gross, Peter Loge, and Rebekah Tromble; and participants in the Social

Movements & Enterprise workshop at the Kellogg School of Management at Northwestern, including organizer Brayden King, as well as Khoa Phan Howard, Anna McKean, Carson Phillips, Rachel Ramirez, Molly Weinstein, and Ruozhou Yan.

A number of other scholars in the broader field have provided indispensable support and guidance throughout the research and writing for this book. Thanks to all of them, especially, Lik Sam Chan, Nathaniel Ming Curran, Stefi Demetriades, Traci Gillig, Kolina Koltai, Stephen Prochaska, Martin Reidl, Aure Schrock, Sonia Shaikh, Silvio Waisbord, and Sulafa Zidani. Additional thanks to the doctoral students I am lucky enough to advise, and who have engaged with the work in this book in various ways: Erique Zhang, Yena Lee, Nash Jenkins, Arcade Salim Zalot-Willis, and Walker Brewer.

At the Center for Applied Transgender Studies, thanks to my co-founders Avery Everhart and Erique Zhang, without whom this work would feel futile. Thanks also to the Center's many Fellows who have provided invaluable support over the last few years, especially Florence Ashley, V Chaudhry, Oliver Haimson, Alex Hanna, Anna Lauren Hoffmann, and Austin H. Johnson.

Of course, I could not have completed this book without the love and support of my family and friends. While in the field I had the great privilege of living with a number of close friends, each of whom kept me grounded throughout the trying process of fieldwork. Thanks to all the Boss Street crew: Stephanie Aguilar, Helen Jorski, Kristen Lombardo, Kayley Marshall, and Jonny Wilkerson. All my love and gratitude to Rachel Moran and Samantha Nesfield, who have stood by me through the best and worst times of my adult life. More love and gratitude than I am capable of producing to my mother Kris, my father Tom, and my sisters Caitlin and Abigail. I love you more than I have words for. Finally, I owe unending thanks to my most beloved, Will, who endured me writing this work twice—first as a dissertation and then as a book. I promise to never write this one again.

Portions of Chapter 3 were previously published in "Movement–Media Relations in the Hybrid Media System: A Case Study from the US Transgender Rights Movement," *The International Journal of Press/Politics* 26, no. 2 (2021): 341–361. Portions of Chapter 5 were published in "Deciding What's (Sharable) News: Social Movement Organizations as Curating Actors in the Political Information System," *Communication Monographs* 89, no. 3 (2022): 354–375. Portions of the appendix were published in "Out of the Tower and Into the Field: Fieldwork as Public Scholarship in the Face of Social Injustice," *International Journal of Communication* 13 (2019): 3512–3528.

1

Making Change in the Networked Public Sphere

Communications (Comms) Director Eric Dyson and I were in a small office on the seventh floor of a Dupont Circle-area coworking space in Washington, DC, which the National Center for Transgender Equality (NCTE) had rented out for the two weeks between moving out of their old permanent offices across the street and into the new ones down on K Street—DC's famous lob-byist corridor. It was early, so no one else from the Comms team had arrived. Eric and I were passing time talking about standup comedy, which Eric did on weekends for fun. He wanted to show me a Richard Pryor routine I had never seen before, so he took to YouTube. Out of habit, I filled the time of his silent searching by scrolling through my phone, jerking my head up as Eric exclaimed "Oh no! He *didn't!*" He looked over at me nervously.

"What?" I asked. My phone dinged before he could reply. My younger sister Caitlin had sent me a screenshot of a series of tweets from President Donald J. Trump, which she had captioned "WTF":

> After consultation with my Generals and military experts, please be ad-vised that the United States Government will not accept or allow . . . [8:55 a.m. 26 Jul 2017]

> . . . Transgender individuals to serve in any capacity in the U.S. Military. Our military must be focused on decisive and overwhelming . . . [9:04 a.m. 26 Jul 2017]

> . . . victory and cannot be burdened with the tremendous medical costs and disruption that transgender in the military would entail. Thank you [9:08 a.m. 26 Jul 2017]

Voices for Transgender Equality. Thomas J Billard, Oxford University Press. © Thomas J Billard 2024.
DOI: 10.1093/oso/9780197695425.003.0001

"Oh *no*," I droned. "I've seen it." Eric's phone rang, and he told me to "get ready" before he answered. "Eric Dyson, National Center for Transgender Equality." A few seconds went by. "The BBC," he muttered to me.

Over the next twenty minutes, Eric and I took frantic calls from reporters looking for comments and interviews. The earliest calls came from European news agencies like Agence France-Presse (AFP) and Sky News, where journalists were already into the full swing of the day. American agencies started calling around the time the rest of the Comms team arrived. NCTE staff darted from office to office trying to figure out what they should be doing. Mara Keisling, Executive Director of NCTE, called everyone into the conference room to set up a centralized "war room." There we coordinated our communications with journalists, policy makers, coalition partners, and transgender community members around a shared strategy. The immediate priority was a press release, which the war room started to jointly draft as we ignored the still-ringing phones.

"The president positioned this in terms of military readiness—trans people hurt readiness—so in our statement and in interviews we need to focus on military readiness and the harm throwing trans people out does," declared Harper Jean Tobin, Director of Policy. "There are 15,000 trans people in the US military, and we need to focus on what throwing out 15,000 qualified service members does. And let's not make this about 'Don't Ask, Don't Tell part two.' That won't help anything, even though journalists will want to paint it as that."

"This isn't Don't Ask, Don't Tell," Raffi Freedman-Gurspan, Director of External Relations, quipped. "It's just, like, *don't serve*."

"Yeah, I like that: This is not Don't Ask, Don't Tell; this is Don't Serve, Don't Serve," Mara rehearsed.

We quickly jotted down the brainstormed phrase to use in the press release. Eric, Communications Manager Jay Wu, and I huddled to craft the final wording before presenting it to Mara for approval. She made a few small changes before approving it. Jay immediately posted it to the website and emailed it out to NCTE's press list. Eric and I resumed answering calls and another staff member mapped out Mara and Harper Jean's busying interview schedules on the white board. Mara's first television interview of the day would be with Reuters TV at 11 a.m., followed by MSNBC, Fox News, and other top news outlets. In the evening, she would be on *Hardball with Chris Matthews*. We quickly noted a problem, though: because NCTE was in a temporary space between rapid-succession office moves, we weren't sure where

Mara's makeup kit was, and her emergency interview suit had gone missing. She would need to go home to change and grab her makeup, and I was tasked with managing her on-the-fly interviews. I grabbed my notebook and my phone, and Eric gave me his phone as a backup. He would communicate with me from the office by email, and I could use our phones to queue up journalists to hand off to Mara.

Mara and I ran downstairs and got in the rideshare car she had called, as she joined a strategy call with LGBTQ media advocacy organization GLAAD, the Transgender American Veterans Association (TAVA), the National LGBTQ Task Force, and other coalition partners. In the meantime, I got a journalist from CBS News on the phone and handed him off to Mara the second she ended the joint call. (Our rideshare driver seemed perplexed by the unfolding events in the back seat, and, I imagine, by the sheer number of telephones in use.) Trump's decision on transgender troops was "dilettante policymaking by whim and tweet," Mara told the journalist before running up the stairs to her apartment for her clothes and makeup. Meanwhile, Eric emailed me that AFP was sending a video team, so they would be arriving to the temporary office shortly after Reuters.

When we returned to the office, I rejoined the war room. Jay filled me in on the spreadsheet system they had set up in my absence to manage the rapidly changing schedule of interviews.[1] Eric reclaimed his phone and took over managing Mara's interviews, while I helped Jay return journalists' calls. NCTE had standing relationships with some journalists because they frequently covered trans topics, like Katy Steinmetz at *Time*, Dominic Holden at *Buzzfeed*, and Nico Lang at Grindr's then-newly-launched-but-now-defunct *Into*. Others NCTE had never worked with before, and the journalists sometimes didn't know anything about the organization other than that having "transgender" and "equality" in the name made them sound like they were probably a good place to go for a quote. An intern at Sirius XM, for instance, called me to get a quote for Tim Farley's talk show, but didn't know exactly *from whom* she wanted the quote; I passed her along to Policy Director Harper Jean, who handled an unanticipated twelve-minute live interview with Tim.

I worked with Jay for the rest of the morning to keep on top of interviews. We wanted to ensure every major news outlet had quotes from NCTE leaders. Around midday, however, we changed tack. At that point most of the major news outlets had been scheduled, and even some unanticipated media outlets like *Elle*, *Harper's Bazaar*, and *Vanity Fair*. Mara declared in her parting shot before heading out of the office to NBC's studios, "We need to make sure trans voices are being heard on this." As staff repeatedly told me, knowing about the transgender veteran who lives in your county is far more important than knowing that, in general, there are trans people in the military.

So, we switched to getting the voices of transgender service members and other transgender citizens in major press outlets, as well as local and community media. Jay, Digital Media Manager Jason Arrol, and I worked with Director of External Relations Raffi and Education Program Director Rebecca Kling to connect news outlets from around the country with local trans people from NCTE's Voices for Trans Equality (VTE) and Families for Trans Equality (FTE) projects. Together, these two projects had established a national network of nearly one thousand "community storytellers" who received media and communication training from NCTE to make them effective spokespersons.[2] These projects mobilized VTE and FTE network members to contact their political representatives, connect them with local reporters, and get their stories placed in local and national media outlets. The VTE project had several veterans on the roll, including frequent collaborators like retired Army Colonel Sheri Swokowski, retired Army Major Evan Young, and Air Force veteran Cynthia DeVille. We connected these VTE veterans with major media outlets to "humanize" the transgender service members who were being coarsely discussed in stories on Trump's tweets. In one case, I worked with journalist Mattie Kahn at *Elle* magazine to secure an interview with Cynthia DeVille that ultimately took the form of a confessional-style video titled "A Trans Air Force Veteran Responds to Trump's Ban."[3] These stories re-centered the transgender service members in question and focused on the material impacts of Trump's proposed policy.

Most VTE veterans, however, were connected with local or community-based media outlets where they lived. Army Master Sergeant Erika Stoltz of Sun Prairie, Wisconsin was profiled in the *Wisconsin State Journal*, which foregrounded her community residency and discussed the fear for her livelihood that she, like other trans Wisconsinite service members, was facing.[4] Another story featured Sheri Swokowski, a resident of DeForest, who made it clear that the "Trump ban on transgender military service hits home for some in Wisconsin."[5] These stories made Trump's proposed ban not just a national policy decision regarding a culturally remote, marginalized group, but a grave decision with material impacts on local community members.

Over the following days, we continued to connect VTE and FTE network members with various media outlets, to push stories over NCTE's social media accounts, and to encourage transgender people on NCTE contact lists to make their voices heard in their communities. The flurry of panicked communications returned to a routine churn, and within a few days the news cycle mostly blew over. Still, conversations continued over social media and in communities as the implications of Trump's tweets were deliberated and the stories of countless transgender veterans and service members were heard, shared, and re-shared.

* * *

As the day of Trump's military ban illustrates, responding to social movement crises in the contemporary media environment requires fast and flexible communication practices. It requires that activists advance their organizational objectives by coordinating outreach through multiple forms of media targeting multiple audiences, all at the same time. And NCTE did this often. The day of Trump's military ban was exceptional because it represented the first time in public knowledge that executive policy was set by tweet; Trump had not communicated with the Department of Defense, meaning DoD lawyers were caught by surprise.[6] But the day of the ban was *not* exceptional in terms of NCTE's communication practices. In fact, it was typical. These were the same communication practices NCTE had previously used to fight against North Carolina's Public Facilities Privacy & Security Act, commonly known as HB2. HB2 required individuals to use public facilities associated with the sex listed on their birth certificate, regardless of their current gender identity, and was partially repealed after widespread public outcry.[7] These were the same communication practices they later used when a memo leaked from the Trump administration's Department of Health and Human Services detailing plans to "define transgender out of existence."[8] These were even the same communication practices NCTE employed daily in their long-term campaigns to advocate for good policies and counter bad ones.

NCTE had honed this set of communication practices through years of patient advocacy and rapid response. Over the past two decades there had been an unprecedented rise in attention to trans people and the issues they face across mass media, new media, and political institutions at every level of governance.[9] This rise in attention to trans issues was largely thanks to the hard work of trans activists, who long fought for the social, cultural, and political equality of transgender people. At the same time, trans people's

cultural visibility and political victories drew the attention of a growing reactionary countermovement. Their oppositional efforts have directed still
more attention to the trans movement in a vicious cycle of magnification. As
a result, trans rights have become, in many ways, the flashpoint *du jour* of the
American culture wars, requiring NCTE, among other trans movement organizations, to be on constant guard.

Yet the rise of the contemporary transgender movement has also
occurred at a very particular time in the development of the media system,
and the contours of the movement have been shaped by this "new" media
environment in important ways. The rise in salience of trans issues in recent decades has been secured less through increasing representation in
mass media (although such representation has certainly increased),[10] and
more through an apparent omnipresence of trans people across the various media and communications streams individuals experience in daily
life. Whereas activists of earlier eras could fight for representation on four
broadcast television networks and in a handful of national newspapers
with confidence that success would mean their issues were experienced
by the vast majority of the population, contemporary activists have no
such assurances. For their issues to be experienced by the majority of
the population, they must secure representation by reaching audiences
through highly individualized flows of content across countless media.[11]
As such, the recent visibility of trans people has been a more *total* visibility, saturating a much larger network of communication channels. And
achieving this has required pioneering new approaches to activism, as seen
in the work done at NCTE.

These new approaches to media activism are the focus of *Voices for
Transgender Equality*. This book's core argument is that contemporary activism is no longer structured around achieving visibility in mass media, as
they have been decentered as the primary avenue for the flow of political information, perspectives, and opinions. Rather, contemporary activism takes
a more holistic approach to activism that seeks influence *across the communication system*. This system includes mass media but extends into local and
community media and into interpersonal communication networks (both
digital and face-to-face). I further argue that the chimaerizing influence of
digital technologies—how they fuse the logics, contexts, and practices of
different media—requires the *concurrent* management of *every* domain
of the communication system. Such system-wide management is necessary

to maintain influence over the flows of political information about trans-gender issues and identities and, consequently, improve the sociopolitical standing of the trans community.

This is a tall order for short-staffed, overworked social movement organizations like NCTE. It's one thing to have a media relations manager (or a team of them if you're lucky) that works with journalists at the major newspapers and broadcast outlets to secure sympathetic coverage. But it's another thing entirely to have a small communications team that works to saturate a diverse ecology of digital news outlets, *and* local media outlets in media markets across the country, *and* both public and private conversations across multiple social media platforms—all of which are, in turn, influencing one another—with voices in support of your cause. Yet this is what NCTE did on the day of President Trump's military ban and on every other day I spent with them. They navigated the complex game of Whac-A-Mole created by the contemporary communication system, in which failing to control the messages in *one* area of the communication system leaves *each other* area open to influence from oppositional forces. To make change, you need to whack every mole simultaneously. You need to master what I call the "politics of flows," controlling the dynamic interrelations of different communication streams and their evolving power relations.

Importantly, NCTE is not the only trans movement organization to engage with the politics of flows. These communication practices are not even unique to the trans movement. Indeed, NCTE's coalition partners and countermovement opponents alike have employed nearly identical approaches. In that respect, I could have arrived at the same argument for this book by studying any number of contemporary social movement organizations. However, the trans movement is special among movements because it emerged from within this unsettled media environment. Unlike many other movements, it did not adapt to the changes wrought by digital technologies; it was forged by them. NCTE is also unique among trans movement organizations, as it has stood at the forefront of this new civil rights movement, leading the charge for transgender equality. This book offers an insider's view of how the trans movement has achieved historic change in a stunningly short amount of time. It also captures firsthand the most momentous battles over trans rights under the uncanny administration of President Donald Trump—an administration defined by the often-disruptive transformations digital media have brought to politics.[12]

Media and Their Publics

To understand this book's core argument, it is necessary to understand both how and why digital technologies have disrupted the business-as-usual of media and politics. Moreover, it is necessary to understand how those disruptions have changed the game for social movements. Achieving social, cultural, and political change means changing the minds of "the public." And there is a foundational assumption among scholars and practitioners alike that "media" are how strategic communicators reach "the public." Thus, media become important terrain that social movements and other similar actors must navigate. But how do we get from influencing media to changing "the public"?

The classic answer to this question comes from German sociologist Jürgen Habermas, who developed the concept of the "public sphere."[13] His basic premise was that there is a formal system of politics, which is the State, and a private sphere of individuals' daily lives. The public sphere exists between the two as common space in which individuals can freely and openly discuss issues of collective concern, identify problems, and evaluate different courses of action. Through engaging in what Habermas called "critical-rational" debate, the citizens who choose to participate in the public sphere develop consensual public opinion, which in turn influences political institutions.

Now, one could be forgiven for thinking this sounds like a fantasy version of how the world works. And Habermas would actually agree that it *isn't* how the world really works. According to him, the liberal public sphere first arose in Europe in the eighteenth century out of interpersonal discussion in public spaces like coffeehouses and salons. It was also given vitality through letters, journals, political newspapers, and other literary materials. However, this idyllic public sphere was short-lived, Habermas argued, because the "structural transformation" caused by the rise of mass democracy transitioned the public sphere into the domain of mass media. This shift to mediation turned individual citizens into passive consumers of political discourse and mere recipients of artificially constructed public opinion. Although a small portion of the liberal public sphere re-emerged whenever individuals engaged in public-spirited conversation, in the twentieth century the commercial mass media of newspapers, magazines, radio, and television *became* the public sphere. This is—at least, theoretically—how influencing media changes the public: Mass media *are* the public sphere, transmitting ideas about the nature of public opinion to audiences. Thus, securing sympathetic representations of your ideas in mass media ensures the public receives your ideas favorably and the political system, in turn, takes them seriously.

Since its first publication, Habermas' idea of the public sphere has been widely critiqued on a number of grounds. Notably, he argued for the existence of a supposedly inclusive *single* public sphere. But as several scholars have noted, the public sphere is not currently, nor has it ever been, actually open to participation by all. Individuals are regularly excluded from participating because of their race, class, gender identity, sexual identity, and other marginalized or oppressed identities. Their exclusion from the public sphere leads to the emergence of subaltern counterpublics, enclave publics, satellite publics, and other fragmented public spheres built by and consisting of the excluded.[14] These counterpublics host their own conversations, discourses, and media outside of those which are considered to be part of "the public." Thus, there cannot truly be a single public sphere.

Instead, there is a constellation of public spheres that together comprise the overarching public sphere we think of when we consider society in its totality. This seems obvious when we think of the public sphere as being based in the interpersonal conversations Habermas celebrated. We all have networks of people with whom we discuss issues of public concern. Those networks are bounded by family ties, friendships, geographic proximity, and shared identity. But the people in our networks also have their own networks, and the people in their networks, in turn, have their own networks. Were we to continue, we could eventually include everyone in the country (and even people outside it) in this patchwork of discussion networks that cut across various kinds of difference.

When we consider media to be its central organizer, though, it may seem less obvious that "the public sphere" is formed by constellations of public spheres—yet it remains equally true. Although we are accustomed to thinking of mass media as means of communication that unify the disparate groups in society, media attention is not uniformly distributed across "the public." Neither is the relevance of every issue discussed in those media, meaning that individuals selectively engage with media depending on how relevant a given issue is to them. Someone may read the *New York Times* every morning, but it's unlikely they read every article in the paper; instead, they only read those they deem relevant to their daily life and personal interests. By engaging in certain "issue publics," but not in others, individuals filter themselves into different sets of public spheres.[15]

This kind of selective sorting occurred even in an era of mass media dominance, but the dawn of the so-called new media that define contemporary life has amplified this dynamic. Given that we live in an era characterized by the ubiquity of digital technologies, it seems necessary to reconceptualize "the public sphere" of today as a complex system of interlinked publics. As digital media theorists Axel Bruns and Tim Highfield argued, Habermas traced the "structural transformation" of the public sphere only up to the era of mass society in the twentieth century, but successive changes in society and in media have resulted in still further structural transformations.[16] Since the twentieth century there have been changes in the nature and organization of audiences; changes in the revenue streams and funding models of news and other media production; changes in the modes, speed, and breadth of media distribution; and changes in individuals' capacity to reach mass audiences with their own personal, non-mass-mediated communications.[17] Collectively, these changes in media and society have led to structural transformations that have taken us from a mass-mediated public sphere to a "networked public sphere."[18]

Within this networked public sphere, media flows differently. The increased ease of production and distribution has led to a boom in the sheer quantity of media outlets. At the same time, both mass and niche media outlets face increasing audience segmentation around specific issues, interests, and topics—and because it is discourse surrounding specific issues that "sparks" publics into forming, media-based public spheres at a sub-national level are proliferating indefinitely.[19] Digital media, particularly social media, further enable people to enter into interpersonally based publics without needing to participate in them face-to-face, and to do so across the community boundaries that often segregate in-person discussion. People also participate in various digital publics simultaneously and non-exclusively, bridging them and serving as conduits for discourses in one public to transfer into other publics. These overlaps and intersections of different publics form what Bruns and Highfield referred to as a "global patchwork of interconnected micro-publics" that comprise "The Public" that was once constituted by mass media.[20]

Transitioning from a mass-mediated to a networked public sphere requires us to reconsider how we think about "media," "news," and the very idea of "political communication" in contemporary society. Traditionally, "media" have been understood quite narrowly, often as corporatized mass media organizations that produce and distribute content to broad public audiences across the country, while "news" has been understood as an informational product produced and distributed by professional journalists working for those media.[21] However, the category of "media" has become destabilized by the introduction of countless technologies that "mediatize" various domains of social, cultural, and political life. Consequently, it has become necessary to decouple "news" from its traditional definition. Instead, we should understand "news" as the product of numerous actors that interact across a variety of media.[22] As political communication scholar Chris Wells incisively argued, the current media environment is far too complex to only account for professional journalism in the public's experience of political communication.[23] The contemporary media system is characterized by new sources of non-journalistic informational content, new means of distributing and consuming this content, and new orienting logics.

Accordingly, we must think of political communication in the networked public sphere not merely as "news" but, as Wells argued, "the continuous flow of facts, opinions, and ideas that help citizens understand matters of potential public concern and identify opportunities for action."[24] People receive facts, opinions, and ideas through complex networks of often highly individualized communicative resources that include traditional news, but also include various actors that shape the information flows of the contemporary media system.[25] In articulating many of these changes, political communication theorist Andrew Chadwick argued for a shift away from the common concept of "news cycles" to a new concept of "political information cycles."[26] Whereas "news cycles" consist of the temporally rigid routines of elite interaction that produce regular news products like morning newspapers and evening broadcasts, "political information cycles" involve new flows of news content as numerous loosely connected individuals, groups, and institutions interact in highly interdependent ways to attract and maintain attention to certain facts, opinions, and ideas, and to assert grounds for their significance.[27] Thus, we can think of our concerns over political communication in the public sphere not merely as concerns with the content of news media distributed to mass publics. Rather, political communication involves the flows of political information among the various publics that make up the networked public sphere.

In sum, the public sphere is no longer dominated by mass media, as Habermas critiqued. Rather, the public sphere currently consists of networked actors of varying sizes and degrees of influence that together shape the flows of information and narratives that inform public political conversation. As such, changing "the public" now requires influencing the flows of information for, from, and among *all* the publics within the networked public sphere.

New Media Logics and New Logics of Activism

The array of transformations that have occurred in the shift from a mass-mediated to a networked public sphere have demanded social movements fundamentally transform how they push for social, cultural, and political change. The strategies pioneered by activists in an era of four major television networks cannot remain effective in a system characterized by high levels of media choice, more horizontal distributions of communicative power, and unprecedented degrees of interpenetration among media of different types.[28] The poles of power in the communication system have changed, and these changes have required that activists change their communication practices for their organizations to succeed.

Scholars' attempts to grapple with these changes to social movement practices have fallen into two broad camps. In one camp are grassroots enthusiasts who have focused almost exclusively on how the affordances of digital technologies allow grassroots or other decentralized activist movements like the Movement for Black Lives, *los indignados*, Occupy Wall Street, and the Arab Spring to "organize without organizations," to increase the visibility of their causes outside of mass media, and to push (with variable success) for change.[29] In the other smaller, camp are organizational transformationalists who have focused on how political organizations use digital media to enhance their organizational capacities and communicate with their stakeholders.[30]

Both grassroots enthusiasts and organizational transformationalists face conceptual and empirical issues, despite the many merits of their findings. The organizational transformationalists, for instance, largely ignore the wider public to instead focus on how organizations relate to predefined constituencies. The grassroots enthusiasts, on the other hand, ignore streams of communication in society beyond digital media, except to construct them as a monolithic "other" that is the "old media" against which "new media" are defined. Per this line of theorizing, the "old" media of television, radio, and newspapers operate according to a dated mass media logic in which professional journalists select and package information in a routine manner based on longstanding news values. The "new" digital media, in contrast, operate according to a network media logic whereby individual media users contin-uously curate information on the basis of their personal opinions, feelings, and experiences and what they think will gain the most public attention in a rapidly changing trend cycle.[31] Ostensibly, social movements find greater traction for their issues under the network logic of social media, while they struggle to gain recognition under the logic of mass media, leading them to adopt digital technologies as their primary media of interest. The problem is that any clear dichotomy between old and new media falls apart under em-pirical and conceptual scrutiny.

The public communication infrastructure is now far more complicated than this argument suggests. Important sources of political communication fall outside of "old" and "new" media and even span the boundaries between them. As media sociologist Sandra Ball-Rokeach outlined in her commu-nication infrastructure theory (CIT), people are embedded in complex "storytelling systems" that span macro, meso, and micro levels—and in the networked public sphere, each level is experienced in both digital and phys-ical space.[32] At the macro level sit mass media, or those media that (1) have an imagined audience of the entire nation, (2) are owned by large national media corporations (whether for-profit or non-profit), and (3) attract large audiences. At the meso level lie local and community media, which have an imagined audience of some sub-national population defined by either ge-ography, social identity, or lived experience. These media also generally at-tract smaller audiences; there is a large drop off in audience size between the smallest mass media outlet and the largest local or community media outlet. Finally, the micro level is where social networks connect people with family, friends, colleagues, community members, casual acquaintances, and others with whom they communicate about personal and collective concerns. These social networks include both the close bonds of people who live daily life to-gether offline and the often-looser bonds of people who are connected only through digital media. Together, these sources of political communication form the informational environments that shape the attitudes, beliefs, and values of individuals and communities.

Perhaps more crucially, another strike against a new–old media di-chotomy is that we do not have an old media system and a new media system that operate in parallel to one another. In his foundational attempt to dispel this notion, political communication theorist Andrew Chadwick argued that we have a *hybrid media system*.[33] That is to say, mass media do not con-sistently act according to their "mass media logic" and digital media do not consistently act according to their "network media logic." The boundaries between the two blur such that mass media often act in accordance with network media logics and social media often act in accordance with mass media logics. Per Chadwick, the overall system is "hybrid" because each often blends features of both media logics in any given instance. Moreover, mass media lean heavily on social media to source information and perspectives, and social media inversely depend on mass media for new information and amplification. Both the technologies and the social practices of "old" and "new" media are deeply entangled.

The concept of the hybrid media system has been broadly applied to the study of political communication and increasingly used to understand the relationship between social movements' digital communications and their subsequent representations in mass media. However, as applications of the hybrid media system concept have become more popular, so too have criticisms of its undergirding premise of "hybridity." The issue with hybridity is, in short, that it requires us to first have two distinct binary categories, followed by the emergence of a new tertiary phenomenon that borrows from both of those categories, in turn producing new practices and dynamics that don't fit neatly into the old binary.[34] While it may once have been the case that "old" mass media and "new" digital media constituted discrete categories that had unexpected meeting points, they are now far too interwoven to be considered distinct.[35] Thus, it is somewhat meaningless to call their logics hybrid; they are in reality fused.

We are now in a post-hybridity age, in which we do not have a *hybrid* media system, but rather what I call a *chimaeric* one. In the biological sciences, a hybrid is an animal that results from the mating of two distinct species, such as a mule, which is the offspring of a male donkey and a female horse. A chimaera, on the other hand, is an animal that is formed when two embryos of the same species, but with two different sets of DNA, fuse together and grow as one.[36] Drawing on this biological metaphor, my shift from "hybrid" to "chimaeric" in describing the media system not only signals the collapse in distinctions between mass and digital media, but also addresses the ways they operate together as one coherent system, rather than separately as two interpenetrating systems.

The emergence of this chimaeric media system has profound implications for the study of social movement communication and the public sphere. As feminist media scholar Bernadette Barker-Plummer argued in her studies of the National Organization for Women's media relations work in the 1960s and

1970s, successful movement media work requires playing within the dominant media logic.[37] And, as Chadwick makes clear, the dominant media logic has fundamentally shifted, requiring movements to adapt their communicative practices to succeed in this new communication system. The concept of the chimaeric media system can help us understand how and why activists make the adaptations they do. By drawing attention to the interconnections among different media and the new logics that drive their interactions with one another, the chimaeric media system reveals new pathways of influence. These new relationships of dependency and influence, in turn, affect how activism is practiced, as movements are forced to contend with merged streams of communication that once would have been distinct. At the same time, maintaining a focus exclusively on *media* fails to consider how unmediated communications affect the flows of political information. Political communication includes the messages that circulate through individuals' communication infrastructures, which include interpersonal conversation—even if those conversations are shaped by media.

A full account of how social movements make change in the networked public sphere must consider all these streams of communication, how they relate, and how activists master the flows among them. Drawing on the concepts I've outlined in this chapter, I offer Figure 1.1 as a map of both (1) the communication infrastructure of the networked public sphere that movements try to influence and (2) the pathways of influence and message flow among its constituent parts. As illustrated in the figure, the messages circulating in mass media strongly influence local and community media and social networks. The messages circulating in local and community media, in turn, reciprocally influence mass media and moderately influence individuals' social networks. For their part, social networks circulate messages within themselves, forming publics in the process. Because they are interconnected, they also circulate messages among *other* linked networks such that they form the "global patchwork of interconnected micro-publics" that Bruns and Highfield argued constitutes "The Public."[38] The publics formed by social networks also influence the local and community media that serve them, while the messages that circulate widely enough through The Public influence those in mass media. But messages don't only circulate in one step increments. They continue to flow. For example, messages can circulate among social networks until they influence local and community media and then, once they circulate in local and community media, reach mass media. Mass media can then amplify those messages by transmitting

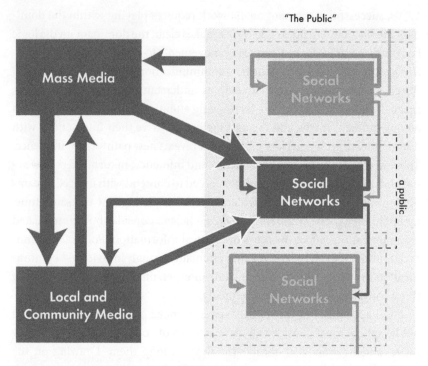

Figure 1.1. Map of the communication infrastructure of the networked public sphere (arrows indicate directions of flow, while line width indicates relative influence).

them to a variety of new social networks. The end result is a system of messages in constant flux as discourse flows from one domain into another.

For social movements seeking to influence the public, this system presents both great opportunities and immense challenges. Activists now have more pathways to receive public attention than ever before, but to ensure that their messages prevail they need to keep alternate messages circulating in the communication system from displacing theirs. For example, activists may succeed in shaping the narratives transmitted by mass media through strong media relations work. However, if alternate narratives surface in social networks and find their way into local and community media, they may ultimately find their way into mass media.

Social movement organizations need to simultaneously address all areas of the communication system in complementary ways. This is what NCTE did on the day of President Trump's ban on transgender servicemembers.

They worked to get their staff quoted in mass media, promote transgender veterans' stories in local and community media, and circulate sympathetic perspectives through social networks. Each area required different strategies and tactics, but each needed to be addressed to saturate the communication system with voices for transgender equality.

Of course, this figure and the summary I provided tell a story about the structure of the communication system. But it says little about the practices that shape it and occur within it. That is the task of the rest of the book. Across its five remaining chapters, *Voices for Transgender Equality* breaks this system apart, looking at how activists manage the social forces and everyday activities involved in making change in the networked public sphere.

Innovation in the US Transgender Movement

If my intellectual interest is in understanding how social movements make change in the networked public sphere, why choose to study the US transgender movement? There are several reasons. The first reason is personal. Before I was an academic, I was a transgender rights activist. Since becoming an academic, I have continuously sought ways to bridge my research and my activism.[39] For me, research and activism are inseparable endeavors. Research is the skill I can contribute to the movement, and the movement is what motivates me to pursue my research.

The second reason is more scholarly. As I've already noted, transgender issues have become the flashpoint *du jour* of the American culture wars. They have been thrust into the center stage of American politics and offer a real-time illustration of the complicated dynamics involved in mediated contests over salient social and political issues. Moreover, the transgender movement didn't adjust to the digital media environment that turned social movement politics upside down; it was born in this digital environment. As I discuss in the following chapter, the organizations that make up the modern transgender movement were all established in the same 2001–2003 post-dot-com boom period and they came of age just as the major social media platforms proliferated in the late 2000s and early 2010s. Drawing on scholarship from organizational sociology, I argue that NCTE experienced "media imprinting" from the digital environment.[40] By that I mean, NCTE took on characteristics reflective of the media environment they operated in at their founding and in their early years, and these characteristics persisted into the time I studied them and will likely persist far beyond. Consequently, studying the transgender movement offers the opportunity to not just study how organizations adapt to the contemporary communication system, but rather to study how they are built to navigate it.

The transgender movement is also an institutionalized social movement, meaning it has a strong network of sufficiently resourced organizations with connections to various social and political institutions. Institutionalization sets it apart from many of the other major social movements that were born in the digital era and which scholars have preoccupied themselves studying. The transgender movement is not a #hashtagmovement, a networked protest movement, or even a digitally enabled movement. It's an old-school social movement in the most traditional sense that just happens to be native to the digital environment.[41] Accordingly, it offers an opportunity to study the implications digital media have for movement activity beyond trendy scholarly fascinations with platform-specific modes of activism.

My specific site of study within the transgender movement was the National Center for Transgender Equality (NCTE) in Washington, DC. NCTE was, in the words of political scientist Anthony Nownes, "the dean of transgender rights organizations."[42] It operated alongside broader LGBTQ rights organizations like GLAAD, the Human Rights Campaign (HRC), and the National LGBTQ Task Force. But its sole focus on transgender concerns and its transgender leadership made NCTE unique among them.[43] Among transgender movement organizations, it had by far the most robust public advocacy program with two departments—Communications (Comms) and Outreach & Education (O&E)—consisting of, at the time of my research, eight staff members focused on media and public communications. These and other factors discussed in the following chapter made NCTE the ideal site at which to study change-making efforts in the transgender movement.

While I discuss my approach to the research that informed this book at greater length in the Appendix, I'll briefly summarize it here. My methods consisted primarily of participant observation at NCTE and interviews with NCTE staff and associates. I conducted my participant observation research in two phases. In the first phase, I studied NCTE for three months in the summer of 2017. During this time, I worked in an intern-like capacity for both the Comms and O&E departments, learning from the inside how the organization approached public communication and why they approached it that way. In the second phase, I returned to NCTE from June 2018 to December 2018. Throughout these seven months, my observations again focused primarily on the Comms and O&E teams, although I also gained access to Policy team meetings. Among the meetings I observed were the daily Comms team morning check-ins, weekly Comms operations meetings, weekly messaging meetings, weekly O&E team meetings, standing meetings for campaigns and special projects, general staff meetings, and ad-hoc strategy meetings.

I took detailed notes during meetings, trainings, rallies, staff interviews with journalists, and various other events. I used those fieldnotes both as data and to inform my construction of interview protocols, which were individualized for each interview subject. Each full-time Comms staff member was formally interviewed twice, as was each O&E staff member, except the Director of External Relations, who was interviewed once due to scheduling constraints. Interviewees included Media Relations Manager Gillian Branstetter, Digital Campaigns Manager Laurel Powell, Communications Director Jay Wu, Interim Communication Director Dave Noble, Education Program Director Rebecca Kling, Family Organizer Debi Jackson, Family Organizer DeShanna Neal, and Director of External Relations Raffi Freedman-Gurspan.[44] Additionally, two Policy staff members were interviewed: State Policy Director Arli Christian and Racial and Economic Justice Policy Advocate Mateo De La Torre.

Beyond staff, I interviewed nine members of NCTE's Voices for Transgender Equality (VTE) and Families for Transgender Equality (FTE) projects, who did important communications work for the organization. These storytellers included transgender individuals (VTE) and the parents or other family members of transgender children (FTE). Five interviewees were transgender members of VTE (Ray Gibson, Benjamin Kennedy, Chloé LaCasse, Leslie McMurray, and Paula Sophia Schonauer), while four were cisgender parents of transgender children (Rachel Gonzales, Jo Ivester, Nicola van Kuilenburg, and Sarah Watson). Interviews lasted between sixty and ninety minutes and were transcribed and then analyzed alongside fieldnotes.

It should be obvious by now that I have not pseudonymized NCTE, their staff, or their VTE and FTE network members in this book, meaning I have not written about them using false names to protect their identities. This decision partly has to do with the fact that it would be virtually impossible to pseudonymize NCTE. The number of national organizations working toward transgender rights is small; those working exclusively on transgender rights issues number, at most, three. They are also the only transgender movement organization in Washington, DC, and their location is an important facet of this book's story. Truly, NCTE stands alone when it comes to the national transgender movement. Pseudonymization of the NCTE staff would be equally ineffective. Because the organization is so small (and each staff member is publicly listed on the NCTE website and in publicly available annual reports), pseudonymization would offer no real protection from the discovery of staff members' identities. Staff were thus made aware of my intentions to name them in my book, and each individually consented to my doing so.

My greater concern was whether pseudonymization would be more feasible and more necessary for members of the VTE and FTE projects. While some scholars have argued that pseudonymization does not always serve the best interests of either researchers or research participants, transgender individuals face a specific form of marginalization based on their identities, and their identities may not be known even to members of their community.[45] "Outing" them could have devastating, if not deadly, consequences. At the same time, those working with NCTE in the VTE and FTE projects are often visibly engaged in public-facing activism, serving as spokespeople for the transgender community to media and political institutions. Thus, I left the choice for pseudonymization among these participants open and their individual preferences were abided. In every case, they elected *not* to be pseudonymized. The final category of individuals for whom pseudonymization might have been a concern is behind-the-scenes collaborators with NCTE. In instances in which their stories have become public subjects of media attention and they chose to be named in stories, I have not pseudonymized them. In all other cases, I have pseudonymized these individuals.

The Way Forward

This first chapter has laid out the theoretical stakes of the book, identified my core thesis, and outlined the structural changes to the contemporary communication system wrought by digital media and the transformations in social practices that have emerged from them. Having encapsulated the system-level argument that *Voices for Transgender Equality* advances, this chapter sets the stage for the rest of the book to unfold by taking apart and deeply analyzing the system's component pieces.

The next chapter, "Welcome to the National Center for Transgender Equality," analyzes three specific contexts that shaped NCTE's work while I was in the field. First, there is the temporal context. I was at NCTE during its "golden age"; it was at its largest, most productive, and most influential, operating at the height of the transgender movement's visibility post-"tipping point." Second, there is the geographic context. NCTE is based in Washington, DC, and its location had a profound impact on what kinds of communicative activities it participated in, what kinds of media it targeted in its activism, and what kinds of issues it chose to engage in. Finally, there is the movement context. The transgender movement is a special case so far as social movement literature is concerned. It is what I have called a "hybrid movement"—a movement that identifies with and operates within multiple social movement fields simultaneously and non-exclusively. Specifically, the transgender movement is simultaneously an independent, autonomous movement of its own *and* a constituent part of the LGBT movement. This hybrid status and the historical process by which the transgender movement became hybrid impacted NCTE's relationships to other organizations operating under the "LGBT" umbrella and the communicative work it was successful at. This chapter addresses each of these three contexts in turn, offering my novel concept of "media imprinting" to make sense of *why* I observed the kinds of activities I did while in the field.

The third chapter, "How Mass Media Still Matter," analyzes NCTE's continued, but evolving focus on mass media. It explores the activities of NCTE's mass media-focused activism and analyzes their organizing logic, explaining how they fit into NCTE's broader approach to making change in the networked public sphere. Some of these activities were mere continuations of best practices inherited from mass media activists of yore, while others innovated on older practices to enhance their efficacy in the digital media environment. Still other activities were wholly new, developed to suit the new kinds of relationships between mass media and social movements made possible by the chimaeric media system. I argue that, ultimately, managing mass media was necessary to ensure that the communication system's central organ was not circulating messages harmful to the transgender movement into the broader communication system and, whenever possible, was instead promoting the flow of pro-transgender messages into the communication channels influenced by mass media. At the same time, managing mass media required managing other domains of the communication system as well. After all, local and community media and social networks succeeded in exerting a surprising degree of reciprocal influence on the content of mass media. I illustrate these dynamics through an analysis of how NCTE managed the transgender passport crisis that emerged in the summer of 2018. During this crisis, individual social media users initiated a storm of mass media attention to a State Department passport policy that NCTE struggled to quell until they finally established control over the discourses circulating in the digital sphere.

The role of digital media in turning relatively minor issues into unlikely national crises was particularly salient with local and community media. Because digital media allow local stories to circulate through networks that span far beyond their intended, geographically delimited audiences, local issues can spread like wildfire across the country. Thus, social movement organizations that want to control the national conversation on their issues need to maintain influence over local media markets across the country. Taking the previous chapter's exploration of the strategies NCTE used to manage relations with media outlets, the fourth chapter, "From Right Here to Everywhere," analyzes the logics underpinning NCTE's unexpected focus on local and community media. I explore the new strategies they developed to make this work more manageable, while disentangling how digital distribution influenced when, why, and how NCTE engaged with local and community media. I pay particular attention to NCTE's Voices for Trans Equality (VTE) and Families for Trans Equality (FTE) projects, which together established a national network of nearly one thousand "community storytellers." These storytellers received media and communication training from NCTE to make them effective spokespersons. They could then be "deployed" to address crises on the ground on NCTE's behalf. I describe when the Alliance Defending Freedom, a far-right Christian legal advocacy organization, tried to instigate controversy over the Decatur, Georgia school district's transgender-inclusive policies and make the issue a national story. Using this controversy, I analyze how and why NCTE employed the VTE and FTE networks alongside more traditional media relations strategies to isolate and contain this serious threat to their control over the national conversation on transgender rights.

From the outside, it could often look like NCTE's communications focused only on mass media and on local and community media because that's where they could be publicly seen representing the movement and fighting for change. You could see Executive Director Mara Keisling's name following a quote in a news article, and Director of External Relations Raffi

Freedman-Gurspan being interviewed on broadcast television. You may notice NCTE's logo on a sign floating in the background of a photo from a protest on the cover of a magazine. But much of NCTE's communications work wasn't directly conducted by them. Much of it was carried out by people NCTE had empowered with the knowledge and resources needed to carry out their activism *for them* in communities nationwide and in social networks (both mediated and unmediated) NCTE couldn't participate in. Chapter 5, "Making Politics (Inter)Personal," builds on the preceding chapter's analysis of the VTE and FTE programs to consider how these programs provided transgender individuals and their family members with the resources they needed to effectively reshape conversations about their sociopolitical issues "on the ground." At the same time, NCTE was able to capitalize on the mass visibility of social media to use network members to create digital news events. These digital news events drew mass and local and community media attention to well-planted digital discourses that then became news media stories. Specifically, I analyze NCTE's Won't Be Erased campaign, which NCTE launched after the leak of Trump administration plans to narrow the legal definition of gender as being either male or female and immutable from birth. Through Won't Be Erased, I illustrate how NCTE crafted a form of "centralized decentralization" that wove the media of the communication system into a coherent cultural narrative that ultimately reversed a major federal policy decision.

The sixth and final chapter, "A Politics of Flows," brings together the forms of activism practiced by NCTE and analyzed in the preceding chapters to consider how these activities converged in a sustained program of work aimed at transforming the political information environment. The chapter argues that such activism can be understood as fitting a "politics of flows," which understands the evolving power dynamics of interrelated communication streams. It further argues that the structure of the contemporary communication system is inextricable from the practices that are developed to influence it, as evidenced by NCTE's work.

Taken together, the six chapters of this book paint a vivid portrait of how relatively small social movements can make big, meaningful changes in politics, society, and culture. All it takes is a new approach to activism that's suited to the networked public sphere.

2

Welcome to the National Center
for Transgender Equality

When I first set foot in the offices of the National Center for Transgender Equality (NCTE) in May 2017, they were located in an unremarkable office block in the Dupont Circle area of Washington, DC—one of the city's historic gay neighborhoods. The building was next to the Founding Church of Scientology. As people walked in and out of the office block to grab lunch, Scientology members would entice them inside for a "personality test." But the Scientologists rarely solicited the people who worked at NCTE. They did not want them. NCTE's offices were in a suite on the fifth floor that they shared with Achieve, a nonprofit education reform organization. NCTE staff stuck to their subleased corner of the office and came in through the tap-to-enter side door. Staff from the two organizations only ran into one another in the shared kitchen or at the document shredders. Relationships in the office were cordial, but distant.

NCTE was a small organization, but it was rapidly outgrowing its corner of the shared office. They had hired over half a dozen staff members in the preceding year, bringing their total staff (minus interns and fellows) up to sixteen. Executive Director Mara Keisling and Deputy Executive Director Lisa Mottet sat side-by-side at desks in a glass-doored office the size of a large walk-in closet. Executive Assistant Lauren Dow sat just outside in a grey-walled cubicle hardly large enough to contain her desk and all her paperwork. Other staff members were tucked in little glass booths only large enough for a desk and a chair. The office interns and I sat on barstools at a breakfast bar attached to the outer kitchen wall because there were no more desks available.

Over the course of that summer, NCTE brought on three more staff members. Two worked remotely on half-time appointments and one was hired to help relocate NCTE to a new office space down on K Street, DC's famous corridor of lobbyists and advocacy groups. The first phase of the move was to temporary offices on the seventh floor of a coworking space catty-corner from their current office. For two weeks, the seventeen local staff, two

Voices for Transgender Equality. Thomas J Billard, Oxford University Press. © Thomas J Billard 2024.
DOI: 10.1093/oso/9780197695425.003.0002

interns, three legal fellows, and I were crammed into a series of glass boxes connected by labyrinthine, stark white corridors. It was from this glorified storage space that NCTE fought President Donald Trump's infamous military ban in which he announced his dismissal of the over fifteen thousand transgender service members in the US armed forces by tweet.

Toward the end of that summer, NCTE finally moved into its new permanent offices on the third floor of the Verizon building on 19th Street. This time, NCTE split an office suite with O'Brien-Garrett, a political fundraising agency specializing in progressive politics, which occupied the north wing. Even half of an office space was expensive, though, so NCTE leased out individual offices to allied organizations like GLMA, an LGBTQ health equity organization, and OutServe-SLDN, a network of LGBTQ military personnel. The offices not leased to tenants were occupied by NCTE staff, grouped by department, surrounding an open bullpen with large built-in desks that looked straight out of a 1980s law firm. Here was where interns, fellows, and a few junior staff members who couldn't fit in the cramped offices clustered. I sat with them right outside the door of the Communications office, where I spent many of my working hours. Within the first few weeks in the new office, O'Brien-Garrett had drawn up plans to erect a barrier between the two organizations. By the time I returned to NCTE the next summer, construction was complete. Interactions between the two organizations were limited to awkward small talk in the shared kitchen that bridged the new walls and passing in the hallway when O'Brien-Garrett staff made morning visits to the single-occupancy gender-neutral restrooms in NCTE's office space.

When I returned to NCTE in June 2018, the organization had expanded considerably once more. At its peak, NCTE had twenty-two staff members, most of whom worked in Policy. Only eight worked in Communications or Outreach & Education, which together coordinated all NCTE's communicative activities. These teams worked in small, unremarkable spaces in which they often felt tolerated but not wanted. Still, from these modest spaces they did work that had profound, far-reaching impacts on the social and political discourse surrounding transgender people and their rights. NCTE achieved these remarkable feats by pioneering communication strategies that capitalized on the powers—and fought the limits—of the networked public sphere to push for transgender rights. That is the story this book tells. But before we can proceed with that story, it's important to place it in its appropriate contexts.

There are three specific contexts that significantly shaped NCTE's work from 2017 to 2018. First, there is the temporal context. My time at the organization was during the "golden age" of NCTE. The organization was at its largest, most productive, and most influential, operating at the height of the transgender movement's visibility post-"tipping point." Second, there is the geographic context. NCTE was based in Washington, DC, and their location had a profound impact on what kinds of communicative activities it participated in, which media it targeted in its activism, and what kinds of issues it chose to engage in activism on. Third, there is the movement context. The transgender movement is a special case as far as the social movement literature is concerned. It is what I have called a "hybrid movement," or a movement that identifies with and operates within multiple social movement fields simultaneously and non-exclusively.[1] Specifically, the transgender movement is a hybrid movement in that it is simultaneously an independent, autonomous movement of its own *and* a constituent part of the LGBT movement. This hybrid status and the historical process by which the transgender movement became hybrid have a significant impact on NCTE's relationships to other organizations under the broad "LGBT" umbrella, as well as on the kinds of communicative work it succeeded and failed at doing. This chapter treats each of these three contexts in turn, helping make sense of *why* I observed the kinds of activities I did while in the field, and setting the stage for the rest of the book to unfold.

Throughout the chapter, I draw on my novel concept of "media imprinting" to organize the various ways that the media environment NCTE was established in and operated in during their early years shaped their approach to activism. My concept of media imprinting borrows heavily from organizational sociologist Arthur Stinchcombe's imprinting hypothesis, which posited that external environmental factors shape not only organizations' initial structures, but also cause those structures to persist over time.[2] Stinchcombe's original hypothesis focused on the industry level, describing why, for example, agriculture was typically performed by self-employed farmers using family labor at the time. Per his argument, agriculture was structured this way because that organizational system was dominant when the agricultural industry began. However, later research focused on the organization level, analyzing why individual organizations retain particular features reflective of the time they were founded. Summarizing this research, organization theorists Christopher Marquis and András Tilcsik defined imprinting as "a process whereby, during a brief period of susceptibility, a focal entity develops characteristics that reflect prominent features of the environment, and these characteristics continue to persist despite significant environmental changes in subsequent periods."[3]

Building on this line of theorizing, I define "media imprinting" as a process whereby an organization, at the time of its maturation, develops characteristics that reflect prominent features of the media environment. The media environment here is understood as consisting of not only the technological infrastructure dominant at the time, but also the place-based media ecology in which an organization operates and the distribution of communication labor that occurs within the organization's industry or field. Per my media imprinting argument, NCTE took on persistent characteristics reflective of (1) the digital media environment dominant when the organization began robust public communication work, (2) the clustering of news media outlets specializing in political news and analysis in Washington, DC, and (3) the public relations-oriented mass media work of the larger LGBT organizations that left other forms of communication work underdeveloped. The three contexts of this chapter address each point, respectively.

Temporal Context: The Golden Age of NCTE

For many people, the transgender movement is a brand-new social movement that emerged overnight around 2013. While it's true that the movement's emergence into public consciousness is a recent development, as with most movements that rapidly appear, it was a long time coming. For the sake of brevity, I won't trace the movement's entire history back to its roots in the 1950s.[4] However, to make sense of how and why NCTE arrived at its "golden age" in 2017–2018, it's important to begin when a truly national movement cohered in the 1990s.[5]

The 1990s were a crucial time for the transgender movement. Collectives of people across the country began to more consistently refer to themselves with the shared label we still use today—"transgender"—and began to form a more coherent community. The community was then largely connected by a circuit of regional social conferences and through community periodicals like *Chrysalis Quarterly* and *Transgender Tapestry*. This newly unified transgender community also began to regularly engage in political activism *as an identity group*. Organizations like Transgender Nation, Transexual Menace, and FTM Alliance were founded during this time, and transgender activists successfully lobbied Minnesota politicians to enact the first state-wide, transgender-inclusive non-discrimination law in 1993. Inspired by their victory in Minnesota, activists attempted to lobby the US Congress for transgender inclusion in the 1994 Employment Non-Discrimination Act (ENDA). However, the lack of a constant, agitative transgender presence in DC hindered the advancement of transgender rights, particularly because gay and lesbian rights organizations refused to push for trans inclusion in civil rights legislation. Thus, transgender activists agreed to institutionalize their movement in DC through an organization called the Gender Public Advocacy Coalition (GenderPAC) in November 1996.

The leadership of GenderPAC was entrusted to veteran activist Riki Wilchins and the organization was initially charged with the mission "to educate society on transgender issues and to advance a legislative agenda in Congress."[6] But Riki and GenderPAC quickly abandoned their mission of advocating for the transgender community, opting instead to advance a mission of "gender rights." This new mission decentered trans people in favor of freeing *all people* from the pressure to conform to gender stereotypes—from the football jock who is reprimanded for crying after a loss to the butch lesbian who is told to dress more femininely at work. GenderPAC's board of directors, which consisted of community leaders across the country, opposed this new direction, as did many in the trans community, and the organization publicly imploded in 2001. The collapse of GenderPAC left a power vacuum and a bevy of unmet advocacy needs for the community.

This political opportunity led to a flourishing of transgender organizations across the country between 2001 and 2003. They included the Transgender Law and Policy Institute (TLPI), the Sylvia Rivera Law Project (SRLP), and the Transgender Legal Defense and Education Fund (TLDEF), all in New York City, and the Transgender Law Center (TLC) in Oakland, California.[7] Among these new organizations, NCTE, founded in Washington, DC, in 2003 by Mara Keisling, had emerged by 2005 as the leader of the modern transgender movement. It became, to borrow political scientist Anthony Nownes' phrasing, "the dean of transgender rights organizations."[8]

NCTE's flagship status emerged in large part due to founder Mara Keisling's professional competencies, connections to other leading activists, and interest in cultivating a national network of support. Mara had made her name within transgender political advocacy at a local level. She ran the Statewide Pennsylvania Rights Coalition (SPARC), which pushed for transgender inclusion in the state hate crimes bill, among other legislative lobbying activities.[9] She traveled to transgender conferences, sharing her experiences and meeting with other activists to deepen their networks of support. At a conference in 2001, Creating Change—a broad LGBT policy conference run by the National LGBTQ Task Force—transgender advocates, including Mara and former GenderPAC board member Donna Cartwright, gathered for a day-long institute.[10] There Mara was introduced by Donna to Lisa Mottet, a cisgender lesbian working on transgender rights law at the Task Force, who later went on to become the organization's deputy director in 2013.[11] Lisa, like Donna, was impressed by Mara and the two worked to convince her to move to DC and found NCTE.[12] From there, Mara worked to earn buy-in from other prominent advocates to serve as board members and supporters, including Donna, who served as the first board chair; Diego Sanchez, a trans man and prominent figure in the Massachusetts Democratic Party, who would go on to serve as Senior Policy Advisor to Congressman Barney Frank; Andy Marra, an Asian-American trans woman from New York, who would go on to serve as executive director of TLDEF; Amanda Simpson, a corporate leader at the major defense contractor Raytheon, who went on to become the first transgender political appointee when President Obama appointed her to the Department of Defense; and Masen Davis, who ran FTM Alliance in Los Angeles and went on to become executive director of TLC and then CEO of the LGBT advocacy organization Freedom for All Americans.[13] Each of these figures saw that Mara's unique qualities suited her to running an organization like NCTE and threw their support behind her leadership.[14]

Mara's particular blend of political experience and glad-handing personality quickly thrust NCTE to the forefront of the transgender movement. Her political education began young, as her father was chief of staff to the governor of Pennsylvania. She pursued a PhD in American government at Harvard University before leaving for a successful career in political polling, including working for political campaigns and legislative lobbying efforts. After transitioning, she shifted her focus to activism. She led the Pennsylvania Gender Rights Coalition, as well as SPARC, fighting for trans-inclusive state legislation.[15] She also had the personality and demeanor to make her a charismatic leader both to trans people and among cisgender politicians. As Lisa characterized her in an interview, "She's quite funny and she just disarms people, and people want to be around her. So that magnetism that she has allows people to be drawn to her . . . including policymakers who still don't quite get it."[16] She also had the professional competencies to back up her claims to leadership. As Donna explained:

[S]he could create the impression somehow that there were three or five Maras—or Mara simulacrum or whatever—who were around because she could project herself in many different settings. She could lobby before Congress, she could talk to the media, she could go out there to the impromptu ... street-level memorial for a trans person who's been killed. She did all of that in those early years, and in that sense, I think, created a fuller personality for a trans organization.[17]

Mara's personal qualities then became directly associated with the image of NCTE, making the organization stand out as a competent and professional authority on transgender policy (which prior organizations like GenderPAC had failed to achieve) and as a leader among the cohort of emerging transgender movement organizations. Yet, Mara's Bugs Bunny-like ability to convincingly play several roles at a time did not change the fact that NCTE was effectively a one-woman show, which was simply not sustainable. By late 2007, NCTE had expanded slightly to a staff of three, as Mara was joined by Stephanie White, as managing director, and the organization's first communications manager, Justin Tanis. But that fall, NCTE's work was stretched far beyond what even three people could manage during what came to be called the "ENDA crisis."

In September 2007, Congressman Barney Frank, sponsor of the Employment Non-Discrimination Act (ENDA), split it into two separate bills. The first bill included only protections for sexual orientation, and the second one included only protections for gender identity and expression. His justification was that—having polled his Democratic colleagues about their support for ENDA—he felt confident a sexual-orientation-only bill would earn enough votes to pass, but trans-inclusion would drive away essential supporters. With no chance of passing a bill protecting only gender expression and identity, splitting ENDA was a calculated act of leaving trans people behind. The Human Rights Campaign (HRC), the largest LGBTQ rights organization in the country, immediately threw their full support behind the transgender-exclusive ENDA bill. In response, NCTE called leaders from other LGBTQ groups, securing seven agreements to sign a letter opposing the sidelining of trans people from ENDA. Within forty-eight hours, over one hundred organizations from around the country signed on, and by the end of the week, roughly three hundred groups had pledged their exclusive support to a trans-inclusive ENDA. The groups formed a coordinated campaign named United ENDA, which Mara headed.

On its surface, the United ENDA campaign failed. The two bills were not merged back together, and the trans-exclusive bill was passed by the House of Representatives (although it failed in the Senate). But the campaign achieved a significant goal for NCTE: it secured their place at the center of the transgender movement and in the machine of Washington social movement politics. The Democratic Party took note, quickly taking steps to incorporate NCTE's platform into their policy agenda. Most significantly, Chair of the Democratic National Committee Howard Dean appointed one of NCTE's founding board members, Diego Sanchez, to the DNC Platform Committee. In that capacity, Diego secured the inclusion of gender identity in nondiscrimination protections as a party priority. In Diego's words, the "gender identity part was no problem in the room because it followed the United ENDA exclamations of 'don't you dare think about taking out trans people.'"[18] As an apology for his actions on ENDA, Congressman Frank hired Diego as a senior policy advisor. In this capacity, he was able to reconcile relations between the congressman and the transgender movement and establish a collaborative relationship between Frank and NCTE on issues, including ID document policies.

With NCTE's status as a movement powerhouse established, the organization expanded. They hired policy counsel (and eventual Director of Policy) Harper Jean Tobin in 2009. Over the following few years, NCTE added mostly policy-oriented staff positions to support their ever-increasing workload. Then, in 2011, NCTE hired Vincent Villano as their new communications manager, elevating him to their first Director of Communications the following year. Vincent's arrival represented a huge expansion of NCTE's communication capacities and coincided with the widespread diffusion of social media, which left its lasting imprint on the organization's media work. As the public became more aware of trans people, NCTE's online traffic increased; 2011–2012 saw a one thousand percent increase in blog traffic and a doubling of Twitter followers.[19] Over that same time, NCTE mentions in mass media tripled as public attention to trans people skyrocketed. Much of the media attention was driven by outside factors, most notably Cher's transgender son, Chaz Bono, appearing on the popular reality television program *Dancing with the Stars*. But it was equally driven by the string of policy wins the movement was achieving, such as the trans-inclusive anti-discrimination laws passed in Connecticut, Hawaii, Massachusetts, and Nevada. NCTE succeeded in increasing their media prominence because of Vincent's professional competencies, developing new programs and practices for managing media work—many of which were imprinted on NCTE strategy long after his departure. NCTE had established itself as journalists' go-to authority on transgender social and political issues.[20]

Over the following years, NCTE steadily grew. Their staff and public standing swelled as they claimed further policy victories at the state and federal levels, and they became established partners for administration of President Barack Obama. Their media profile likewise increased as Mara became a regular feature in mass media news broadcasts on transgender issues. Then came a wave of unexpected public attention to trans people and the trans movement as *TIME* magazine declared the arrival of the "transgender tipping point" in their June 2014 cover story—which featured Mara.[21] Following this increased visibility, trans people became more prominent targets of conservative attacks. Across 2015 and 2016, numerous state legislatures proposed so-called bathroom bills that sought to criminalize transgender access to spaces of public accommodation. The most significant of these bills was the Public Facilities Privacy & Security Act (better known as HB2) in North Carolina, which Governor Pat McCrory signed into law in March 2016. The debate leading up to the law's passing and the blowback to its signing elicited significant attention in the national press. This attention made transgender people and their access to gendered spaces subjects of national conversation.[22] NCTE, accordingly, engaged in significant media work around HB2, including sending Mara to North Carolina to be arrested in a sit-in at the state legislative building.[23]

During the wave of bathroom bills, NCTE experienced significant internal changes. In the summer of 2015, NCTE's Policy Advisor for Racial and Economic Justice, Raffi Freedman-Gurspan, left the organization to become the first openly transgender staff member at the White House, working under President Obama. Later that same year, Vincent Villano left the organization, leaving NCTE without any communications staff. NCTE replaced him with three new staff members in three separate positions. In February 2016, NCTE hired Jay Wu, who had been a Press Assistant at the US Department of Health and Human Services, as their new Media Relations Manager, and they used Vincent's thirty-one-page exit memo detailing his policies and procedures as a how-to guide for the organization's media work.[24] In March, a mere seventy-two hours before the passage of HB2 in North Carolina, Rebecca Kling joined the organization as their Community Storytelling Advocate. In this role, she worked to train trans community members how to tell their personal stories in impactful ways that advanced NCTE's policy objectives, and to connect them with opportunities to do so. In July 2016, Jason Arrol joined NCTE as Digital Media Manager, running the organization's social media and serving as an in-house media content creator.

Jay, Rebecca, and (later) Jason worked together as NCTE's first Communications (Comms) team, spending much of their first year focusing on the unfolding crisis in North Carolina surrounding HB2. For Jay, that meant building on Vincent's established practices and developing more collaborative relationships with journalists at media outlets nationally and in North Carolina. For Rebecca, responding to HB2 required identifying trans people in North Carolina willing to speak publicly about their experiences, training them in storytelling and policy, and connecting those storytellers with policymakers and media outlets. (This program would become institutionalized over the following year and given the formal name of Voices for Trans Equality, or VTE.) Once Jason joined, he built out the social media side of NCTE's campaign against HB2 and created original graphics and video content so that NCTE could serve as their own primary source of information about the policy outside of mass and local media.

As this new Comms team began to fall into a rhythm of work that foreshadowed their eventual formal strategy, they began to operate more independently of the Policy team. Until this point, the policy shop had been the heart of the organization, and the Comms staff served as a megaphone for the Policy team's work. But now communication was becoming a strategic goal for NCTE. The Comms team worked in concert with the Policy staff on HB2, but they also worked parallel to them by taking on the momentous task of shaping public opinion on transgender rights. NCTE hired Eric Dyson as Director of Communications to supervise Jay and Jason in February 2017 and Raffi Freedman-Gurspan returned from the White House to supervise Rebecca as Director of External Relations in April 2017. Finally, shortly after I entered the field in the summer of 2017, NCTE hired Debi Jackson and DeShanna Neal—both cisgender mothers of transgender children—as family organizers to build out the Families for Trans Equality (FTE) program. FTE was a companion program to VTE that provided the same training and resources to the parents, guardians, and siblings of trans people (usually trans youth). Debi and DeShanna worked under Rebecca's supervision within the new department of Outreach & Education (O&E) that Raffi headed.

Beyond routinizing NCTE's team-based communication work, the fight over HB2 in North Carolina catalyzed the organization's expansion into new modes of political advocacy. NCTE was originally founded as a 501(c)

(3) nonprofit social justice organization. The legal classification of 501(c)(3) meant that NCTE served an ostensibly "educational" purpose where it concerned politics. As such, NCTE was legally limited in engaging in political lobbying. Additionally, they were legally prohibited from engaging in "political campaign" activities or partisan political speech.[25] The organization's political speech was therefore usually broad, focusing on specific policy concerns and on the material conditions faced by transgender people in the United States. NCTE's interactions with elected officials were limited to serving as informational resources. And the organization's interactions with media made no official endorsements or denouncements of elected officials, candidates, or political parties. However, after the series of bathroom bills swept the nation—especially after Governor McCrory went up for reelection following the passage of HB2—NCTE felt they needed an arm that *could* engage in partisan political speech. As Mara explained, it felt detrimental to NCTE's mission to not be able to say how people should vote if they want to protect trans rights.[26] In October 2017, NCTE launched a 501(c)(4) political advocacy organization called the NCTE Action Fund.[27] Through the Action Fund, they were able to endorse candidates, support or oppose ballot measures, ask candidates to make pledges on transgender issues, and post partisan political messages to their social media profiles. With these newly available activities, NCTE became an even bigger force in institutional politics.

The organization and launch of the Action Fund coincided with President Donald J. Trump's first year in office. He quickly made opposing transgender rights a cornerstone of his federal policy agenda. Particularly following the historic gains achieved under President Obama, Trump's agenda was a major setback for the movement, and it detrimentally impacted the everyday lives of at least one million trans people across the United States.[28] At the same time, President Trump's relentless assault on transgender people allowed NCTE as an organization and the transgender rights movement as a movement to newly engage within the mainstream of liberal politics. There was increased public interest in transgender issues among those who opposed Trumpian politics, and there was an attendant increase in public allyship for the trans community among previously apathetic liberals and progressives. As a result, NCTE was finally brought into the inner circle of the progressive coalition in DC, and mass media outlets began to run sympathetic stories about the trans community more regularly, depicting them as hapless victims of an antagonistic administration. Nowhere was the shift in public opinion more evident than in the public response to President Trump's ban on transgender military service. People who previously had not cared about transgender issues suddenly cared about them because they could be held up as exemplars of President Trump's social authoritarianism.

In the nine months between my two rounds of fieldwork at NCTE, Director of Communications Eric Dyson departed the organization, as did Digital Media Manager Jason Arrol. Veteran LGBTQ rights activist Dave Noble joined as an interim director until a permanent replacement (Jay Wu) was found. NCTE also hired Gillian Branstetter, a former journalist, as Media Relations Manager, and Laurel Powell, a former political staffer, as Rapid Response Communications Manager (later, and more accurately, retitled Digital Campaigns Manager). Their arrivals signaled an increasing prioritization and professionalization of communications work in the organization. NCTE's now-complete Comms team's work was quick and flexible, making their responses to incidents like the military ban much more successful. The value of this team and their partners in O&E was quickly evident in their ability to increase media attention and mobilize constituents.

I describe this period as the "golden age" of NCTE not because it was the time I was there and therefore it must have been the best. Rather, I do so because it was the time during which the organization exceeded every metric of success. NCTE had more staff than ever: twenty-two employees across five departments (Comms, Development, Operations, O&E, and Policy) and the executive office (see Table 2.1). They had a larger budget, with an annual revenue of over $3.8 million.[29] They also could be effective on both the policy front *and* the public front, and the teams responsible for each seamlessly coordinated with one another. NCTE was on the defensive from the Trump White House and conservative movement actors emboldened by his administration. Still, NCTE appeared more frequently in a greater number and variety of media outlets. They also had larger numbers of VTE and FTE members willing to expand their influence in the digital media environment. Perhaps most importantly, NCTE started to enjoy the benefits of a far more sympathetic public.

I also describe this period as the "golden age" of NCTE because it didn't last. Despite the staff at NCTE achieving incredible feats, the time I conducted fieldwork at NCTE was rife with internal tension. Long-simmering issues of racial justice boiled over and staff pressures for a union were met with heavy resistance from the executive leadership team of Mara and Lisa. At the heart of these tensions were a number of incidents involving the hiring and retention of staff of color, and the treatment of staff

Table 2.1. NCTE staff (by department) during the organization's peak in 2018

Department	Staff Member	Pronouns	Race/Ethnicity	Position
Executive Office	Mara Keisling[†]	she/her	White	Executive Director
	Lisa Mottet	she/her	White	Deputy Executive Director
	Dylan Yellowlees[†]	they/them	White	Executive Assistant
Communications	Dave Noble	he/him	White	Interim Communications Director
	Jay Wu[†]	they/them	East Asian	Deputy Communications Director, then Director of Communications
	Gillian Branstetter[†]	she/her	White	Media Relations Manager
	Laurel Powell[†]	she/her	White	Rapid Response Communications Manager, later retitled Digital Campaigns Manager
Development	Jami Westerhold	she/her	White	Director of Development
	Daniel Shad	he/him	Southwest Asian	Development Manager
	Lauren Dow	she/her	White	Executive Assistant, then Development Associate
	Alex Roberts[†]	he/him	Black	Workplace Inclusion Manager
Operations	Patrick Paschall	he/him	White	Director of Finance and Operations
	Tucker Duval[†]	he/him	White	Operations Manager
Outreach & Education	Raffi Freedman-Gurspan[†]	she/her	Indigenous/Latina	Director of External Relations
	Rebecca Kling[†]	she/her	White/Jewish	Education Program Director
	Debi Jackson	she/her	White	Family Organizer
	DeShanna Neal	she/her	Black	Family Organizer

Table 2.1. Continued

Department	Staff Member	Pronouns	Race/Ethnicity	Position
Policy	Harper Jean Tobin[†]	she/her	White	Director of Policy
	Arli Christian[†]	they/them or she/her	White	State Policy Director
	Ma'ayan Anafi[†]	—	—	Policy Counsel
	Luc Athayde-Rizzaro[†]	he/him or they/them	Latino	Policy Counsel
	Mateo De La Torre[†]	he/him	Latino	Racial and Economic Justice Policy Advocate

Note: Names and pronouns listed represent those used at the time I left the field. These may have changed in the intervening time. Staff member names marked with [†] identified as trans and/or nonbinary at the time I left the field.

of color during their time with the organization.[30] In one incident, Hope Giselle, a Black transgender woman with a long history of activism and a considerable public profile, was temporarily hired as an organizer for the TRANSform the Vote campaign, NCTE's get-out-the-vote effort. Within weeks, Hope left the organization following a day of closed-door meetings with Mara and Lisa, the contents of which were, of course, not shared with staff. In another incident that happened shortly after my departure from the field, Lissette Miller, a Black Nicaraguan trans person hired to serve as an outreach coordinator for the 2020 US Transgender Survey, was fired without cause.[31] These incidences were the latest in a longstanding pattern of race-based retention issues. As staff members of NCTE wrote in an open letter published in *Out* magazine:

> Since 2012, the organization has watched at least 35 employees begin and end employment, 21 of whom are people of color. Fourteen of those employees expressed strong complaints of racism within the organization, including by expressing those feelings to NCTE's board of directors. At least four people of color were told to sign nondisclosure agreements; no white former staff member of NCTE has reported doing the same.[32]

These racial inequities produced several forms of harm. First, they harmed the individual staff members of color who were mistreated during their employment and in their terminations. Second, they harmed the wider staff collective, who struggled to navigate the racial tensions produced by executive leadership as they worked together to center racial justice in their teams' programs. Finally, they harmed the organization's relationships with other movement organizations (especially organizations focusing on racial justice) and the transgender public it claimed to represent (especially trans people of color whose trust in the organization was rightly diminished).

These issues were a partial impetus for the staff's unionization efforts, which they pursued through the Nonprofit Professional Employees Union (NPEU). While executive leadership publicly claimed to support the formation of a union, their actions indicated otherwise. They dragged out the process of voluntary recognition and made cosmetic changes to office culture as a means of convincing staff that a union wasn't necessary.[33] In August 2019, following Lissette's dismissal, staff staged a walkout in protest, refusing to attend the all-staff meeting Mara called to discuss the firing.[34] The next month, discouraged by leadership's lack of action following the walkout and their decision to hire a crisis communications firm, staff formally requested Mara and Lisa submit a timeline for their departure from the organization within the next eighteen months—a request that was forwarded to the Board.[35] Rather than comply with the request, however, Mara and Lisa countered with an offer for staff to take a ten-week buyout. When only a few staff members accepted this severance package,[36] Mara and Lisa extended the offer, clearly indicating their desire to rid themselves of the organizing staff members rather than address their concerns. Nearly all staff members accepted this extended offer. The organization was left with only Mara, Lisa, the new Deputy Executive Director for Policy and Action Rodrigo Heng-Lehtinen, two cisgender members of the Development team, one cisgender member of the Operations teams, and Policy Director Harper Jean Tobin, who would ultimately resign shortly before Christmas 2019.[37]

Publicly, Mara and Lisa framed the buyout as a generous act. As they presented it, executive leadership advanced a new long-term strategic plan to "modernize [NCTE's] operations," including its race-based practices. Staff who "disagreed with the new direction were given the chance to accept buyouts."[38] The NPEU responded with an unfair labor practice charge against NCTE, arguing that the discharging of all staff in the bargaining unit constituted retaliation.[39] A month later, 440 transgender community leaders published an open letter in *Out* condemning NCTE,[40] shattering what remaining public trust the organization held. By mid-December, the now-six-member NCTE unveiled "The Plan Forward," a document detailing plans to recruit new staff; hire "diversity, equity and inclusion coaches"; and scale up policy work back to their former capacity.[41] The success of that plan remains to be seen, even as of this book's writing.

The precipitous decline of NCTE made the golden era I witnessed, and that I analyze in this book, special. Unfortunately, it is unlikely to be duplicated because NCTE is no longer the same organization. And beyond the internal changes at NCTE, the transgender community's place in American society has evolved since December 2018, when I left the organization. The specific temporal context of my observations made the work I describe and theorize in this book possible and greatly enhanced its success. And while the dynamics of activism in the networked public sphere I've laid out apply more widely than at NCTE, the specific events that informed my argument were also shaped by the place in which they occurred.

Geographic Context: The View from Inside the Beltway

In dissecting Qatari news company Al Jazeera's failure to break into the US market, global media scholar Will Youmans argued that each city the company attempted to establish bureaus in constituted a "media port of entry."[42] Each city was its own "media capital" in which media companies of the same type cluster. Washington, DC, is the capital of political news media; New York City is the capital of broadcast news and magazine publishing; and San Francisco, the epicenter of Silicon Valley, is the capital of digital-first media. But each of these cities, beyond being home to a particular sector of the media industries, has its own "anthropological terrain." That is, they each have "unique characters, histories, and social, cultural, and political currents that differentiate them in total from other places."[43] Each of these capitals serves as a media port of entry for foreign media companies, like Al Jazeera, attempting to enter the US market. What determines a company's success is how well they assimilate into the anthropological terrain of their port of entry.

Youmans' concept of media ports of entry helps explain how the geographic context in which a social movement organization operates shapes their forms of activism and how successful they are at attaining their goals.

For example, queer media theorist Vincent Doyle explained that the gay and lesbian media advocacy organization GLAAD had eleven different chapters, with two main ones in New York City (GLAAD/NY) and Los Angeles (GLAAD/LA).[44] Each chapter did work based on the kinds of media companies located in their respective cities. GLAAD/NY primarily focused on pressuring news media organizations to change their reporting on gays and lesbians, while GLAAD/LA pressured film and television studios to improve the quantity and quality of gay and lesbian representations in entertainment media. Eventually, however, the NY and LA chapters voted to merge into one national organization and Los Angeles became their unified headquarters. Accordingly, the organization increasingly focused on the entertainment industry and all but ceased pressuring the news media. In short, they were imprinted by their place-based media ecology.

NCTE was founded in Washington, DC, because the transgender movement needed proximity to federal policymakers and a presence on the national political stage. After the implosion of GenderPAC, the movement only had local organizations scattered across the country. NCTE's presence in DC meant their work focused almost exclusively on formal politics with a "capital P"—institutional politics—rather than the still-very-important lowercase-p politics—the informal politics of everyday life. After all, DC is an industry town, and their industry is capital-P politics. And DC is the media capital for politics, as reflected in the news media outlets specializing in political news and analysis that cluster in the city. Consequently, NCTE's activism targeted news outlets and other media specializing in the production and distribution of political information. Only rarely and under special circumstances did NCTE engage with entertainment media.

At a deeper level, NCTE's activism was shaped by their location in Washington because NCTE assimilated into that anthropological terrain. This political media capital shaped everything about the organization, from what stories counted as "newsworthy" to which narratives attracted journalists' attention and how they navigated the DC-specific social dynamics that governed news-making processes inside the Beltway.[45] As journalism scholar Nikki Usher has argued, place exerts a major structuring influence on newsmaking. Place provides the material setting for news, serving as a "location for action" for the stories it tells. Place also sets where journalistic action is taken, and where social meanings are made. Journalists, audiences, and institutions interact within these settings, build news-gathering routines, and construct shared cultural meanings. Place even exercises cultural, economic, and symbolic power by situating journalism's relationship with social and political institutions, distributions of resources, economic imperatives, and flows of capital.[46] Thus, in shaping the political news media that congregate in and around the capital, DC also shaped NCTE's activism in important ways as they sought to assimilate into the norms that drove this media capital.

The influence of Washington, DC, as a physical setting and as a cultural context was evident in NCTE's activism. For example, NCTE drew on the symbolic power of physical space in their activism. DC contains buildings, monuments, and other physical markers of political power that carry material and symbolic weight. They are where power is exercised, and they visually represent the power vested in government. Consequently, these locations have become common stages for political activism and backdrops for political news stories.[47] When staging their activism, NCTE often planned events that used these landmarks as centerpieces. For instance, NCTE held rallies and protests in Lafayette Square in front of the North Lawn of the White House, so that the White House could be seen in the background. In other protest events, NCTE occupied the atriums of congressional office buildings, demonstrated on the lawns of Capitol Hill in the shadow of Congress, rallied on the steps of the Supreme Court, and unfurled a transgender pride flag on the steps of the Lincoln Memorial. The organization even held Facebook Live broadcasts outside the buildings of federal agencies like Immigration and Customs Enforcement (ICE). In an interesting merger of institutional political advocacy and consumer activism, NCTE digitally projected pro-transgender messages of resistance onto the side of the Trump International Hotel in Federal Triangle. NCTE's media activism leveraged the physical-symbolic power of place to reinforce the organization's proximity and access to the political institutions that govern the nation. Simultaneously, this physical-symbolic power made NCTE's activism more newsworthy by playing into political news media's penchant for spectacular stories.

Another notable way that DC geographically and culturally shaped NCTE's activism was the central role of networking in achieving political influence. Like most "industry towns," Washington has a notable "networking culture." Within such a culture, the size and diversity of a person's interpersonal networks of professional contacts determine their level of power and importance.[48] Accordingly, networking is the central organizing social activity for the city. As anyone who has lived in DC will tell you, every conversation you have with a new person will start with a discussion of what you do for work and how many people you know in common—even if you're just trying to hang out at a bar or celebrate a friend's birthday. This networking dynamic most famously plays out among congressional staffers and other government employees trying to climb the political ladder,[49] but it's just as common among activists working in social movement organizations. Within NCTE's activism, DC-style networking resulted in a broad approach to coalitional politics, with the organization attaching their name to a wide array of amicus curiae briefs and sign-on letters from partner organizations related to different political issues.[50] In return, NCTE's own briefs and sign-on letters received a wealth of support from a diverse set of movement organizations. Their support established NCTE as belonging to a particular class of activists and as a key player in the progressive coalition. Such a reputation ensured their own activities had further reach in times of need because network contacts could quickly close rank with them.

NCTE also deeply invested in building networks with congressional staffers and federal agency staff to ensure access to important policy-making processes. Often networks were built through queer-centric networking events and employee resource groups, which helped NCTE staff meet and build relationships with government employees who could be resources later. Other times, the relationships were a bit more personal. For example, NCTE's Director of Development Jami Westerhold was married to a senior policy advisor in the office of Congressman Dan Kildee, providing an "in" on Capitol Hill. Such network contacts were crucial to NCTE responding to the turmoil of the Trump administration's anti-trans agenda. For example, NCTE was alerted by an insider that the Trump administration planned to roll back Section 1557 of the Affordable Care Act, which provided transgender people federal protections from discrimination in health care. This heads-up allowed NCTE to coordinate a "Protect Trans Health" campaign opposing the action for *over ten months* before the planned rollback was even announced. In turn, the need to build and maintain these relationships influenced how NCTE engaged in activism on certain issues. For example, when public panic broke out over whether trans people were being denied gender marker changes on their passports, NCTE wanted to ensure they didn't harm their ability to wield influence later. They checked with their contacts at the State Department before publicly commenting.

In still other cases, NCTE built networks through the so-called revolving door of politics. Most commonly, the "revolving door" describes the tendency for congressional staff to leave government service to work as lobbyists and sometimes return to government service later, but the same dynamic occurs in the advocacy sector.[51] Staff often leave social movement organizations to take positions on the Hill or in the administration. They then leave at the end of a term and return to their movement or to become regular political commentators for the Washington press corps. For example, as I noted previously, Raffi Freedman-Gurspan left NCTE to join the Obama White House, only to later rejoin NCTE (bringing with her a stunning network of government connections), before finally leaving NCTE again in 2018 to join the National Democratic Redistricting Committee. Raffi's network connections improved NCTE's ability to influence politicians and shaped how they engaged in activism.

While several of the ways that DC geographically and culturally shaped NCTE's activism were neither good nor bad from a normative perspective, some were normatively bad. Most notably, the city of Washington, DC, is a city divided. There are, in many ways, two cities. One is the predominantly white and universally privileged world of capital-P politics that I have already described and that most people think of when they think about Washington. The other is the predominantly Black and historically disenfranchised community native to the city, which has its own rich and distinct culture. The former is built upon geographic, social, cultural, political, and economic segregation from the latter and, more specifically, on the establishment of a Black working underclass that keeps the city running.[52] When I say that NCTE assimilated into DC's anthropological terrain, I necessarily mean they assimilated into the norms of the first city I described, including adopting the norms of white professionalism and hierarchical power structures that are required by the city's political industry and are premised on racial inequality.[53] Indeed, NCTE's assimilation to these norms allowed the organization to operate at a breakneck pace within the elite power system, but it also, as I described earlier in this chapter, marginalized their employees of color and ultimately led to the organization's collapse.

DC's cultural context also shaped NCTE's media work, as they adapted their communications to suit political journalists' proclivity for punditry. Pundits are expected to give facts meaning by explaining, interpreting, and making predictions based on them.[54] NCTE often fulfilled this pundit role by donning the mantle of activist-as-analyst for media outlets loathe to dive into the intricacies of transgender policy on their own. The organization's punditry most commonly took the form of a response when a law or policy was announced or leaked. A journalist would contact NCTE's Media

Relations Manager Gillian Branstetter with a request for a quote or an interview, and she would connect the journalist with one of NCTE's policy staff or with Mara. The NCTE spokesperson would explain to the journalist what the law or policy ostensibly did, discuss how or why that law or policy was relevant to trans people, contextualize the law or policy, and speculate about its likely effects on the trans community. The journalist would then assemble a completed story in which NCTE interpreted transgender politics for a public often ignorant of and apathetic to transgender issues. For instance, a leaked memo emerged from the Trump administration's Department of Health and Human Services detailing plans to change the legal definition of sex in a manner that would "define transgender people out of existence."[55] Gillian was inundated with reporter requests for someone to explain the meaning of the administration's decision. One such request came from *MSNBC*, which aired an interview with Director of External Relations Raffi, in which she characterized the leaked memo as part of a pattern of targeted harassment by the Trump administration and predicted the failure of the proposed policy if it was brought before the courts. This punditry procedure became routinized for NCTE, and determined which topics NCTE regularly spoke on, as well as how they discussed issues facing the trans community.

NCTE's location in DC led them to primarily focus on the news media that reported on national politics in ways that suited the culture of the city, but this place-based media logic also carried over into the communications work they did in local media markets across the country *outside* DC. In these places, like in DC, they focused almost exclusively on the "informational" media serving each locale. That is, NCTE focused on local news broadcasts, local and community newspapers, and local talk radio stations rather than on local interest magazines, religious broadcasts, and lifestyle media. For example, when Executive Director Mara traveled to Kalamazoo, Michigan, NCTE booked her on the local NPR affiliate WMUK to discuss the state of transgender equality.[56] Because of NCTE's acclimation to DC media culture, they considered these media most relevant. Moreover, NCTE mimicked DC-based political journalists' tendency to address local needs and interests through a national political lens, attempting to balance, as Usher put it, "where the Beltway and the Heartland meet."[57] Of course, NCTE cared about the political specificities of each locale, but at the end of the day, their media work attempted to ensure that local political stories were made into exemplary instances of national political currents, and conversely that national political stories were made into explanations for why local events were happening.

Within DC, dynamics were also changing. Newsrooms went virtual, eschewing physical offices for online collaborative software like Slack. In response, journalists for major press outlets became freelancers writing from their homes or rented co-working spaces.[58] The "Washington press corps" became much less DC-based. NCTE frequently worked with national political reporters who were only actually in the city once or twice each year. Yet even amidst these transformations, you couldn't throw a stone in DC without hitting at least one journalist. NCTE did everything they could to tap into this professional network, particularly the surprisingly large and tight-knit network of queer reporters in the city.[59] For instance, Media Relations Manager Gillian spent many of her early days at NCTE setting up coffee meetings with reporters, such as Caitlin Emma at *Politico*, Chris Johnson at the *Washington Blade*, and trans journalist Katelyn Burns at *Rewire News Group*, to build out a network of connections who could be counted on to include NCTE's work in their reporting. Once NCTE moved into their new offices on K Street, they were also a mere block away from *Vox*'s DC headquarters. So, when Gillian had the chance to visit their offices with State Policy Director Arli Christian, who was being interviewed on camera, she had the video producer give us a tour and tell us about *Vox*'s work. At the end of the interview, Gillian spoke with the producer about different projects he was working on that she could help provide a "trans angle" on. From then on, *Vox* was not just NCTE's neighbor—they were a network connection waiting to be tapped. In this way, geographic proximity became social proximity, and these social relationships could be used to achieve organizational goals.

All these DC-specific network dynamics combined to produce a particular approach to communication-focused activism distinct from that of other organizations in other movements or in other cities. NCTE's activism was distinct from Los Angeles-based LGBTQ media advocacy organization GLAAD. GLAAD's work was centered around pre-release consultation with entertainment media companies to ensure the positive representation of LGBTQ people.[60] NCTE's activism was also quite different from the Asian Pacific American Media Coalition, whose work focused on using media policy as a lever of influence.[61] Of course, as this book details in depth, NCTE's activism also extended far beyond the domain of mass political news media. However, NCTE's activism was shaped and continually informed by their presence in Washington, DC. The imprinting of DC culture on the organization led to an enduring emphasis on the media that constituted people's political information networks and a particular approach to discussing the issues trans people faced.

Movement Context: The Promise and Perils of Being a Hybrid Social Movement

As I noted toward the beginning of this chapter, NCTE was founded in the same period (2001–2003) as other transgender organizations, including the Transgender Law Center and the Transgender Legal Defense and Education Fund. These organizations collaboratively advanced transgender rights initiatives across the country, forging a network that birthed what I have described elsewhere as the "modern transgender movement."[62] The modern transgender movement was independent of (and often acted in opposition to) the LGB movement, from which trans people were excluded.[63] For several years, the independent transgender movement worked to shore up its relationships with other civil rights movements, like the women's movement, and to build small, mostly local, institutional power.

While the transgender movement achieved modest successes on their own, the leaders of the movement realized that they could be more effective if they could persuade the LGB movement to advocate for their needs, as the LGB movement had amassed more resources and a greater degree of institutional power over their longer history. Accordingly, much of the transgender movement's independent operations focused on transforming the policy positions and advocacy practices of the LGB movement. As the largest LGB movement organization and the main driver behind federal gay rights legislation, HRC was the ultimate target of the trans movement's inclusion efforts. Eventually, in August 2004, HRC's board of directors voted to only support the Employment Non-Discrimination Act (ENDA) if it were trans-inclusive moving forward, and the organization changed its mission statement to include trans people. It was a small victory, though, considering HRC made no such promises about the federal hate crimes bill they were pursuing, nor any pro-transgender sub-national legislative and policy efforts. Moreover, even after including transgender people in their mission statement, HRC lobbyists played Janus. They met with congressional staff alongside representatives from transgender movement organizations (most often NCTE) and professed their support for trans-inclusive legislation. Then they returned to those same congressional staff later and told them they did not *actually* support trans inclusion.[64] The transgender movement organizations, for their part, were not ignorant of HRC's duplicitousness. They were aware of the tenuous relationship they had to the LGB movement and worked toward trans inclusion in LGB policy advocacy alongside building up their own movement power and their own policy positions. As Mara explained in an interview:

> We were insisting on there being a trans movement *and* we were insisting on the gay rights movement being an LGBT movement—and that the T be a real part of it. But we were still insisting that there be a trans movement. That LGBT organizations exist, but that there be trans organizations.[65]

The transgender movement tried to derive as much benefit from the LGB movement as possible, but transgender movement success would not look like LGB movement success, so it needed to stand on its own two feet.

When the "ENDA crisis" I described earlier in the chapter hit, following Congressman Barney Frank's announcement that he was splitting ENDA into two separate bills—one including only sexual orientation and another including only gender identity—the transgender movement's power was put to the test. The United ENDA campaign, headed by Mara and NCTE, united transgender organizations to oppose the move, but it also brought approximately three hundred LGB groups from across the country together to oppose Congressman Frank and to oppose HRC for supporting him. In the aftermath of the crisis, in which HRC's standing within the LGB movement took a massive hit, LGB organizations more earnestly became LGBT organizations. They brought transgender rights into the fold and included transgender organizations in their alliance system. But while transgender movement organizations were eager to work with the newly LGBT groups to expand their power base, they remained fundamentally mistrustful of them. The transgender movement became what I have called a "hybrid movement"—a movement that identifies with and operates within multiple social movement fields simultaneously and non-exclusively.[66] Specifically, the transgender movement is a hybrid movement in that it is simultaneously an independent, autonomous movement *and* a constituent part of the LGBT movement; it comprises its own field of movement organizations *and* it participates in the field of LGBT movement organizations.

Movement hybridity was a strategic necessity for the transgender movement. Without participating in the LGBT movement, they would have fewer resources and less access to political institutions. However, without independence they could not trust their interests would be represented. But hybridity created significant strategic challenges, as well. Specifically, transgender movement organizations (most often NCTE) had to jockey with the far larger LGBT organizations, like HRC and GLAAD, for public recognition and authority as spokespeople for the transgender community. In particular, HRC was constantly overstepping boundaries trying to claim ownership over all things transgender, even when they had done little to actually advance transgender rights. For example, when a coalition of organizations led by Equality North Carolina successfully campaigned for the overturn of HB2 (with quiet, on-the-ground support from NCTE), HRC parachuted into North Carolina to hold a press conference claiming victory.[67] In another instance I witnessed firsthand, NCTE held a rally in front of the White House to protest the memo leaked from Trump's HHS detailing plans to "define transgender out of existence." HRC showed up with a small army of staff and interns carrying large signs emblazoned with their logo. They immediately posted themselves directly behind the podium, in front of NCTE's banner.[68] It looked like an HRC rally on television broadcasts, despite the fact they had not organized it. So, in some cases, participating in the LGBT movement was an advantage for the transgender movement because it provided resources. In other cases, it was a disadvantage because it cost the trans movement ownership and authority over their issues.

This tenuous hybridity emerged more-or-less immediately following the ENDA crisis in 2008, but the legalization of marriage equality by the Supreme Court in 2015 exacerbated things. LGBT movement organizations like HRC had justified their existence and obtained funding on the fight for marriage equality. With marriage equality now the law of the land, these groups needed new fights on which to justify their existence and fundraise. The arrival of the so-called transgender tipping point the year before marriage equality provided them with a much-needed public purpose. But the work these organizations did on transgender issues was more public relations than it was activism. They avoided hiring more transgender staff and refused to add programs dedicated to transgender rights. They didn't even build meaningful relationships with transgender communities to collectively fight for change. Instead, they hired a few high-profile transgender spokespeople and began regularly featuring transgender rights battles in their press releases and fundraising appeals.

The apparent transformation of LGB movement organizations to LGBT organizations worked on the press. Journalists increasingly turned to these far larger organizations for commentary and insight on transgender rights issues. Their cisgender constituencies continued to financially support these organizations as expressions of solidarity with their transgender siblings. But transgender community members and movement organizations weren't persuaded. Many of the trans and trans-adjacent individuals recruited by LGBT organizations to work on transgender advocacy quickly left when they realized they couldn't do meaningful work, joining organizations like NCTE instead. For example, Debi Jackson and DeShanna Neal were originally recruited in 2016 to establish HRC's "Parents for Transgender Equality National Council," which was to train and mobilize parents of trans children to fight against policies targeting trans youth, much like NCTE's Families for Trans Equality (FTE) program. It quickly became apparent to them, and to other parents involved, that HRC was only interested in treating them as brand ambassadors and including their stories in fundraising emails. When the parents pushed to do actual activism, HRC ignored them. So, Debi and DeShanna resigned from HRC's Council, asked HRC to remove all the promotional materials containing their names and pictures (as well as those of their children), and joined NCTE as family organizers. In their roles leading FTE, they could actually do the kinds of work they thought the National Council was going to welcome.[69] These kinds of migrations became common, leading to an influx of talent at transgender movement organizations.

The problem remained that the press, particularly national news media, often accepted the authority of LGBT movement organizations on trans issues even when the trans community didn't. There was a robust trans movement with its own organizations, but the press didn't always turn to them. It thus became a problem for the movement that *trans voices* weren't being heard on *trans issues*; "LGBT" voices were speaking over them. These voices always discussed transgender rights issues as "LGBT rights" issues, obscuring their trans-specific nature. The problem of LGBT voices drowning out trans voices became so persistent that staff at NCTE expressed excitement when news headlines about trans rights issues expressly mentioned "transgender" in the headline instead of "LGBT." Of course, as I'll continue to demonstrate throughout this book, NCTE often succeeded at influencing the national news media. In fact, they were stunningly successful in many instances. They just didn't hold as much of a monopoly on press influence as one might expect of the leading organization in the transgender movement. The fact they had to share control over the national media conversation caused them to innovate and find their own avenues of influence. Specifically, it led NCTE to invest in working with local and community media outlets (Chapter 4) and in the often invisible, but nonetheless influential work of building a mobilizable base of communications-trained trans people across the country (Chapter 5).

In contrast to the public relations-oriented mass media work of the larger LGBT organizations like HRC (dealing with news media) and GLAAD (dealing with entertainment media), NCTE built out a multipronged approach to communicative activism that sowed influence throughout the American communication system. This multipronged approach produced NCTE's distinctive focus on "trans voices," which prioritized the cumulative sociopolitical effects of mass transgender visibility over the political benefits of heightened visibility for themselves as an organization. However, if the transgender movement hadn't been pressured to contend with national LGBT organizations' mass media dominance, they likely wouldn't have taken such an approach. In short, the hybrid nature of the transgender movement imprinted upon NCTE's activism as it shaped and constrained the avenues of influence most open to them.

Conclusion

The three contexts discussed in this chapter shaped NCTE's activism by informing the development of the communication strategies this book analyzes. The temporal context of the 2017–2018 period during which I was at NCTE informed my observations because it was the "golden age" of NCTE. During this time, NCTE had the largest staff in its history, and the most devoted to media and communications work. It was also operating at the peak of the transgender movement's visibility, while fighting against a highly unpopular presidential administration that was targeting trans people. These qualities were distinct to this period, meaning that I was observing NCTE when they were able to engage in a greater number of communicative activities successfully.

The geographic context of Washington, DC, informed the activism NCTE pursued and the approaches to communication they took as the organization assimilated to the anthropological terrain of the city. DC is the media capital for the national political press. Accordingly, NCTE shaped their communication practices around the norms and priorities of the mass news media. This included driving which media outlets NCTE considered relevant targets for their activism, which issues were worth engaging on, and which narrative qualities influenced journalists. NCTE's proximity to centers of national political power also shaped their activism, as they needed to conduct their activism while maintaining the social and political relationships necessary to have influence in the city. These challenges gave NCTE's activism a distinct flavor that set them apart from other organizations in cities whose physical and cultural environments produced different organizational styles.

Finally, NCTE's activism was shaped by the broader context of the transgender movement. That is, NCTE's work was shaped by the fact the transgender movement was a "hybrid movement"—simultaneously its own independent, autonomous movement *and* a constituent part of the LGBT movement. NCTE needed to work around the large LGBT organizations that tried to claim ownership of trans issues in the wake of marriage equality. It was forced to capitalize on the benefits of alliance with LGBT organizations while also resisting being steamrolled by those same organizations. They carved out as much influence over mass media as they could, while also working to control the local and community media and the interpersonal networks that LGBT organizations largely ignored.

Taken together, these three contexts illustrate how NCTE was shaped by media imprinting, causing NCTE to engage in the forms of activism I outlined in the previous chapter and unpack in stages in the following three chapters. Building on this initial understanding of *why* I observed what I did while in the field, the next chapter considers NCTE's work targeting mass media outlets. It explores how and why mass media remained a significant focus of the organization's activism, even in a technological environment in which mass media were increasingly decentered as the media of politics, and in a political environment in which the transgender movement faced countless challenges (from both allies and opponents) to influencing mass media.

3

How Mass Media Still Matter

For many people, activism is synonymous with social media. When they imagine an activist, they think of someone participating in hashtag campaigns like #MeToo, posting links to petitions from websites like Change.org, and changing their profile pictures and social media banners to widely shared activist symbols like the raised fist. To be fair, when you sit in meetings at activist organizations, you'll hear discussion about how to maximize social media engagement, increase follower counts, and "go viral." Social media are widely conceptualized by professionals, academics, and laypersons as *the media* of activism. Yet, even in this age of social media dominance, mass media figure prominently in activists' goals. When they use media to affect change on a priority issue, their first objective is to get their issue on CNN or the front page of the *New York Times*.[1] Regardless of the issue, activists assume that visibility in mass media will change public opinion and influence policymakers.

The problem is that mass media visibility is hardly the silver bullet solution activists think it is. As political sociologist Sarah Sobieraj has thoroughly demonstrated, activists' efforts to secure mass media representation are largely futile because journalists don't want to reward what they view as "calculated media work," and the failed pursuit of media attention often comes at the expense of other, potentially more impactful, activities.[2] Even when activists do attract mass media attention, it's often not particularly effective at driving desired policy outcomes. Yes, mass media help "set the agenda" for policymakers, but mass media alone is unlikely to persuade them to adopt activists' preferred solutions or implement changes.[3] On top of that, negative media attention can be disastrous for movements' ability to achieve their goals.[4] So, if mass media attention is hard to get and not particularly effective, why do activists still expend so much effort targeting mass media in their pursuit of sociopolitical change?

Before setting foot in the National Center for Transgender Equality (NCTE), I had a hunch about what the answer was. I reckoned that activists were driven not by a genuine belief that they could sway public opinion

Voices for Transgender Equality. Thomas J Billard, Oxford University Press. © Thomas J Billard 2024.
DOI: 10.1093/oso/9780197695425.003.0003

through mass media, but by a desire for "symbolic legitimation." A long literature of communication research has argued that mass media serve a legitimating function in society. Mass media ordain certain issues and identities as worthy of consideration and cast others as irrelevant.[5] Drawing on my own previous research, which showed that mass news media coverage often delegitimated transgender claims in the political arena, I suspected that trans activists fought for positive mass media attention as an appeal to that old world order of mediated significance.[6] Of course, in the digital age mass media no longer hold the monopoly on legitimation they once did; issues often ascend to social and political prominence through the digital media sphere.[7] But in the same way that journalists at the *New York Times* still value the symbolic weight of placement on the front page of the print newspaper because of what it represents historically,[8] I hypothesized transgender activists would value mass media attention. I believed that mass media could symbolically legitimate this new, emergent movement and the marginal and poorly understood identities it represented. If I was right, then activists' continued and ineffectual pursuit of mass media wouldn't be some nonsensical whim. It would be a deliberate choice guided by a clear and strategic logic of symbolic legitimation.

Quickly after arriving at NCTE, I realized my reckoning was wrong—and so was much of the extant theorizing on contemporary mass media-focused activism. As I began to see in my daily observations, mass media were less central to NCTE's communications work than I expected. NCTE's mass media work also remained strategically important for material, not just symbolic, reasons. After tossing my hypotheses aside, I returned to political communication scholar Andrew Chadwick's contention that the "old" media of "television, radio, and newspapers are still, given the size of their audiences and their centrality to public life, rightly referred to as 'mainstream.'"[9] Of course, "new" media are claiming a space in the media system as unlikely purveyors of news, developing a "new mainstream" that extends beyond mass media. But mass media are also adjusting to fit this new mainstream by "adapting, evolving, and renewing their channels of delivery, working practices, and audiences."[10] Given the success of their adaptations, evolutions, and renewals, mass media remain central powerbrokers in a complex and dynamic communication system that includes "new" media.

Once I considered the idea that mass media remain central powerbrokers in the contemporary media system, NCTE's activities began to make more sense. NCTE didn't assume mass media were a silver bullet that could reach "the public." Rather, mass media influenced the rest of the communication system, and they were deeply interpenetrated with other forms of media, such as local and community media and social media. If NCTE ignored mass media in their communicative activism, open pathways to public discourse would be exploited by opponents and competitive allies. Thus, to control the messages circulating in the communication system, they needed to maintain control over mass media discourses. But to influence mass media required leveraging the tools of digital media in new and often unexpected ways.

This chapter explores the organizing logic of NCTE's mass media-focused activism. It explains how mass media strategies fit into NCTE's broader approach to making change in the networked public sphere. Some of these activities were mere continuations of best practices inherited from mass media activists of yore, while others innovated on these strategies to enhance their efficacy in the digital media environment. Still other activities were wholly new, developed to suit the new relationships between mass media and social movements enabled by the chimaeric media system. Ultimately, I argue that managing mass media was necessary to ensure that the communication system's central organ was not circulating messages harmful to the transgender movement into the broader communication system and, if at all possible, was instead promoting the flow of pro-transgender messages to the various communicative avenues influenced by mass media.[11] At the same time, managing mass media required managing other domains of the communication system, such as local and community media and social networks, which exerted a surprising degree of reciprocal influence on the content of mass media.

The Mass Media–Movement Relationship

In his foundational work on movement–media relations, media sociologist Todd Gitlin portrayed a media system that could easily be confused for our current one.[12] The media system had recently been transformed by technological changes and institutional consolidation, which increased the speed and efficiency of communicating messages to the broad public. Suddenly "floodlit" by this new system, movements needed to change their means and modes of communication to successfully affect the social and political order.[13] Gitlin was discussing broadcast television, though, decades before the advent of social media. For him, the commercial nature of mass news media and the attendant profit-oriented practices of newsmaking precluded certain types of visibility for social movements. Mass news media would never carry social movements' critical messages about the dominant order, but rather would always marginalize them and portray them as dangerous. They would engage in "ideological domestication . . . taming and isolating ideological threats to the system," only incorporating the critiques of movement actors who betrayed their core radical identities to be more palatable to the system that mass media worked to protect.[14]

Feminist media theorist Bernadette Barker-Plummer aptly called this understanding of movement–media relations the "strong hegemony" model, and it dominated critical studies of media and political activism for decades.[15] However, the strong hegemony model was built on a weak empirical foundation and a rigid theoretical worldview. Although Gitlin justified his model through an impassioned analysis of the New Left, analyzing how mass news media marginalized the concerns of Students for a Democratic Society, scholars studying other social movements compellingly illustrated that movements often hold far more power than the strong hegemony model suggests.[16] To more accurately characterize the dynamics observed in these movements, Barker-Plummer offered an alternative "dialogic" model that describes the sustained patterns of collaborative interaction among social movement actors and mass media actors that form movement–media relationships.[17] According to her model, social movements and mass media enter into strategic relationships in which they try to understand and employ one another's discourses. Journalists try to understand social movements' messages so that they can incorporate their perspectives into their social and political reporting, while social movement organizations try to learn journalists' storytelling conventions so that they can craft messages that fit into their reporting. Over time, these two sets of actors form mutual dependencies; journalists become dependent upon social movements for newsworthy information, and social movements become dependent upon journalists for the transmission of their messages to the public.[18]

Most research on social movements and media activism has produced findings consistent with Barker-Plummer's dialogic model. If social movements succeed in building dialogic relationships with the press, they can (contra Gitlin) affect mass media content to advance their own objectives by shaping how journalists frame stories and ensuring coverage of stories that would otherwise go unreported. Of course, the activist–mass media relationship remains asymmetrical because journalists hold much more power.

After all, journalists can far more easily find information and perspectives from non-movement sources than social movement organizations can find non-journalistic routes to mass visibility;[19] achieving mass visibility through social media is rarer than most people think.[20] Still, scholars have shown that so long as movement organizations construct their working practices around journalists' needs, they can shape news content.

Over time, activists have established a standard "toolkit" of strategies to shape news content.[21] First, organizations must understand the criteria of "newsworthiness" held by journalists and editors—what makes something "coverable" as news? Extraordinary events are newsworthy, and so organizations stage "pseudo-events," such as demonstrations, rallies, and press conferences to attract press attention. The arrival of novel information is also newsworthy, and so organizations publish research reports containing new information about the populations and causes they work to advance. Second, organizations must learn journalists' work routines and informational needs. Organizations need to know journalists' print deadlines so they can give them material with ample time to be written into their story. Organizations need to know what format journalists can most easily receive information to include in their stories so they can write their press releases accordingly. And organizations need to know what kinds of information journalists are most likely going to be looking for so they can provide it. (Often journalists will be looking for statistical information and other such verifiable facts, beyond mere opinion.) Third, organizations must designate well-trained spokespersons or media "principals," who know how to be interviewed and how to serve as authoritative figures on the issues the organization advocates for. Finally, organizations must establish trusting relationships with journalists sympathetic to their movement. Once a relationship has been built, the journalist will know they can depend on the organization to help them do their job more efficiently and the organization will know they can depend on the journalist to represent their interests favorably. Then, when organizations construct their messages in ways that resonate with the existing cultural and political environment, and actively respond to the maneuverings of their competitors and institutional elites (like politicians), they can effectively shape the mass news media.

For a long time, NCTE had no professional communications team capable of performing all these strategic activities. As I discussed in the previous chapter, NCTE hired its first full-time communications staffer, Vincent Villano, in 2010, during transgender peoples' rapid ascent in visibility. Prior to Vincent's arrival, NCTE had largely worked with LGBT media outlets across the country because those were the media outlets available to them. Because those outlets' target audiences were LGBT people, they reported on trans issues when mass news media didn't. In the select instances in which NCTE worked with mass media, they were usually approached by earnest journalists who were intent on finding trans perspectives. But when Vincent joined the organization, the organization's media strategy changed. In part, this was because public attention to trans people was increasing. Candis Cayne became the first transgender actor to have a recurring role in a primetime television program in 2007, Thomas Beatie became known around the world as "the pregnant man" in a media circus that began in 2008, Cher's son Chaz Bono underwent a very public gender transition between 2008 and 2010, and Kye Allums became the first transgender athlete to play NCAA basketball in 2010, among other major moments of transgender visibility. And with a rise in public intrigue about trans people, news media began writing more stories about transgender topics. To help them do so, journalists came knocking on NCTE's door.

Vincent was also especially good at his job, managing most media relations activities on his own. Although he came into the position expecting to do more digital organizing, Vincent quickly adapted to his circumstances and shifted the majority of his efforts to managing relationships with reporters working in the national press.[22] Faced with a deluge of press inquiries from journalists clearly lacking awareness of transness, he created a guide for reporters on how to talk about trans issues and identities and began sending the guide to everyone who contacted NCTE. He also established relationships with prominent journalists who had begun regularly writing on trans issues, making NCTE their go-to source for quotes and analysis. The year after Vincent joined NCTE, the organization released their report (coauthored with the National LGBTQ Task Force), "Injustice at Every Turn: A Report of the National Transgender Discrimination Survey," which presented findings from a national survey of almost 6,500 transgender adults.[23] Vincent incorporated the report into his routine media relations work. He presented journalists with the first quantitative data summarizing transgender experiences in the United States. By the time Vincent departed the organization in 2015, mass news media were regularly running stories on transgender topics by collaborating with NCTE.

In his time as communications manager, Vincent implemented professional media relations at NCTE that aligned with Barker-Plummer's dialogic model and set a precedent for the organization. Once he was gone, NCTE ensured their communications staff included individuals with similar media relations expertise. His first replacement was Jay Wu, who was brought on to serve in the communications manager role in February 2016. Jay joined the organization from Obama's Department of Health and Human Services, where they had worked as a press assistant, which made them familiar with the routine work of media relations.[24] When Jay was elevated to the position of Deputy Communications Director, the communications manager position was divided into two new roles. In early 2018, a Media Relations Manager and a Rapid Response Communications Manager (later renamed the Digital Campaigns Manager) were hired. The rapid response position primarily handled social media content and the communications work for NCTE's Action Fund, while the media relations position took primary responsibility for the mass media work that had taken up most of the communications manager's time. Gillian Branstetter brought a new kind of expertise and strategical approach to this new media relations role from her work as a professional journalist. With her journalism experience, Gillian understood how journalists could be influenced, and she brought a network of journalists and editors with whom she had professional relationships. She also had a clear vision of what the value of mass media work would be for NCTE.

Under Vincent and Jay, most of NCTE's engagement with mass media had been reactive; that is, NCTE had been responding to journalist inquiries and riding a wave of externally driven media attention. But with Gillian at the helm of media relations, NCTE aimed to take a more active role in "steering the conversation" around transgender issues and providing thought leadership for the whole movement.[25] Mass media was an inevitability that needed to be addressed, a force that could either be resisted at their own peril or be directed to their advantage. As Gillian commented in an interview, NCTE needed to be "very wary of where media is moving" for fear of being "dragged along by it."[26] At the same time, NCTE's power to redirect the flows of mass media attention was limited; they couldn't just push the stories that mattered to them and squash those that didn't. In Gillian's words, "we are a bunch of queer people in an office in DC and the media will generally move around us more than we will move it."[27] Thus, Gillian and the rest of the Comms team needed to develop a strategy for managing the ambivalent nature of mass media as both a force that needed to be steered and one that could not be driven. In short, NCTE needed to contend with the power asymmetries inherent to movement–media relationships.

The organization's approach to managing this power asymmetry was a strategy of redirection—a kind of mass media *jujutsu*. To explain my metaphor, the Japanese martial art of *jujutsu* takes as its core philosophy the idea that one should not resist their opponent's force or return with their own force. Rather, they should manipulate their opponent's force to their own advantage by redirecting it elsewhere. NCTE might not always have been able to control which issues mass news media reported on, but it could capitalize on journalists' general ignorance of trans topics to steer the direction their reporting took. Much of Gillian's work in this vein involved preparing NCTE's expert staff to engage with mass media in ways that were directive, rather than acquiescent to the press's extant agenda.[28] Her directive approach involved teaching Policy staff and executive leadership how to maneuver interviews to attract journalists' attention to different, more sympathetic facets of the issue they were reporting on. For example, Gillian prepared Director of External Relations Raffi Freedman-Gurspan for an interview about transgender candidates in the 2018 election with *Reuters* journalist Daniel Trotta. She helped her craft language to pivot away from Trotta's intended framing of transgender candidates as some new phenomenon worthy of attention for the sole reason they were unlikely or uncommon (or, worse yet, as test balloons for public support of transgender rights). She encouraged the use of "nothing-about-us-without-us language," emphasizing that the value of transgender candidates was that "for too long" transgender people have "been kept" from "the table where policy decisions are being made."[29] Gillian's language situated transgender candidates as challenging a history of systematic exclusion, making their running for office a success—independent of the eventual outcomes of their elections. Perhaps most importantly, her language ensured the resulting story was more than a mere fluff piece about the supposed "novelty" of transgender politicians.

NCTE also redirected mass media's own force against itself by capitalizing on the dynamics of what political communication scholars call "intermedia agenda-setting."[30] Mass media outlets often engage in horizontal surveillance by looking at the stories being covered by their peers. In response, they cover those same stories for fear of losing shares of the "informational market" to their competitors.[31] Most famously, newspapers across the country look to the *New York Times*, but in the digital media environment even smaller outlets can initiate a wave of copycat coverage across the country.[32] Such intermedia agenda-setting provides a useful entry point to the wider mass media system for social movement organizations because some mass media outlets can more easily be influenced to run particular stories; perhaps one outlet employs an especially sympathetic journalist or has a beat focusing on movement-relevant issue. In multiple instances, NCTE secured coverage of a story in a more influenceable outlet and let intermedia agenda-setting run its course, prompting other, less influenceable outlets to follow suit and publish their own coverage. Cascading coverage allowed NCTE to preserve its sparse resources by expending small, manageable efforts that could have desirable domino effects, instead of wasting energy on large, herculean efforts that were unlikely to pan out. In this *jujutsu*-like way, NCTE's expert management of the dialogic movement–media relationship turned mass media into the very tool through which NCTE exerted influence on other mass media.

The Traditional Tactics of Media Relations

In early August 2018, Gillian was contacted by Evan Urquhart, a transgender reporter at *Slate* magazine with whom NCTE regularly worked. Urquhart was working on a "back-to-school-special" article about trans children returning to the classroom. He was hoping Gillian could provide him with data from NCTE's 2015 US Transgender Survey (USTS) about trans youth's experiences in education.[33] Unfortunately, the USTS had only surveyed transgender *adults*, so the only data NCTE could make available pertained to respondents' reflections on their past (rather than current) experiences in school. That data wasn't useful to Urquhart, but Gillian wasn't going to let the opportunity to help shape his story slip away. Instead of providing numerical data, Gillian connected Urquhart with the Maison family in Michigan, who were part of NCTE's Families for Trans Equality (FTE) program and whose transgender daughter Corey was returning to school for eleventh grade after a year of homeschooling. The final article, "Facing Bullies and Court Battles, Transgender Kids Head Back to School," was built around Corey's experiences and it also included quotes from her father, Eric.[34] The end result was a story about the Trump administration's targeting of transgender youth that was anchored in the experiences of actual trans people, and the fears instilled in those who love them.

This incident was entirely typical of NCTE's routine media relations practices. It also demonstrates several ways that the traditional tactics of mass media relations continue to be used by contemporary social movements.

For one, it illustrates the draw that novel data have for journalists, making the publication of research reports an important tool for influencing mass media content. It shows how movement organizations influence media content by providing access to specialized insights and analyses that journalists can't get from non-movement sources. It also demonstrates the value of well-developed collaborative relationships with journalists, and particularly with journalists sympathetic to the movement, for influencing news stories. Perhaps most importantly, it shows how conducting media relations can produce substantial impacts on the form of mass media content. Not only can organizations influence journalists through providing informational subsidies that shape the facts of their reporting, but they can also influence them through providing what public relations scholars Daniel Jackson and Kevin Moloney have called "editorial subsidies"—strategic messages that shape the core argument of their reporting.[35]

These tactics shaped much of the organization's daily interactions with journalists across a variety of issues, often starting with journalists' data needs. As I noted earlier in the chapter, NCTE first conducted the National Transgender Discrimination Survey (NTDS) in collaboration with the National LGBTQ Task Force in 2011. The NTDS provided the first large-scale quantification of transgender experiences and quickly made NCTE the primary source of data on the transgender community for journalists. NCTE then followed up the NTDS with the USTS in 2015, this time surveying over 27,000 transgender people in the United States. When I was in the field, the USTS was perhaps the most-cited NCTE resource, far surpassing press releases, rallies, and one-on-one interviews with staff members—although it was often cited in combination with those other resources. Oftentimes journalists would call Gillian (and, before her, Jay) to verify statistics from the USTS reports, giving NCTE the opportunity to ensure the accuracy of their claims, and also shape the story they were telling.[36] Gillian would almost always offer the journalists access to a relevant NCTE staff member for an interview or offer to connect them with a member of NCTE's Voices for Trans Equality (VTE) or FTE programs. In either case, NCTE would be able to center transgender people and their experiences in the story.

The survey also helped NCTE set the press agenda on transgender issues. By making data on transgender issues available, NCTE encouraged journalists to take trans issues seriously. Moreover, the inclusion of relevant data in a story on a particular policy helped demonstrate the importance of that issue to audiences that would otherwise not be inclined to care. The USTS data were an entry point for journalists writing on transgender issues, particularly those who were new to covering trans topics or who were writing a one-off trans story. Journalists frequently asked Gillian if there was more recent data than from 2015, as data have a decently short shelf-life. The organization began planning a new wave of the survey to collect data journalists would find compelling, which was originally slated to launch in 2020 but was postponed until late 2022.[37]

Another resource NCTE provided as part of their routine media relations work was their style guide, which briefed journalists on the appropriate language and discourse for discussing transgender identities, and issues that transgender people face. Although Vincent first issued a journalistic style guide during his tenure as the communications manager, the guide remained, in Gillian's words, "very bare bones."[38] It was also being constantly updated because, as Gillian remarked, style guides "are not rule books, they are mirrors."[39] It needed to be continuously updated to reflect changes in how the transgender community understood and communicated itself. For example, the proliferation of the term "Latinx" as an inclusive alternative to Latino/Latina or Latin@ prompted NCTE to discuss internally whether they felt the term was appropriate to use. Having eventually decided it was, they updated the style guide accordingly.[40]

Style guides were an important NCTE resource for two main reasons. First, journalists often needed guidance on appropriate transgender terminology and on introductory concepts relating to transness—especially if they had never reported on trans topics before. Journalists who were worried about marginalizing trans people frequently called Gillian, and she sent them the style guide to soothe their anxieties.[41] Second, as Gillian explained in an interview, NCTE was in a "unique position to set the tone on language" because of their trusted relationships with journalists.[42] Journalists often didn't know what language to use, and because they trusted NCTE, they accepted their advice. Of course, NCTE's style guide was limited in its influence on journalists' reporting in that they had to actively seek it out by visiting NCTE's website or working with Gillian. Nonetheless, having this shareable resource helped journalists feel comfortable turning to NCTE for assistance, increasing their dependency upon the organization for resources and enabling a dialogic relationship.[43]

The most widely used resources NCTE produced for journalists were also the most routine: press releases. Although it may seem surprising—

particularly given common criticisms of press releases as hopeless acts of screaming into an inattentive void—on the whole, press releases remain stunningly successful at securing mass news media coverage of issues.[44] According to some estimates, as many as one in ten news articles is initiated by an organizational press release, and organizational press releases often provide language that is directly adopted by news outlets covering controversial social issues.[45] For NCTE, press releases provided a routine churn of stories and public statements for journalists to report on. When situations arose that NCTE determined significant enough to warrant a public statement, Gillian would draft a perambulatory explanation of the issue and its significance. She wrote it in the style of a news lede, followed by a quote from one of NCTE's media "principals." Gillian would then post the press release to the NCTE website and email it to NCTE's journalist distribution list, which would usually be enough to drive at least one news outlet to cover the story, even if only a small one.[46] From there, Gillian would target outlets that frequently covered trans issues or picked up NCTE's press releases and would reach out to journalists with whom she or the organization had a strong relationship. These efforts succeeded in drawing journalists' attention to the importance of events like the announcement of a new policy by the Trump administration.

Of course, the sheer fact that NCTE issued a press release would not ensure coverage; it also had to be well-written in the appropriate news style, and it had to include a compelling quote that offered the right balance of analysis and opinion. A successful press release also provided a distinct motivation for why the issue was significant enough to the public. In short, it needed to fit into the narrative frames in which journalists wrote political stories. During the administration of President Trump, NCTE most often succeeded in ensuring coverage of their issues by fitting their press releases into the mass news media's metanarrative about the administration's attacks on marginalized groups.[47] That is to say, reporters' individual stories about political events in the United States generally fit into a journalistic narrative about the impacts of Trump's antidemocratic, oftentimes fascistic administration. In response, NCTE wrote their press releases in ways that mirrored this tendency, representing individual transgender political events as examples of Trump's villainous crusade against the marginalized. Through crafting messages that resonated with the popular narrative of the contemporary political environment, NCTE secured more attention from a broader range of outlets.

In one such case, NCTE issued a press release following Attorney General Jeff Sessions' announcement of a new policy that would no longer grant asylum to individuals fleeing domestic or gang violence. In the morning Comms team check-in the day after Sessions' announcement, Media Relations Manager Gillian, Deputy Communications Director Jay, Director of External Relations Raffi, Policy Director Harper Jean Tobin, Interim Communications Director Dave Noble, and Digital Campaigns Manager Laurel Powell discussed how best to respond.[48] Raffi felt strongly that the statement should emphasize that the Trump administration's action "flies in the face of all convention" regarding both domestic violence and asylum policy, and make clear the specific harms it would do to the transgender people who disproportionately experience such violence. Although NCTE would ordinarily draw on USTS 2015 data to illustrate the extent of violence trans people face, asylum-seeking was not captured in the data. Instead of using quantitative data, Gillian crafted the statement around the stories of two women: Roxsana Hernandez and Alejandra Barrera. Roxsana was a trans woman from Honduras who fled to the United States after experiencing sexual violence from gang members, only to die in ICE custody. Alejandra was a trans woman from El Salvador who likewise faced violence from criminal gangs and was still detained by ICE at the time. The statement emphasized that the attorney general's decision "could be a death sentence for untold numbers of LGBTQ migrants" like Roxsana and Alejandra and was yet another instance of the Trump administration's prejudice becoming policy.[49] With executive director Mara's approval, the statement was released, attributed to Harper Jean.

Admittedly, NCTE's press releases failed at garnering significant mass news media attention just as often as they succeeded. Their modest success rate was true even when the press releases did everything "right," including fitting transgender rights issues into broader political metanarratives. There were a variety of reasons for their failures. Sometimes the issues competing for precious attention in the news cycle meant a story got "crowded out."[50] The timing of other important social and political issues (or even major weather events) could mean a trans issue didn't make the cut. Still other times journalists held opaque ideas about what made stories newsworthy, leaving NCTE guessing as to why a particular story wasn't getting covered.[51] Whatever the case, certain issues would just not get picked up. For example, one year to the day after President Trump announced his plan to ban transgender troops from the US military, the Department of Veteran Affairs (VA) proposed a rule prohibiting the VA's medical benefits package from covering transition-related surgeries for trans people. In justifying this rule, they reiterated earlier prejudicial claims about the mental health of transgender people and the frivolousness of transition-related care Trump tweeted out when announcing the ban. NCTE issued a press release denouncing the administration's continued efforts to target trans people and take away "life-saving care" from transgender veterans.[52] Yet, despite the timeliness of the proposed VA rule being announced on the anniversary of such a momentous news moment for transgender rights and the story sitting at the nexus of three of journalists' favorite fascinations—trans people, veterans, and transition-related surgeries—the press release got no bites. As one journalist told Gillian when she followed up with them about writing a story on the issue, "we talked it out in an editorial meeting and agreed that it was too wonky."[53] Given that most of the setbacks to (and victories for) transgender rights were byzantine matters of federal policy, the issues NCTE tried to get covered were often considered "too wonky."

Less visible from the outside, but closely related to NCTE's crafting press releases, was their creation of "messaging documents"—internal guides for how to talk with reporters about issue areas such as health care, sex work, and hate crimes. Although press releases and messaging documents were different, both represented efforts to package communications that would subsidize journalists' needs for information, analysis, and competing perspectives. In contrast to press releases, which were often drafted to instigate press attention, messaging documents were created so NCTE was prepared when journalists approached them with a story they were already working on.[54] In these reactive situations, NCTE was far more successful in shaping mass media coverage.

Although messaging documents were internal guides for staff rather than external ones for journalists, they helped ensure that the statements staff gave in interviews met journalists' needs sufficiently to be included in their stories. NCTE could expect press inquiries to focus on a key policy issue relevant to transgender people, such as health care, immigration, sex work, violence and hate crimes, military service, bathrooms, gender markers on ID documents, nonbinary identities, and trans children in school.[55] Gillian therefore gathered executive leadership and members of the Policy and Comms teams to "hammer out" prepared strategic talking points for each issue area.[56] The finalized, semi-standardized messaging documents included policy-relevant information, analysis, and organizational perspectives. These meetings were auxiliary, however, to the weekly messaging meetings in which more time-sensitive messaging issues pertaining to subjects currently being discussed in mass media were resolved. While formal messaging documents were not generated out of these regular meetings, summarizations were sent out after each for staff to reference.

For Policy staff who were routinely interviewed by journalists, these documents were a valuable resource. Messaging documents helped ensure that they advanced NCTE's strategic objectives and gave journalists what they needed well enough to influence their coverage. Racial and Economic Justice Policy Advocate Mateo De La Torre, for example, expressed in an interview that the messaging documents were great references because his issue areas experienced a rapid increase in media attention, thus putting him in contact with reporters more frequently.[57] State Policy Director Arli Christian indicated similarly, noting the difficulties they faced when being interviewed by journalists. They recounted one instance in which Gillian had helped prepare them for the call, but had to exit the interview part way through to speak with another journalist, leaving Arli to answer questions without messaging resources:

> They got super into weeds on ID stuff, and it got technically complicated. They wanted to know, like, when you live in this state, but you were born in this state, and you need to get a court order, how does that work? What goes on? . . . And I was constantly kind of struggling in my head of like, "is this too much information?" . . . I do think it was the right information to give them, but it was tricky to sort of frame those really complicated questions in a way that talks about our talking points of why this is important.[58]

For Gillian, the messaging documents served an inverse function. They allowed her both to feel certain that Policy staff could manage the interviews she set up for them without hour-long prep sessions and to feel confident that she had the intricacies of policy down when providing journalists quotes herself. As she summarized, having messaging documents "helps me get reporters what they need, which is quotes, as relatively fast as possible without having to throw a brick into the insanely busy schedules of our team."[59]

Significantly, the effectiveness of NCTE's press releases and messaging documents depended upon the organization's relationships with journalists they hoped to influence. While NCTE worked with a variety of journalists, as I noted in the previous chapter, the organization's geographic proximity and cultural values influenced which journalists they truly valued. At the same time, NCTE sought to work with journalists they could count on to get the story "right"—representing transgender issues and identities accurately and sympathetically. Sometimes this trust was established through a personal relationship between an NCTE staff person and a journalist. For instance, NCTE frequently worked with Katelyn Burns, a journalist for *Rewire News Group*, who is a transgender woman and who often reported on transgender issues. As it happened, she also lived across the hall from her friend Laurel, who was NCTE's Digital Campaigns Manager. In fact, the only time during my fieldwork when I saw Burns in person was at a party thrown at Laurel's apartment.[60] Other times trust was established because a journalist was queer and mostly wrote on queer topics. For example, NCTE often worked with journalists like Nico Lang, Mary Emily O'Hara, Samantha Allen, John Paul Brammer, Lucas Waldron, and Evan Urquhart.

NCTE also built enduring relationships with straight, cisgender journalists carving out a niche for themselves by covering trans topics. For example, Gillian set up a coffee meeting with Caitlin Emma, a policy reporter for *Politico*. Emma had previously published stories regarding complaints transgender students had filed with the Department of Education and worked with Jay when they were communications manager. Gillian took advantage of her proximity to Emma in DC to develop a stronger relationship. As Gillian commented in an interview:

> Building relationships with reporters and pressing flesh and getting out of the office—it's something that I'm getting more comfortable to do. . . . Certainly, the relationship between me and reporters is transactional, but I also want to build trust with them, and I want to get to know them and get into what they need and to make sure that we're [providing it.] And I'm getting to a space, too, where reporters that we've worked with numerous times, I'll say, "Hey, we just saw this study. We just saw this story. Here's this federal policy that came out. You might be interested in this," and just shooting them over email.[61]

Building these relationships immeasurably increased NCTE's ability to get stories covered the way they wanted them covered.

Media Relations Gets a Digital Facelift

In August 2018, the Department of Labor issued a new directive that government contractors could legally fire people for being transgender if the
decision was motivated by religious beliefs. It was the latest in a long line
of similar "religious liberty" exemptions to nondiscrimination protections
from the Trump administration, following the Supreme Court's ruling in
Masterpiece Cakeshop v. Colorado Civil Rights Commission, which held that
businessowners could refuse certain public accommodations to individuals
based on the First Amendment. NCTE, of course, issued a press release
denouncing the directive. The three-hundred-word press release, written in
the style of a news report, described the directive, explained what it meant,
and closed with a two-paragraph quote from Policy Director Harper Jean
Tobin criticizing the policy for promoting employer prejudice. The press release was emailed directly to the journalists on NCTE's press list and posted
to the organization's website.

A very different version of that same press release was also posted to
Twitter. The tweeted version was shorter, consisting of only three threaded
240-character tweets followed by an image of a quote attributed to Harper
Jean. In contrast to the informational tone of the press release, each tweet
in this version made bold, emotive claims, such as "This directive—and the
corresponding removal of information from the Department of Labor website about LGBTQ protections—is a direct attempt to undermine our rights,
and we won't stand for it."[62] The emotive tone of the tweets was intended to
encourage individuals to share NCTE's tweets by retweeting them because
emotionally charged content gets reshared far more often than informational
content.[63] NCTE was also keenly aware that journalists' perceptions of what
issues are newsworthy are shaped by social media. A statement circulating
well on social media increased the likelihood of it being picked up in mass
media.[64] Thus, ensuring the tweeted press release was primed for widespread sharing increased its odds of getting journalist attention. As Interim
Communications Director Dave commented in an interview, "you have a
much narrower target of reporters who are going to see a press release" versus
see social media chatter, so it's important "to get the kinds of people in the
world to follow and to engage with your shorter post" to maximize attention
to the message.[65]

The stark differences between the press release sent directly to journalists
and the version shared to social media reflect different fundamental logics.

Traditional mass media practices are driven by different forces than the attention cycles of the contemporary digital mediasphere. To put it simply, mass media are driven by the routinized selection and packaging of ostensibly "objective" and novel information by professional journalists in accordance with long-standing news values. By contrast, social media are driven by the near-immediate curation of personal opinion, emotional expression, and disclosures of subjective experience by lay citizens in accordance with rapidly changing trends.[66] But to make matters more complicated, mass media and social media cannot be depended upon to consistently act according to their respective logic because they no longer operate as distinct media spheres. Rather, in the chimaeric media system, the two spheres are fused into one. Mass media and social media each act in accordance with network media logics *and* mass media logics at the same time.[67] This fusion of logics can be seen in the case of NCTE's press release about the Department of Labor directive. Some journalists covered the Department of Labor's new directive because they received NCTE's emailed press release, which suited the norms of traditional movement–media interactions and provided new information on an important policy decision. Others covered it because they saw NCTE's Twitter release, which adhered to the communicative norms of social media and provided emotionally charged content around which to build a story.

These changing dynamics of journalist attention—whereby new media logics often drove the practices of mass media institutions—required that NCTE adapt traditional tactics of media relations practiced by activists of bygone eras. NCTE gave these tactics "digital facelifts" by incorporating digital technologies into their practice in ways that either afforded new means of maintaining relations with mass media or increased the ease of doing so.[68] Beyond press releases, digital facelifts were given to a host of other media relations tactics, such as the press conference, a long-standing tool for political actors to secure journalistic attention. Everyone is familiar with the image of the press conference: a prominent speaker stands at a podium in front of an institutional seal or outside an impressive building, while journalists with videographers in tow wave microphones to capture answers to a barrage of questions and cameras flash capturing photos of the speaker. Press conferences have historically served as important "pseudo-events," or preplanned events manufactured for the sole purpose of being reported on.[69] In the digital age, however, press conferences often take on a very different form. For NCTE, press conferences were digital events by design. The conference was still expected to attract journalists' attention, but it was expected that they would notice it over *social media* and not attend in person. One pragmatic reason for this shift was that the journalists in the Washington press corps were increasingly located *outside* of Washington, so it would be hard to get journalists physically in the room. Another reason was that NCTE's press conferences were generally focused less on providing journalists with information and analysis and more on displaying outrage and indignation. And digital media were where those messages played best.

On July 17, 2018, for example, NCTE held a press conference launching their Protect Trans Health campaign, which they ran jointly with the Transgender Law Center in Oakland, California.[70] The campaign focused on mobilizing resistance to the Trump administration's planned rollback of Section 1557 of the Affordable Care Act, which provided transgender people federal protections from discrimination in health care. The press conference was held in a large chamber in the front area of the AFL-CIO headquarters in DC. The chamber had vaulted ceilings and a glass wall facing the street with sunlight streaming in. Opposite it stood a giant stone and gold mural that ran the length of the wall, featuring laborers in their trades with a man, woman, and child centered. This mural was the imposing backdrop to the podium from which Mara and other leaders in the LGBTQ movement and allied movements delivered prepared remarks to the press. But only a handful of journalists were actually in the room; the rest of the gathered crowd consisted of staff from the participating organizations and local allies who were there to show support. The main audience for the press conference was journalists following online. While the speakers delivered their comments to the crowd, NCTE's Digital Campaigns Manager Laurel Powell live-tweeted their comments. I used an iPhone to broadcast the press conference over Facebook Live on NCTE's official account, as an intern shot photos of the speakers with another iPhone and emailed them to Laurel for her to include in the live tweeting. Staff from each participating organization shared or retweeted NCTE's social media content in real-time from the press conference.[71] While a handful of journalists experienced the press conference in the room, the vast majority experienced its digital mediations.

NCTE approached rallies similarly, treating the physical gathering of people in one place as a dramatic opportunity for digital distribution rather than a site of newsmaking. For example, after the leak of the Trump administration's plans to narrow the legal definition of gender as being either male or female and immutable from birth, NCTE became the center of an impromptu media campaign under the banner of Won't Be Erased. As part of this campaign, NCTE organized a rally in front of the White House with partner organizations.[72] In contrast to the Protect Trans Health press conference, the Won't Be Erased rally was incredibly well-attended by journalists, partly because of how large a story the campaign already was, having launched in the *New York Times*. Like the Protect Trans Health press conference, several speakers addressed the crowd (and the press) from a podium with the White House framed behind them. Also like the press conference, I used an iPhone to broadcast the rally over Facebook Live on NCTE's official account, where it was shared over two thousand times and reached an audience of over two hundred thousand viewers. Combined with the social media posts of the other organizations and attendees at the rally, the gathering of several hundred individuals covered by a dozen journalists spread to hundreds of thousands of people, including hundreds of online journalists. The overwhelming spread of the rally across social media made it a significant news story even to journalists jaded by daily protests outside the White House.[73]

NCTE also gave digital facelifts to more splashy and theatrical forms of media activism that political sociologist Sarah Sobieraj has described as ineffectual and counterproductive. But the "street theater" displays Sobieraj witnessed among activists trying to attract journalist attention during presidential campaign events were ineffective because they didn't play to the logics guiding the serious journalists convening at campaign stops. In the chimaeric media system, where more dynamic media logics reign, those same "direct action" tactics can often be much more effective. During my time in the field, NCTE sought to experiment with the renewed possibilities of direct action attention-grabs. As part of the Protect Trans Health campaign, for example, NCTE spent considerable time planning performative direct actions that would draw dramatic attention to the threat the Trump administration posed to transgender people. NCTE viewed these tactics as an extension of the legacy of queer activism, recalling the work of groups like ACT UP and Queer Nation.[74] At other events, they viewed them as part of a contemporary "moment" that prized such actions, looking to the example of the Claremont United Methodist Church, which earned international media attention for displaying a manger scene in which Jesus, Mary, and Joseph were caged, as a commentary on family separation at the southern US border. NCTE also looked to the "Baby Trump" balloon depicting the President as a screaming orange baby holding an iPhone, which was flown over London during an official visit. As Gillian explained, "It wasn't really nuanced political commentary, but it amplified Britain's message, which is that you are unwelcome here. And it played in the media like hell."[75] Importantly, NCTE understood that mass media attention would not necessarily be directly garnered by the action, but they viewed the action as content that would circulate well on social media. Eventually, they knew that high enough circulation in social media would guarantee *some* mass media attention.

Ultimately, NCTE never enacted a direct action plan as part of the Protect Trans Health campaign, as other priorities took over and as public attention to transgender health care dwindled. The Protect Trans Health campaign was also partly subsumed under the Won't Be Erased campaign, which became an overarching banner under which to discuss the myriad ways the Trump administration sought to strip rights from trans people. But when the Won't Be Erased campaign kicked off, NCTE decided to incorporate elements of direct action into their media work. As Communications Director Jay explained the plan in an interview:

> It was very much a photo stunt . . . The idea behind it was to have like a big splashy "fuck you" to Donald Trump. And, you know, we won't be erased. We are here. Like, sort of an establishment of trans presence in the nation's capital and, therefore, in the United States.[76]

The final plan was to unfurl a series of 150-foot plastic tablecloths in blue, pink, and white along the steps of the Lincoln memorial to form a giant transgender pride flag. Just after 1 p.m. on October 29, 2018, NCTE gathered over two dozen volunteers and staff members on the steps, grouped people into teams responsible for each banner, and began the unfurling. Meanwhile, I was shooting video from beside the reflecting pool and members of the Comms team took photographs.[77] The video and photos of the unfurling were posted to NCTE's social media accounts. From there, the story was picked up by news media, such as *The Hill*, as NCTE hoped might happen, which covered the direct action as a news hook before diving into the details of the Trump administration's policy attacks and their consequences for trans people.[78]

Of course, most of these digitally facelifted tactics depended on new modes of digital news production and distribution for their success. The journalists who were likely to pick up a news story from NCTE's social media feeds were not necessarily going to work for the largest mass media outlets. Indeed, they often reported for smaller, digital-first outlets.[79] However, NCTE understood that coverage in smaller online outlets often served as entry point for getting their story covered more widely. Sympathetic journalists who paid close attention to NCTE would circulate stories of their activities via social media to journalists working at other news outlets. These stories spread through the intermedia agenda-setting process I described earlier in the chapter. Because social media conversations drive what stories news outlets cover,[80] there was often a "hall of mirrors" effect. A story run in a smaller, digital-first outlet was then picked up by prominent individuals (both trans and cis) on social media, drawing further press attention to the story and resulting in more social media discussion. Social media and mass media would feed on each other in a mutually enforcing cycle. Thus, the adaptations of older mass media relations tactics for the digital news environment helped NCTE direct attention to issues that otherwise might go uncovered and secure coverage that would not otherwise result from traditional media relations work.

Opening Up the Media–Movement Relationship

As I've shown throughout this chapter, the dialogic relationship between social movements and mass media described by feminist media theorist Bernadette Barker-Plummer persists in an evolving form. It continues to structure the modes of activism of movement organizations. Yet, at the same time, the movement–media relationship is changing in important ways. There are several assumptions that underpin the dialogic relationship between mass media and social movements that the emergence of digital technologies has unsettled, destabilizing the dialogic relationship. The result is a more "open" relationship that requires different modes of activism, motivated by different goals, to successfully engage in mass media work.

The first unsettled assumption that underpins the dialogic movement–media relationship is that building relationships with specific journalists makes it possible to attain coverage in mass media outlets. That is to say, the dialogic model assumes that if a movement organization wants, for strategic reasons, to get their stories consistently covered in the *Washington Post*, they can achieve that by building positive working relationships with journalists employed by the *Post*. The problem with this assumption is that dramatic changes in the journalism industry in the last few decades mean journalists are rarely at any one outlet for very long. For some journalists, high turnover and frequent layoffs at news outlets across the country mean they change employers as often as every few months.[81] For others, the on-going "flexibilization" of labor under late capitalism means they can only find precarious work as a freelancer, selling individual stories to news outlets.[82] In either case, movement organizations can't "choose" which outlets to get covered in by strategically working with specific journalists. Indeed, during my time in the field, NCTE often worked with individual journalists who they could count on the "get the story right," even while not knowing if or where they could place the final story. For instance, NCTE regularly worked with Nico Lang, a queer journalist who had frequently covered transgender issues as a freelancer for outlets including *HuffPost*, *The Daily Beast*, *Salon*, and *Rolling Stone*. In June 2017, Nico joined Grindr's newly launched LGBTQ news outlet *Into* as a full-time politics reporter, where he worked with NCTE on countless articles. But by January 2019, only a few weeks after I left the field, Grindr shut down *Into*, sending Nico back to freelancing and adding uncertainty back in to NCTE's work with him.

The second unsettled assumption of the dialogic movement–media relationship is that "the mass media" is a coherent and identifiable category of media outlets. That is, it assumes a set of "mass media" that movement organizations are aware of, that they consistently target, and that serve a defined mass audience that organizations want to reach. The problem with this assumption is that, in the digital age, the delineation between mass and not-so-mass media is a blurry one, and it is often hard for movement organizations to know which outlets serve which audiences. Indeed, one of the key features of the evolving communication system that most affected NCTE's mass media relations work was the seemingly endless proliferation of smaller, digital-first news outlets. These outlets—such as *Vox*, *Rewire News Group*, *HuffPost*, *Buzzfeed News*, *Slate*, and *Politico*—form a secondary ring of mass media outlets around the central figures of the legacy press, like the *New York Times*, *Washington Post*, *Los Angeles Times*, *Boston Globe*, and *Chicago Tribune*. While these secondary outlets are significantly smaller, they still qualify as "mass media" because of the breadth of their reach; they are simply *less* mass. The *Washington Post* has over 6.5 million likes on Facebook and over eighteen million followers on Twitter, and the *New York Times* has nearly eighteen million likes on Facebook and over 50.5 million followers on Twitter. By comparison, *Buzzfeed News* has over three million likes on Facebook and over 1.3 million followers on Twitter, and *Vox* has almost three million likes on Facebook and one million followers on Twitter (as of the time of writing). These mass-but-simply-less-so outlets differed from the legacy press in other ways that mattered for NCTE's media relations work.

Smaller, digital-first mass media outlets tended to present a more transparent left-leaning perspective on news issues, both in their selection and their framing of stories they found newsworthy enough to report on.[83] Relatedly, as became evident in my fieldwork, the journalists who worked for these outlets were more often sympathetic to transgender issues and invested in developing relationships with NCTE.[84] These secondary outlets were more likely to run in-depth reports on policy issues and news features on important social and political issues because they had more active, politically interested audiences. In contrast, legacy mass media outlets were far more likely to run "breaking news" style reports but leave out a nuanced social and political analysis.[85] The coverage provided by digital-first news outlets was also more closely linked to the agendas of social media, which "spend a lot more time discussing social issues such as birth control, abortion, and same-sex marriage . . . than the traditional media."[86] Due to all of these factors, digital-first news media had a strong intermedia agenda-setting effect on the legacy press, making coverage in these smaller digital-first outlets an important way to gain coverage among the larger legacy outlets.[87] As I've already noted in this chapter, NCTE often relied on this intermedia agenda-setting process to turn coverage in smaller mass news media outlets into coverage in larger ones.

The third and final unsettled assumption that underpins the dialogic movement–media relationship is that mass media are movement organizations' primary route to public attention and movement organizations are mass media outlets' primary source of movement-relevant information and analysis.[88] The problem with this assumption is that digital technologies have altered the balance of power between activists and journalists such that neither has a monopoly over the resources needed by the other. On the one hand, movement organizations now have innumerable mediated paths to visibility to the mass public. Organizations leverage social media for mass visibility, for instance, by sharing movement-relevant information directly with interested audiences, who in turn spread that information through their own networks.[89] NCTE did this often and with great success (as I discuss further in Chapter 5).

On the other hand, social media platforms allow journalists to acquire information and perspectives from a wider range of sources with greater ease. Individual users with high profiles post first-hand accounts of newsworthy events and opinions that serve as proxies for public sentiment.[90] Often NCTE would try to take advantage of the heightened profiles of these new actors, such social media influencers, to amplify their message, attract the attention of mass media, and increase the spread of coverage they received in smaller mass media outlets. In fact, on June 6, 2018, the Comms team convened an hour-long meeting, open to all staff, in which the gathered participants brainstormed which "social media influencers and validators" NCTE should cultivate relationships.[91] These influencers were often helpful in bringing attention to NCTE's issues. For example, when a joint *Vox/ProPublica* investigative report on ID documents that NCTE helped shape (as I discuss later in this chapter) was released, Laverne Cox tweeted out the story to her over half-million followers.[92] In other instances, these influential actors elevated by digital technologies played more disruptive roles, derailing journalists' attention. In such instances, NCTE found themselves *decentered* as the mass media's primary source for transgender political information, analysis, and perspectives, ceding ground to other (often less strategic) actors. In these ways, the transactional and codependent relationship between mass media outlets and social movement organizations assumed by the dialogic model has unraveled.

In short, the three assumptions that underlie the dialogic understanding of movement–media relationships don't hold as consistently as they once did. This is not to say dialogic relationships do not still exist; this chapter has demonstrated that they do. But it is to say that the relationship between movement organizations and media is no longer dyadic. Rather, it is at best triadic and more often completely networked, as both movements and mass media have become more deeply entangled with other streams of communication in contemporary society. This new "open" relationship is less exclusive, and its openness affects how and why movement organizations engage in mass media work. Organizations now manage their relationship with the press by managing the messages circulating in the digital sphere, while trying to shape mass media content before it starts circulating in the digital sphere. Because the content of social media influences mass media, the successful management of mass media messages requires both direct influence through routine media work targeting journalists *and* indirect influence by steering digital media conversations. Organizations must accomplish these goals through simultaneous communications with different audiences governed by different norms.

The next section isolates one specific case from my time in the field that illustrates these new dynamics in action. In late July 2018, Condé Nast's LGBTQ-focused digital news platform, *them*, published a story claiming the State Department was "retroactively revoking" transgender citizens' passports.[93] The story was based on two isolated experiences, roughly a month apart, in which transgender women were denied renewal of their passports. Both had posted about their experiences on Twitter and received significant attention.[94] This initial report was then picked up by other (non-LGBTQ-focused) news outlets and became a significant public scandal for several weeks, despite NCTE's efforts to tamp down on the story and correct widespread misunderstandings about the passport policy. Then, in mid-September, NCTE became aware via Twitter of concerning-seeming (albeit substantively negligible) changes to the section of the State Department's travel website dedicated to gender marker changes on passports.[95] Getting out ahead of the story, NCTE succeeded in steering the narrative on transgender passport policy, ultimately even pressuring the State Department to reverse the changes to their website.[96] NCTE's management of the panic over transgender passport policy reveals the complex ways the chimaeric media system has transformed how organizations work to influence the networked public sphere and manage mass media content.

The Panic Over Transgender Passports

On June 29, 2018, Danni Askini, a prominent transgender activist, then based in Seattle, Washington, tweeted that she was denied renewal of her US passport pending proof of US citizenship and her gender transition.[97] Her tweet went out to her roughly thirty-five hundred followers but quickly spread beyond her immediate network. By July 2, her post had been retweeted almost ten thousand times, liked almost seventeen thousand times, and was being discussed by almost eleven thousand people on Twitter alone. This online discourse centered on concerns that, as a prominent trans woman, Askini was being targeted by the Trump administration. Although there was no evidence to support this interpretation, it produced real fear among trans people, fueling the spread of her tweet. Then on July 25, another prominent trans woman shared a similar story. Janus Rose, a New York-based technologist and writer, posted to her over five thousand followers that her passport was "retroactively invalidated" by the State Department.[98] She even quote-retweeted Askini's original tweet, explicitly linking their denials.

By Friday, July 27, social media attention to the issue had reached critical mass. NCTE's Media Relations Manager Gillian raised the mounting tension in the morning Comms check-in. Digital Campaigns Manager Laurel seconded, noting that several people had tagged NCTE on Facebook and Twitter regarding the issue. Laurel suggested releasing an unofficial statement—"Just something on social saying, 'hey, we're aware of these reports. We're looking into it, and we'll share more as we get it.'"[99] Then-Interim Communications Director Dave asked how many people had tagged NCTE to gauge whether attention was low enough to avoid commenting. Gillian responded by noting that the number of people tagging NCTE was much smaller than the number seeing the information. NCTE had an opportunity to calm their fears, assuring everyone that there was no change in policy and that they were looking into the reports. With trans people's fears quelled, hopefully attention to the issue would die down and it would escape the notice of journalists and the Trump administration. NCTE leadership's position was to not shine a spotlight on a "non-issue" for fear of turning it into one. By the end of the day, however, Condé Nast's LGBTQ-focused digital news platform, *them*, published a story on the women's experiences, amplifying the social media conversation.

The *them* article, written by Mary Emily O'Hara, claimed the State Department was "retroactively revoking" transgender citizens' passports and fit the story into the mass news media's metanarrative about the administration's attacks on marginalized groups.[100] While O'Hara's story included exclusive interviews with both women, the "sources" of the story were their tweets, which were embedded throughout the story. Indeed, O'Hara's framing of the issue came directly from the tweets, linking the two cases together in the same manner Rose had done on Twitter. As trans people, Rose and Askini were accepted as experts on the issue even though they lacked specific knowledge of the policy situation at the heart of their personal experiences. NCTE was not contacted for the story, despite their longstanding positive working relationship with O'Hara and their expertise as authors of the passport policy. As such, no alternative explanation for their isolated experiences was offered. The article turned Askini and Rose's isolated personal experiences into a transgender rights issue, which further fueled panicked chatter on social media.

Within twelve hours, at least six other news outlets picked up O'Hara's story, including Washington-insider darling *Axios*, online women's magazine *Bustle*, progressive Univision subsidary *Splinter* (aggregated by *MSN*), and queer online news magazine *LGBTQ Nation*.[101] These outlets further amplified the issue, and each used the original tweets as the source of the story and reflected their unchallenged framing. In fact, most news outlets that picked up O'Hara's story replicated the quotes in the original story without secondary verification or additional sources. At this point, NCTE realized the story would not be contained and they urgently needed to respond. Gillian convened the Comms and Policy teams to draft a response. By Saturday, July 28, the response was posted to Twitter, where it circulated among the news-making tweets, and emailed to journalists.[102] As Laurel explained in an interview, the statement "was just put out under social media [rather than as a formal press release] because that was where the concern was coming from."[103] Like many corrections to misinformation, however, NCTE's statement spread slower than the original story, both in news media and on social media.[104]

NCTE's statement provided a counter-frame for the original accounts, but it wasn't as compelling. It simply stated that the policy had not changed, and that Askini and Rose's cases involved "unusual circumstances and bureaucratic mistakes."[105] Although the statement was technically correct, it relied on people trusting NCTE as policy experts more than they trusted Rose and Askini as affected people. In the midst of a fear-driven social media panic, the calm tone of the statement was less noteworthy than the frenzied tweets of community members. While several members of the trans community with upward of ten thousand followers each retweeted NCTE's statement, as did the largest LGBTQ rights organization in the United States (the Human Rights Campaign), few news outlets updated their stories or ran new stories about the statement. The counter-frame of the reported events offered by NCTE failed to meet the criteria of newsworthiness that would ensure press attention to it because, in Gillian's words, "our statement poured water on the fire they were building, and they couldn't say, 'This thing you just read 600 words on actually isn't happening.'"[106]

From NCTE's perspective, the framing they offered was best because their role was to step in as a policy authority to ensure trans people that they could still change the gender marker on their passports. As Gillian commented in an interview, Askini and Rose were "taken as an authority because of their following."[107] Where this authority is presumed to apply to policy, it can present major problems because:

> if there's a bunch of headlines out there about the State Department turning trans people away when they go to renew their passports, then most trans people just won't renew their passports. They aren't going to look up the line and letter. So, we needed to do that.[108]

State Policy Director Arli was particularly sympathetic to Askini's choice to go public with her story. Nonetheless, they regretted the consequences of her and Rose's publicity. Even though "by Department of State policy, it was nothing new," there was a large amount of "community attention that came on these stories" because they each had a "very large platform."[109] The end result was widespread fear. Gillian felt this was especially true because "to most people, two points make a line."[110] She continued:

> they [journalists] saw a narrative taking shape, but that can be the danger of getting all your news from social media, right? Suddenly everything looks like a crisis. But the end point is, you know, if you crowd source to, what is it, 100 million Twitter followers and ask for two people who have had a similar experience, no matter what the experience is, you're going to find at least two people.[111]

At the same time, Gillian saw this as further evidence of a point she had been making to her colleagues: "we don't drive the public conversation in the way maybe we would hope . . . when NBC and CBS are calling, it's too late."[112] For people used to fighting to convince journalists to cover their issues at all, as veterans at the organization were, clamoring to respond to mass media attention driven by other trans people was an uncomfortable task.

At the Monday morning Comms check-in media relations manager Gillian thanked everyone for their work over the weekend on the passport crisis, remarking there was "a surprising amount of press on the story."[113] She continued with a soft reprimand:

> It's been numerous times since I've been here that we've said, "Well we don't want to talk about X. We don't want to talk about X because it will make noise about it." But we need to start recognizing when the water breaks that we risk not looking like leaders in our community by staying silent.[114]

Policy Director Harper Jean agreed and apologized for encouraging NCTE's silence. Gillian made clear she was not looking to assign blame, she just wanted to use the incident as an example. Indeed, it did become an example, and NCTE referred to this incident when considering the timeline of their future actions. As Arli mentioned to me in an interview, "I wish we had said something a little bit earlier because I actually do think if we cut this a couple days earlier, we could have nipped a lot of the panic."[115] NCTE learned the cost of finding themselves at odds with the logics of the chimaeric media system.

The dynamics of the passport crisis, while hardly new to NCTE, stood in sharp contrast to the dynamics of their other work on ID document issues. The passport story was published quickly and, perhaps ironically, by a journalist with whom NCTE had a longstanding relationship. But the story broke while NCTE was in the midst of a long-term collaborative project on ID documents with journalists at *Vox* and *ProPublica*, with whom NCTE was eager to build new relationships. NCTE's involvement with these journalists—Lucas Waldron and Ken Schwencke—began in April 2018 when they interviewed Racial and Economic Justice Policy Advocate Mateo De La Torre.[116] Waldron and Schwencke kept in touch with NCTE over the following months, and on July 30, the same day NCTE's statement was finally beginning to be picked up, Arli was interviewed from *Vox*'s DC offices. The interview covered the patchwork of gender marker change laws and policies in the United States and their consequences. To Arli and Gillian's relief, it did not include questions on the passport issue. As the interview concluded, Gillian asked the on-set producer when and where the final video would appear, but he didn't know.[117] The article finally appeared on August 16, *five months* after first contacting NCTE.[118] In the midst of a slow-burn project working directly with journalists to serve as a resource and shape their narrative, the sudden emergence of the passport crisis over Twitter was a major disruption to NCTE's media work.

Amid a traditional dialogic relationship with journalists, NCTE was caught off guard by how relationships with other journalists could work in a new media system. Gillian had expected O'Hara would contact her prior to running a story like the passport one, but she didn't; the dynamics of their dialogic relationship broke down. In response, NCTE found an alternative mode of influencing coverage. The press was attributing Askini and Rose expertise on the grounds of their trans identities while denying NCTE's policy-based expertise. In response, NCTE decided to influence Askini and

Rose's communications and thus indirectly affect the press's framing. As Arli told me, Rose "had qualms about the fact her story got so much publicity," so they talked her situation through with her and explained the common policy reasons behind her seemingly uncommon situation.[119] NCTE similarly made itself a resource to Askini. As Gillian noted, Askini only wished to have her problem resolved and was being inundated with interview requests with which she didn't want to deal.[120] Although NCTE preferred journalists to come directly to them, but because they didn't, NCTE found a way to capitalize on their sourcing routines. NCTE offered to help Askini with the policy and getting her issue resolved and had her redirect interview requests to them. Askini went on to make a public Facebook post scaling back her claims and noting her case was unique, and her post was even picked up alongside NCTE's statement in *LGBTQ Nation*.[121] By the end of the week, the passport issue seemed to have been resolved and NCTE was once again in control of the public narrative on transgender ID documents.

The initial passport crisis recalibrated NCTE's responsive dynamics. When news began circulating that the passport crisis might not be over on Wednesday, September 12, NCTE took immediate action, lest journalists again source the story from Twitter. Around 8 p.m., Media Relations Manager Gillian sent an email to the Comms and Policy teams reporting that users on Twitter had noticed concerning modifications to the State Department's website offering instructions on changing passport gender markers. She outlined the major changes, the most concerning of which was that "a U.S. passport does not list the bearer's gender identity" and the sex marker on a passport requires "medical certification of sex change" to alter.[122]

Director of External Relations Raffi Freedman-Gurspan responded, "Not good. Let's discuss tomorrow." Almost immediately thereafter, Comms staffer Laurel replied, "I'm curious if someone from Policy can review. If this is as significant as it sounds, we may want to respond ASAP."[123] Policy Director Harper Jean responded later, noting the Foreign Affairs Manual (FAM) State Department employees used to process passport applications had been "renumbered and very slightly revised." However, when compared side-by-side, the policies and procedures had not changed. The changes Gillian noted were to the "information for travelers" page. She added that she or Policy Director Arli should call the State Department in the morning and ask what prompted the FAM and travelers page changes. Beyond that, she advised monitoring the conversation on Twitter and perhaps "repeating or refreshing our previous statement" that nothing had changed.[124]

The Comms team members were less willing, after the Askini and Rose incident, to treat the recent changes as nothing new. Laurel and Deputy Comms Director Jay both expressed an urgent need to respond, with Laurel writing, "while I trust your reading of the policy more than some random person on Twitter, it's going to be significantly harder to tamp this down than it was before."[125] Even if NCTE was right about the policy, they needed to think about how it would look to journalists and the digital public. While Laurel may have trusted Harper Jean's analysis more than "some random person on Twitter," others likely wouldn't. Gillian instructed everyone to "jump on the Comms line" to discuss.[126] On the phone, everyone agreed an immediate response was necessary, but the team debated the balance between ensuring policy accuracy and specificity versus managing the fear and outrage of the community. There was clear awareness that the framing needed to reflect truth *and* be compelling. It needed to speak to the press *and* to the community on social media. Policy Director Harper Jean articulated that the important thing was to let everyone know the policy hadn't changed, and they shouldn't worry. Laurel and Gillian were more insistent that it didn't matter the policy hadn't changed if the public believed it did and was acting like it had.

There was also a secondary debate about if the website changes were a deliberate attempt by the State Department to make acquiring accurate passports more difficult for trans people. Everyone agreed that the community would think so, and NCTE had previously denounced the Trump administration deliberately erasing information on LGBTQ resources from government websites. And, of course, journalists would want to fit this into their metanarrative about Trump's attacks on marginalized groups. Media Relations Manager Gillian asserted confidently that "they're trying to obfuscate policy and confuse people"—and that framing would grab journalists' attention.[127] Policy Director Harper Jean more conservatively countered by suggesting using the public page to explain that the policy was revised to "emphasize restrictions and deemphasize trans people's rights."[128] She strongly urged that NCTE should not attribute ill motives, because NCTE still needed to maintain a productive working relationship with the State Department. The team settled on her framing of the issue, as it struck a balance between the empathetic messages circulating in social media conversations and technical accuracy. The end conclusion was essentially to note what the changes were and describe why they were suspect (without specifically assigning intent) because it fit the trend of erasing LGBTQ resources. NCTE urged people to exercise their rights without fear of any changes in policy. By 11:47 p.m., the statement was drafted by Gillian, approved by leadership, sent out to journalists, and posted to NCTE's social media accounts. Their tweet tagged the Twitter user who first noted the changes to ensure the statement would circulate among the burgeoning conversations.

The next day, several news outlets picked up NCTE's statement, including *The Advocate*, *Rewire News Group*, *The Daily Beast*, and culture and politics magazine *Rolling Stone*.[129] Each cited NCTE as the source of the story and stuck closely to NCTE's framing. Each article led with the newsworthy hook the Trump administration had made changes to government websites, indicating potential targeting of the transgender community, but subsequently presented NCTE's point that trans people could still update and renew their passports. Moreover, because NCTE had incorporated the discourse circulating on social media, only one of the published articles included social media actors as additional sources.[130] NCTE then circulated their message further through social media, where they could continue to speak to multiple audiences while controlling the discursive field, thereby limiting the emergence of counter-frames. In the Comms team check-in on September 13, Gillian mentioned she tagged the "usual suspects" of journalists in the statement on Twitter. Laurel suggested doing a Facebook Live with Executive Director Mara, basically rearticulating the statement, followed by a live Q&A with Arli. Laurel added that they also should do a "Twitter chat" with Arli. These social media activities let NCTE simultaneously put trans faces to the issue and ensured accurate policy information would circulate online.[131]

Later that day, Gillian exclaimed from the Comms office: "State backed down!"[132] Once the Comms team and Mara were all in the office, Gillian explained that Kate Sosin, a journalist at *Into* with whom NCTE frequently collaborated, had forwarded her an emailed statement a press officer in the Bureau of Consular Affairs sent them. It walked back the changes, with instructions that it "may be used on background, attributable to a Department of State Official." The statement confirmed the policy had not changed, apologized for "any confusion" and "inadvertently including some language which may be considered offensive," and promised to immediately reverse the changes made to the website. Mara thanked "everyone who hopped on this." The team's rapid response secured enough press attention and consequent pressure to change the State Department's actions, earning NCTE both a media win *and* a policy win in one fell swoop.[133]

The assembled group drafted NCTE's statement announcing the State Department's apology. Policy Director Arli was particularly excited to frame the apology as a win for NCTE, while Comms staffers were less convinced. As Gillian said, "It's a win for us because we are nerds and because this is our job."[134] For everyone else, it was merely a momentary relief that the worst had not yet happened, although it still could. Laurel asked them if NCTE wanted to reconsider doing the Twitter chats and other social media activities. Mara immediately replied, "No." As she said later, "this an ongoing problem. This is like our fourth fire alarm."[135] Doing the Facebook Live and Twitter chat would offer an opportunity to shut down and redirect the "chatter," as Laurel called it, on social media by taming the community's emotions. By 12:27 p.m., NCTE had tweeted a statement that spoke directly to the trans community and press.[136]

That afternoon, *Rewire News Group* and *The Daily Beast* updated their stories to include the State Department's statement after receiving confirmation of the apology directly from the Department by email.[137] Following those updates, *Bustle* published an article titled "Passport Language for Trans People Changed Overnight—Then was Reversed after Criticism," detailing the events of the preceding twenty-four hours.[138] The next day, *them* published an article on the events, this time written by John Paul Brammer and centered solely on NCTE's statements. It even directed readers to NCTE's recent Facebook Live and the upcoming Twitter Q&A.[139] The issue of passports had finally subsided, and this time NCTE had retained control of the public narrative on transgender ID documents.

Lessons Learned

The passport crisis in 2018 exemplifies the core argument of this chapter. It demonstrates why managing mass media is necessary to ensure that the contemporary communication system circulates messages aligned with an organization's aims, and that failing to do so can have detrimental effects on public discourse. At the same time, the passport crisis shows how managing mass media requires managing community media and social media because they can have intermedia agenda-setting effects on mass media outlets. Moreover, this case is particularly illustrative of my argument because it breaks cleanly into two parallel parts: one in which NCTE fumbled the dynamics of the chimaeric media system and failed to control the mass media agenda on transgender rights issues, and one in which NCTE successfully navigated those same dynamics to maintain control over the mass media agenda.

The passport crisis also reveals features of contemporary newsmaking that have been transformed by the emergence of digital media and their network logics, and that have required social movement organizations to innovate their practices. The first feature is the temporality of issue emergence in contemporary newsmaking. The rapid attention cycles of social media now drive the speed of newsmaking. As a result, the content of social media often informs the emergence of issues and their coverage as issues of political significance. Considering that social media provide journalists with immediately available sources, the conversations happening on social media often become the social and political issues represented in mass media.[140] This was evident in the first part of the passport crisis; Askini and Rose posted tweets that quickly reached a mass circulation. Within two days of Rose's tweet, O'Hara had written and published a news story sourced entirely from their tweets. Once that story was published, it took less than twelve hours for another half-dozen stories to appear from other outlets. For movement organizations to successfully influence mass media under these conditions, they must adjust the temporal rhythms of their media work to suit those of social media. Accordingly, when word of changes to the State Department website reached NCTE, they worked quickly to preempt individual actors with large digital presences from drawing attention to the issue, getting their own statement out over social media within mere hours. The tweets containing NCTE's statement became sources for the news outlets that reported on the changes.

The second feature of note is that individuals' personal experiences, and their subjective understandings of those experiences, are now newsworthy in their own right—even when those understandings may not reflect the true nature of an issue. Movement organizations are not used to this kind of communication. Their impulse is to lean on their policy expertise to validate their claims and be taken seriously as legitimate sources by journalists.[141] They much less frequently invoke their identities as constituents of their movement to justify their value as sources.[142] NCTE was no exception, and they expected their policy analysis to drive how journalists and the public perceived the passport issue because they were "the experts." However, in the contemporary media system, expertise is often "crowdsourced" from figures with digital prominence regardless of the "factualness" of their commentary.[143]

The basis on which these figures are deemed legitimate commentators is that their identity or their individual experiences relate to the topic being reported.[144] Such was the case with Askini and Rose, whose tweets overrode NCTE's analysis to become the dominant interpretation of events. NCTE thus found themselves in a position in which competing criteria for expertise had to be met to ensure their voices were represented. When the passport issue reemerged in September, NCTE adjusted course, putting the faces of transgender staff members out over social media to discuss the issue. These staff members could speak simultaneously as trans people *and* experts—striking a balance such that appeals to their transness as a source of expertise did not jeopardize appeals to their policy expertise.

The final feature of note in contemporary newsmaking is that the emotional charge of public communications is far more important to making them newsworthy than the "newness" of the information they provide. In the traditional relationship between movements and media, movement organizations provide journalists with novel and trustworthy information that meets their criteria for coverage.[145] In the new communication system, news is more often *affective*, meaning what makes an occurrence newsworthy is the emotional charge of the event as represented by the source, regardless of its veracity.[146] The fear that drove social media conversations surrounding Askini and Rose's situations, for instance, made their situations newsworthy. NCTE's calm-voiced assurance that everything was fine wasn't as newsworthy, and thus failed to command journalists' attention. Movement organizations are conventionally more restricted in their ability to communicate with affective charge than private citizens with large digital platforms, much less to such a degree that the news story centers on the emotiveness of their communications. Yet, when informational novelty isn't enough to win mass media attention, organizations must balance these two competing criteria of newsworthiness in ways that appeal to journalists *and* the social media sphere. Accordingly, when the passport issue reemerged, NCTE grappled with how to represent the trans community's rightful fear in a way that would make their statement newsworthy, while ensuring attention was paid to new information about the policy.

These various features combine to produce a communication environment that makes mass media not *less* important, but important in *new* and *different* ways. And this environment demands movement–media relations that are more complex and dynamic than the classic dialogic model suggests. Because the content of social media influences mass media, successfully managing mass media requires direct influence through routine media work targeting journalists and indirect influence by steering digital media. At the same time, local and community media have become important in ways they previously have not been. Media coverage that would once have only been visible to a small group of people (such as readers of niche LGBTQ outlets) now circulates to wider audiences where it gets picked up by mass media. Mass media attention then begets even more social media and local and community media attention in a vicious cycle of amplification. Now, if movement organizations don't manage mass media effectively, the modest influence they have on local/community media and social media will be overwhelmed by the more powerful agenda-setting forces of mass media. They are forced to control all these streams at once.

The need to manage mass media has necessitated a shift beyond the traditional forms of media relations movement organizations have historically relied upon. As I've shown, the traditional media relations strategies of building relationships with sympathetic journalists, providing them informational and editorial subsidies, and adapting public communications to suit the demands of their workdays still occur. But now movement organizations must manage a greater number of actors across a broader sphere of public conversations. Doing so has required that movement organizations give digital facelifts to old media relations tactics, as well as develop altogether new tactics.

Understanding the new dynamic of the communication environment sets us up for the following chapter, which considers how local and community media circulate both within their niche audiences of interest and through national (and even transnational) networks. These local and community outlets thus have a dual character in the contemporary media environment—they make every local issue also a national issue, and every community issue relevant issue to the wider American public. The dual character of local and community media requires new approaches to activism as movement organizations seek to manage local media markets and community media outlets across the country all at once. They must manage them simultaneously for fear not only of what intracommunity consequences may occur in the wake of coverage, but also of how that coverage may circulate in decontextualized ways beyond the community. Much of this work requires new tactics that allow organizations to operate everywhere all at once, even if they only have a small team in one corner of the country.

4

From Right Here to Everywhere

On December 11, 2020—near the close of a year defined by a national wave of protests surrounding the murders of George Floyd and Breonna Taylor at the hands of the police—Oklahoma City Police Sargent Clifford Holman murdered Bennie Edwards, a sixty-year-old Black man who experienced schizophrenia and chronic homelessness. *Newsweek* published an article reporting the murder the day it happened, and the Associated Press ran a single wire story four days later. The AP story led with the fact that Edwards had been charged with stabbing a postal worker six years prior to his murder.[1] No other mass media outlets covered the story. Local outlets like *The Oklahoman* and the *Norman Transcript* provided the only coverage.

On the day of Edwards' murder, my partner Will and I were living in Los Angeles. Because of the lack of national media attention, I was completely unaware of the events unfolding in Oklahoma City. So too was Will, who is from Oklahoma City and lived there for the first eighteen years of his life before moving to Missouri for college and, eventually, to Los Angeles with several of his closest friends from home. The following day, several of Will's Oklahoma City-raised, Los Angeles-based friends shared an Instagram post by *Territory OKC*, a digital culture magazine in Oklahoma City, to their stories.[2] The post was a photo of Edwards in a salon chair, smiling and holding a bouquet of flowers. The accompanying text reported his murder and shared a community member's fond memories of him selling flowers on their street. Will's friends had seen people back home share the news, and so they shared it too. When Will and I saw their stories, we shared the post to our stories as well.

I noticed, though, that none of *my* friends had posted about Edwards' murder—even activists in the Movement for Black Lives and others who shared similar stories daily. Like me, they hadn't seen the story because it hadn't been covered by national mass media. Once I posted *Territory OKC*'s post to my story, though, that changed. Soon afterward, my sister in Baltimore shared it, colleagues in my PhD program in Los Angeles shared it, and activist friends in Washington, DC, shared it. Then I noticed my sister's

Voices for Transgender Equality. Thomas J Billard, Oxford University Press. © Thomas J Billard 2024.
DOI: 10.1093/oso/9780197695425.003.0004

college friends from Charleston, South Carolina share it from her story, and friends-of-friends began sharing it, too. Slowly throughout the day, my Instagram filled with more and more followers—none of whom were in or from Oklahoma City—sharing the story.

This is perhaps a strange anecdote from my life to share but it illustrates a central argument of this chapter: There is a duality between local news and national circulation. Local media provide important attention to social and political issues for the local communities they serve, yet those stories circulate through networks that span far beyond their intended, geographically delimited audiences. The *Territory OKC* post my partner and I shared was intended to be seen by people in Oklahoma City. And it was. But it was also seen by people—like my partner and his friends—for whom Oklahoma City media are "local" because of their social connections, even though they are no longer located in proximity to the outlet. Digital media afforded them the ability to remain connected to "local" media from afar. These people, by curating an otherwise "local" story into their social networks, which are full of people for whom the story is *not* local, fueled the story's national spread. So, this "local" story did not stay local.

Edwards' story illustrates the duality between what I call "placefulness" and "placelessness."[3] By "placefulness," I mean the specific quality of local media that locates stories within a social world based in geography. Local media tell stories about people with whom readers experience commonness because of their shared location and because of the social proximity they assume comes from that shared location. "Placelessness," in contrast, refers to the quality of community media that universalizes human experience by locating stories in a social world based in collectively held, but fundamentally *imagined* identities.[4] Community media tell stories about people with whom readers experience commonness because of shared social identity (over and above any geographic differences) and because of the sameness of experience they assume comes from that shared social identity. Confusingly, both placefulness and placelessness happen simultaneously; digital media have rendered placeful media *also* placeless. This duality has important implications for the activism of organizations like the National Center for Transgender Equality.

National social movement organizations like NCTE must now manage local and community media in new ways. Previously, they could focus on national mass media and leave local media to local activists.[5] And this need has required organizations to develop innovations in strategy that allow single-location organizations to "be everywhere." They must maintain constant presence in and influence over local and community media markets across the country. I describe these organizations as "single-location" because "national" organizations are not actually national in the sense that they work everywhere in the nation. As I demonstrated in Chapter 2, NCTE was a Washington, DC-specific organization. It was shaped by the geography *and* culture of DC as a city. The same holds for other ostensibly national social movement organizations.

From NCTE's single location of Washington, DC, it needed to continuously manage the narratives circulating in local and community media across the United States. "Being everywhere" all the time served NCTE's strategic aims well because they did important communicative work for the movement at the local level. At the same time, the demand to simultaneously operate at local and community levels made NCTE's work more difficult, particularly when crises flared locally or within a community but, due to the changing media environment, threated to spread far beyond their immediate context and cause domino crises elsewhere in the nation. Building on the previous chapter's exploration of NCTE's mass media strategies, this chapter analyzes the logics underlying NCTE's focus on local and community media. In it, I explore how the new strategies they developed made this work more manageable and disentangle how the digital distribution of local and community media influenced when, why, and how NCTE engaged with these media.

"Local" and "Community" Media: What's the Difference?

What's the difference between local and community media? And why do their differences matter? Scholars of journalism don't necessarily agree on answers to those questions. Journalism studies has increasingly focused on local news outlets, the importance of place to the production and consumption of news, and the central significance of identity and community membership to individuals' personal media consumption practices.[6] Across these lines of inquiry, "local" and "community" have been used interchangeably. Local is most often defined solely in opposition to "national," and some scholars further refine "local" news with terms like "hyperlocal" to refer to outlets serving small towns or neighborhoods within cities.[7] In other contexts, "local" is used to refer specifically to the *people* an outlet serves, rather than the geographic space—but even so, those people are understood to occupy shared physical space.[8] This latter understanding of local is virtually identical to that of "community" news media. Journalism scholar Jock Lauterer, for example, defined "community newspapers" as those that "serve people who live together *in a distinct geographical space* with a clear local-first emphasis on news."[9] Here, "local" journalism is integral to the development of place-based "community."[10] Media serving communities *not* based in geography are generally not referred to as "community" media, but rather as the media of a particular identity group, such as "the Black press" or "gay and lesbian media."[11]

In the interest of clarity, I will break from this blurred understanding of "local" and "community" media. Specifically, I separate them into two distinct kinds of non-mass media, while understanding that they share orienting logics that are important for understanding how and why social movement organizations remain concerned with them. In using the term "local media," I refer to any subnational media outlet that defines its audience as those individuals belonging to a bounded geographic region and that produces content presumed to be of near-exclusive relevance to those individuals. Examples of local media include local television network affiliates, such as ABC affiliate KOCO 5 in Oklahoma City, Oklahoma; local public broadcasting radio, such as KOAC in Corvallis, Oregon; and local newspapers, such as the *Marietta Daily Journal* in Marietta, Georgia. As the anecdote I opened this chapter with showed, "local" media are often consumed by people who are from the geographic area they serve, but who do not currently reside there. As such, my understanding of local media aligns with what journalism theorist Kristy Hess calls "geo-social" news—news that serves a group of people embedded in social relationships with a geographic center, but that circulates in ways that are not geographically exclusive.[12]

In contrast, I use the term "community media" to refer to any media outlet that defines its audience as individuals belonging to a specific social identity group, and that produces content both of specific interest to and in the expressive norms of members of that identity group.[13] Examples may include *The Root*, an online magazine oriented toward Black audiences; *Out*, a print and online magazine oriented toward LGBTQ audiences; *The Forward*, an online newspaper oriented toward Jewish-American audiences; and *Indian Country Today*, a digital news outlet oriented toward Indigenous Americans.

These communities are distributed across the country. As such, the media serving them have no basis in a single geographic locale, but neither can they be lumped with "mass media" because they do not aim to serve "the mass audience." Rather, they aim to serve specific subgroups and assume that members of those subgroups are the only ones engaging with their content, or at least are the only ones with the cultural understandings necessary to fully decode their messages.

Additionally, some media may be both local *and* community, as I have defined them. These media are oriented toward individuals belonging to a social identity group *within* a specific geographic region. These media may include local community media, such as Chicago's LGBTQ newspaper the *Windy City Times*, and what media system theorist Sandra Ball-Rokeach calls "geo-ethnic media," or media targeted to a particular ethnic group enclaved within a locale, such as Los Angeles' Korean community newspaper, the *Korea Times*.[14]

One might reasonably ask, given the distinctions I've drawn between local and community media, why are they woven together in my argument? Why are they distinct enough that they must be conceptually separated in this way, and yet similar enough that they should be analyzed together? In part, my answer is that the innovative activism strategies developed and deployed to affect local and community are nearly identical. Activists seek to "ground" their movement issues for different subnational audiences by locating them in the daily realities of social worlds. At a broader level, however, local and community media have experienced the same effects of digital media distribution on who engages with their content and how. In particular, the "enclave" quality of these media has mostly disappeared.[15] The geographic enclaves that once defined local media have been breached by the global distribution of web-hosted content. Meanwhile, the social enclaves that once defined community media have been breached by the curatorial dynamics of digital media, which allow social contacts from one community to make in-group media visible to out-group members. At the same time, people increasingly experience the "local" world through its digital mediations, which ultimately renders local and community media similar, at least as it concerns the "imagined" nature of the collectivities they serve.[16] As a result, local and community media increasingly look alike and function similarly, even as they conceptualize their audiences as having different origins.[17]

NCTE Everywhere, All the Time

For the better part of 2018, NCTE's Racial and Economic Justice Policy Advocate Mateo De La Torre toiled away on what was internally referred to as the "police scorecard." This "scorecard" was a report analyzing the policies of the twenty-five largest police departments in the country.[18] The seventeen policies of relevance included departments' treatment of transgender individuals on issues including the listing of pronouns on forms, arrangement of police transportation, and sexual misconduct toward transgender people in custody. The final report was a mammoth 111 pages of deep analysis and model policy proposals.

When deciding how to roll out this report, NCTE extensively debated the relative merits of focusing on local versus national media. In a special strategy meeting held in mid-September, Media Relations Manager Gillian Branstetter opined that "this could be a national news story and it deserves to be so."[19] The story would be how police departments across the country failed the transgender community in egregious ways, and how those failures are built into the structures of policing. But as Mateo explained to me in an interview, "for this particular case, it wouldn't really move our cause forward." Rather, he said, "a localized push will drive change and will get [police departments'] attention, because it's no longer some DC wonks telling a small county sheriff in Iowa what to do. That's not going to work."[20] As NCTE's staff deliberated their roll-out strategy for the report, they came to agree that a focus on local media outlets would be best. By focusing local media outlets' attention solely on the portion of the report analyzing policies in their own local police department, they could simultaneously "shame" those departments into changing their policies and provide local advocates with a resource to keep up the pressure for change.[21] NCTE ultimately decided to work with different media in each locale, developing twenty-five unique press lists (each consisting of local outlets in a police department's jurisdiction). It also sent out customized press releases for each press list and provided local transgender advocates in each jurisdiction with media toolkits for working with those outlets. The workload to customize press lists and toolkits was immense, but it led to a more impactful rollout.

This example of NCTE's local media work, while only one of many, illustrates a salient reality: Political battles over transgender rights, like those over other civil rights, are often waged at the state and city level, rather than nationally. Because the policy landscape for much of NCTE's work was local, national advocacy offered little recourse for the issues trans people face in the United States. Therefore, targeting local press to influence had a greater political impact. This may seem like an unremarkable observation, but the centralization of local media efforts I witnessed at NCTE is relatively new among national organizations. That is, national organizations have only recently started to directly engage in local and community media activism. They previously depended on local activists and advocacy groups to handle their own local issues. National organizations also now dedicate significant resources of money, skills, and time to this work, on par with or surpassing those they dedicate to mass media work. Especially considering (1) that many are pronouncing the death of local media, (2) that media serving minority social groups are facing existential financial threats across the country, and (3) that local and community media reach such smaller audiences than mass media, this degree of investment in local and community media by national organizations is striking.[22]

NCTE was so dedicated to local and community media because, as Director of Outreach & Education (O&E) Raffi Freedman-Gurspan noted in an interview, they helped "put out all the fires that are going on" around the country. NCTE might not be able to be there or dedicate a staff member to work on every local issue, but their local and community media programs could rapidly and flexibly respond to crises wherever they (predictably or unpredictably) arose.[23] In contrast to their mass media work, however, NCTE's local and community media work did not center on NCTE's media principals or even NCTE as an organization. Although NCTE staff would often be offered as sources to local and community journalists (as with the police scorecard), journalists were more often connected with members of NCTE's Voices for Trans Equality (VTE) and Families for Trans Equality (FTE) networks. These networks allowed NCTE to respond rapidly and flexibly.

The VTE and FTE projects together established a national network of nearly one thousand "community storytellers" who received media and communication training from NCTE to make them effective spokespersons.[24] Where it concerned media, these projects connected community storytellers with local reporters, getting stories about them placed in local and national media outlets, and getting their op-eds placed in state- and community-level media. These storytellers served as extensions of the organization, allowing NCTE to reach and monitor the furthest corners of the country, even while their relationships to NCTE remained obscured from public view. Preparing storytellers to be effective in this role necessitated training, of course, which NCTE's O&E team provided.

The O&E team included Education Program Director Rebecca Kling, who oversaw the VTE and FTE programs and took primary responsibility for the VTE network, and Family Organizers Debi Jackson and DeShanna Neal, who reported to Rebecca and together managed the FTE network. Once prospective VTE or FTE members were identified, they were trained. In-person trainings usually were run either at one of the transgender conferences held across the country, at which NCTE regularly held panels, or on an ad hoc basis before major political events. These events included the special session of the Texas legislature in 2017; the 2018 referendum on an anti-transgender "bathroom bill" in Anchorage, Alaska; and state or federal lobby days.[25] Other trainings occurred via webinar because network members were distributed across the entire country, making in-person trainings more difficult.[26]

The "core" training covered what Family Organizer DeShanna referred to as "general advocacy" or "storytelling" training.[27] This training consisted of teaching basic strategies for effective narrative communication for media interviews, and every VTE and FTE member went through this training prior to becoming a full member. Further trainings for members, which were offered on an ongoing basis, covered how to communicate about more specialized content or how to navigate specific situations. For example, some trainings covered useful talking points about access to sex-segregated facilities or section 1557 of the Affordable Care Act, which protects citizens from discrimination in the provision of health care.[28] These trainings expanded the basic skills network members were provided by giving them language and resources to apply those skills in more effective and targeted ways. Once prospective members were identified, screened, and trained, they became active members of VTE or FTE. Active members had access to continued training and important advocacy resources, such as op-ed templates, talking point guides, and—in the case of FTE members who were parents of trans youth—access to a secret Facebook group. At this point, they began to be regularly "deployed" by NCTE for media appearances and interviews. VTE and FTE members were most frequently connected with journalists and other media professionals writing stories or shooting videos about transgender issues. Having a stock of network members to connect with local and community media made NCTE more responsive to political crises. For example, they could nearly instantaneously respond when President Trump's announced his plans to ban transgender service members from the military (as discussed in Chapter 1). In most instances, the deployment of VTE and FTE members through local and community media was reactive, rather than proactive.[29] Once a political or social crisis hit a locale, NCTE would connect VTE and FTE members with local media to tilt public discourse in favor of the transgender community. As O&E Director Raffi remarked in an interview, "we are able—really under extreme time turnarounds—to activate our storytellers to come out in the media and tell their stories."[30]

Being effective at activating storytellers in the face of crises depended on "being everywhere, all the time." For NCTE, that meant having accessible storytellers in as many places as possible. Sometimes, though, NCTE found themselves without any storytellers to activate when a crisis struck, either because they didn't have anyone there or because the people there weren't willing to do media work in that specific instance. For example, when Anchorage, Alaska held a referendum on an anti-transgender bathroom bill in 2018, there was only one person in the VTE network located in the state. Given the rabid anti-trans sentiment at the heart of public debate on the proposition, he wasn't comfortable sharing his story in local media. Rebecca, as manager of the VTE network, went to Anchorage, "built out a lot more connections," and quickly set up a reliable team of storytellers to mobilize in local media on the issue.[31] Other parts of the country were also sparsely represented in the VTE and FTE networks. For example, NCTE had only one or two storytellers in Montana, which meant more media work would fall on their solitary shoulders if a crisis arose, and they had none in Idaho.[32] However, because crises had yet to break out there, NCTE was less immediately concerned with expanding their lists in those locations.

The uneven distribution of storytellers across the country was partly attributable to general population trends; trans people aren't distributed evenly across the country,[33] and so neither were NCTE's storytellers. But the uneven distribution was also based on NCTE and their coalition partners' attempts to predict where anti-trans policies would soon likely be on the docket. NCTE called these anticipated locales of interest "priority states." They included, at various times, Arizona, Florida, Georgia, North Carolina, and Texas. Because NCTE wanted to be prepared for battles there, the VTE and FTE networks included a greater number of members from these states.[34] During my time at the organization, NCTE also worked to increase the number of storytellers in Maine in anticipation of a pending battle, and in Massachusetts to combat the 2018 Massachusetts Gender Identity

Anti-Discrimination Initiative (often referred to as "Question 3"), which sought to overturn the state's transgender-inclusive nondiscrimination law via referendum.[35] Despite their uneven coverage, together the VTE and FTE networks included members in over forty states and a number of US territories, making the programs effective at covering most of the country's media markets.[36]

Managing the work of the networks was a momentous task. NCTE did not simply task VTE and FTE network members with putting their training into action on their own or give them a target and leave them to accomplish the mission, as though they were Charlie's Angels. Far from it. NCTE actively managed the VTE and FTE networks' activities, using them to extend the organization's reach and strengthen the impact of its messaging. In fact, managing the VTE and FTE networks were Family Organizers Debi and DeShanna's *full time jobs*, and it was most of Education Program Director Rebecca's job, too. Media Relations Manager Gillian Branstetter was often actively involved with coordination, as well. Altogether, this management required getting storytellers access to journalists working in relevant media, preparing them for interviews, and helping them draft and pitch op-eds and letters to the editor. NCTE staff also shouldered immense emotional labor as they helped storytellers process traumatic experiences and cope with the psychological stress of communicating about them publicly. This is not to say that NCTE could always provide one-on-one guidance in dealing with local and mass media, given the sheer volume of work nationwide. Instead, they could most actively support the storytellers who were working in areas NCTE *needed* them to, while making strategic decisions about when to dedicate their full resources to storytellers elsewhere. As Rebecca commented in an interview:

> If someone from San Francisco—where at a state, county, and city level there are good protections—was still really interested in sharing their story, I probably couldn't offer the same level of one-on-one line edits that I might for a "Yes On 3" op-ed [defending Massachusetts' trans-inclusive nondiscrimination law].[37]

Nonetheless, the goal of the VTE and FTE networks was to have ubiquitous presence across the country. Thus, even in cases in which there was less urgency to place storytellers in local and community media, Rebecca "would absolutely provide resources as much as I was able to with those other responsibilities."[38] The reward for the team's strenuous work was mediated presence "on the ground" in communities all across the country.

"Grounding" the Transgender Experience

At the time I interviewed her in November 2018, Leslie McMurray was a sixty-year-old, white, trans woman living in the Dallas suburb of Coppell. She had long blonde hair, a warm smile, and a soothing cadence perfected over decades working in radio before she was fired for coming out as trans. She was something of a superstar on the VTE roster because her media career had made her a strong writer and an even stronger public speaker. Leslie appeared in media often because she was skilled and instantly likeable. When she did, she would frequently mention that she owned a house in Coppell and frequented local businesses in the Dallas area, like supermarkets and cinemas. As she explained to me in an interview:

> [Texas is] a very red state, but Dallas is a blue little marble in the middle of this horrible red state that offers protections. So, I may mention that [I live in Coppell], and it may hit closer for people that live in Texas reading it to say, "Gosh I didn't know my state was like that," versus [someone in] Chicago saying, "God, I'm glad I don't live in Texas."[39]

By embedding her story—and her existence—in a local context for a consciously local audience, Leslie made her point resonate with people in her community.

While Leslie was particularly conscious of the value of rooting her narratives in her connection to her local community, this same dynamic undergirded *all* NCTE's local and community media work. Effective storytelling humanizes the teller by appealing to what they share in common with their audience, which may be agnostic or even antagonistic to them. NCTE's storyteller training implicitly encouraged personal narrativizing rooted in the mundane and ordinary experiences of community life—and it did so for strategic purposes.

VTE and FTE provided NCTE with the logistical benefit of being "everywhere, all of the time." In a basic sense, they helped the organization manage the overwhelming volume of local and community media work that needed to be done across the country. But they did more than simply

provide a nationwide presence. VTE and FTE helped "ground" the transgender experience in the immediate lifeworlds of individuals nationwide,
thereby increasing the impact of their mediated presence. That is, the presence of transgender storytellers in local and community media made transgender concerns relevant to the daily lives of otherwise disinterested people
by showing that they affected people in their immediate social surroundings.
And this was an immense asset to NCTE in responding to local political
crises and in pressuring specific local institutions. But it also, more importantly, was an asset for trying to achieve more long-term, durable social
change by improving public attitudes toward transgender people and convincing the public that transgender concerns mattered.

Staff at NCTE often bemoaned that mass media coverage had the unin-
tended effect of making transgender people seem like a "new" (and over-
whelmingly white) phenomenon. Trans concerns risked being approached
like a non-issue whipped up into political spectacle, or a "problem" found
solely in the big cities on either coast. As Family Organizer Debi commented
in an interview, people often perceived transgender existence as "a red state/
blue state thing."[40] Coverage in local and community media, particularly off
the coasts and out of major cities, helped overcome that presumption. As
Debi explained, "having local stories get covered . . . is important because,
again, it disproves the notion that this is just liberal ideology in strong-
held blue areas and [shows] that people are impacted everywhere."[41] Media
Relations Manager Gillian expressed similar sentiments, commenting that
"when [people] see [transgender issues] in their neighborhood, when they
see it being covered by reporters who live in their cities, the impact is more
directly felt by trans people."[42] Local and community media offered both a
counterweight and a complement to mass media coverage. They reached
where mass media couldn't, while also providing coverage that countered the
negative perceptions mass media sometimes caused.

Local and community media also addressed different audiences than
mass media, ensuring transgender messages were received by a wider range
of people. For instance, when NCTE's Executive Director Mara Keisling
was in Kalamazoo, Michigan for work travel, Gillian arranged for her to be
interviewed on the public affairs program on WMUK, the local public radio
station.[43] Gillian deduced that "those local audiences can have a really big
impact on their lives just in changing the conversation and reaching folks
that we aren't going to reach by being in the *Daily Beast* or being in *Slate*."[44]
The added layer of local connection to an audience that storytellers like Leslie

McMurray brought to a story only deepened that impact. Of course, securing coverage in local and community media was very rarely as easy as calling up a local reporter and handing them a storyteller. NCTE's most successful local and media community work was reactive, not proactive.

As Interim Communications Director Dave Noble explained, attempts to place "evergreen" stories about trans people—human interest stories without a specific connection to an ongoing political, cultural, or social controversy—nearly always failed.[45] For example, throughout 2018, NCTE's Comms team worked to place "evergreen" stories about storytellers in local Arizona media. Although there was not yet a political crisis in Arizona, NCTE anticipated that one could soon be sparked by Republican control of the state government. If they could seed the local media with stories about trans Arizonans, maybe they could get out ahead of transphobic policies. Unfortunately, despite their pitching, NCTE got zero bites from local media. It wasn't until news about the Arizona Court of Appeals hearing a case challenging Phoenix's transgender-inclusive nondiscrimination ordinance hit that NCTE successfully placed storytellers in local media. As Dave reasoned:

> It'd be fantastic to get more papers for their Sunday whatever section to talk about just, "Hey, let's profile this family and what they're doing here in our state." But there are fewer newspapers and fewer newspapers have those kinds of reporters that do that kind of work. And when you can tie that to a breaking-news-relevant thing, it's easier to get those stories shared.[46]

Education Program Director Rebecca expressed similar experiences working with local media:

> Pitching stuff is really hard and is sort of a thankless task and we are much more likely to get something placed if a reporter reached out and asked us for a reactive response. . . . If there's not something otherwise happening in the news, it's tough to get stuff picked up.[47]

For local journalists, storytellers put a human face on the political issues they wrote about. Beyond that singular purpose, they were useless. Thankfully, journalists' interest in finding storytellers who would be relatable to local audiences gave NCTE an opportunity to connect them with VTE and FTE members who could do that well.[48] But journalists' concern with political issues meant NCTE needed to structure their storyteller work around externally driven news cycles. They could only rarely *make news* with storytellers. In short, the presence of storytellers in local media served primarily to make news stories relevant to local publics by providing a sympathetic narrative hook.

Similar dynamics pervaded NCTE's community media work. NCTE placed storytellers in community media to make transgender concerns directly relevant to—rather than additional to or external from—the concerns of social identity groups. This was particularly important for racial, ethnic, and religious groups in which (a) ignorance of or opposition to transgender identity was more common or (b) transgender identity was understood as a problem of "other people." For example, NCTE expended considerable energy placing storytellers in evangelical Christian media in hopes of combatting the widespread transphobia in evangelical communities.[49]

However, in contrast to local media, community media was often less interested in helping audiences see trans people as their neighbors and more interested in seeing trans people as valuable members of identity-based communities. Fundamentally, this narrative shift required communicating about trans issues and identity in the language internal to a given community—in some cases quite literally. For instance, NCTE worked to place Latinx storytellers in Spanish-language media and other media targeting Latinx communities not necessarily to overcome transphobia, but to overcome cultural differences in understandings of transgender identity relative to non-Latinx Americans. In Spanish, for example, it is less common to use the term *transgénero* (a literal translation of "transgender") and more common to use *transexual* (in English, "transsexual," a term widely considered outmoded) to describe trans people.[50] The use of *transgénero* often flags to Spanish-speaking audiences that the speaker is an outsider, or as least an "Americanized" Latinx person. As Racial and Economic Justice Policy Advocate (and NCTE's only native Spanish speaker) Mateo explained:

> There's very limited education around the difference between *transgénero y transexual*. Transitioning is a word that not many people use. People will describe the action of transitioning before using the word transition. They'll say like, "*o, el cambio*" [the change], "*o, la cirugía*" [the surgery], "*o, el proceso*" [the process], you know? They won't necessarily say, like, "*la transicion*" [the transition], you know? . . . And "*identidad de genero*"

[gender identity], *"género y sexo"* [gender and sex]—people know what it is, but there's generally very little education around what the difference between those two is.[51]

In other cases, in media serving other communities, storytellers communicated about trans issues and identities not literally in a different language, but in different "codes"—expressive norms internal to a community. Oftentimes, there are sets of assumptions, unspoken understandings, and expressive modes shared among a community that, if a speaker doesn't get them right, reveals they do not belong. An NCTE staff member would be an obvious outsider when included in a story, thereby reinforcing the "otherness" of transgender concerns. By contrast, storytellers revealed themselves to be insiders, making trans concerns more relevant to a community. As Ray Gibson, a sixty-one-year-old VTE member remarked in an interview, "I am a Black man who happens to be transgender. I'm not a trans man who happens to be Black."[52] Through articulating his experiences as a trans person in the context of his Blackness, he could speak more directly Black publics, who identified with him in a more meaningful way.

Moreover, when dealing with historically marginalized communities, NCTE placed storytellers in community media to bridge the oppressions that transgender people faced with other forms of oppression experienced by other groups. In doing so, NCTE hoped to make those individuals who were politically engaged around their own identities understand the relevance of transgender issues to their own fights for equality. For example, Mateo did an interview with *El Tiempo Latino*—a local Latinx media outlet based in Washington, DC—about the connection between family separation at the border and the experiences transgender people face in Immigration and Customs Enforcement detention.[53] In the interview, he emphasized how the impact that confinement has on vulnerable people is clear, and that is an impact being experienced by a variety of Latinx people—trans people included. As Mateo explained:

> The Spanish media is more interested in the Latinx part of the community, so that's a significantly larger focus of my conversations [with them]. . . . If I'm talking about the same topic with Spanish media [rather than English media], I'll have to explain both incarceration and trans identities and then highlight the Latinx piece.

Although not unique to the Latinx community, emphasizing the relevance of transgender concerns to broader community concerns was often necessary.

At another level, community media provided the only means of getting certain transgender stories told. Mass media have historically paid little attention to transgender communities, and they have even more consistently ignored the issues facing racial and ethnic minority communities.[54] Thus, while mass media could sometimes be coaxed to cover issues facing white trans people, they were far less receptive to the specific concerns of trans people from other minority groups. By focusing on community media, NCTE could work toward greater visibility of transgender people who face secondary marginalization due to other facets of their identity,[55] and in so doing draw attention to under-addressed members of the community. In Media Relations Manager Gillian's words:

> These kinds of papers and these kinds of websites [that focus on specific racial and ethnic communities] tend to be covering stories and covering communities that aren't getting coverage in the rest of the press and if we can help direct them towards the impact of transgender people within this community, of the issues faced by transgender people within those communities, then I absolutely want to make sure we're doing that, too, because even within communities folks can be marginalized, folks can feel unseen, and we need to be making sure that we're addressing that, as well.[56]

Community-level attention would then elevate transgender concerns in new arenas, making transgender concerns relevant to more people, including those for whom transgender people might not be part of their geographically local social world.

Of course, NCTE's efforts to embed transgender people's stories within the social realities of local and community publics required them to make strategic decisions about *which* storytellers to prioritize for different media opportunities. As Education Program Director Rebecca explained to me in an interview, she tried to steer clear of evaluating stories or storytellers as "good or bad" and instead focus on "impact." In her words, she asked: "Will this person's story and will their experiences connect to an issue—whether it's general support of trans people or whether it's a specific policy issue—in a way that's going to impact a reader who maybe isn't familiar with that issue?"[57]

Historically, activists have appealed to notions of "respectability" when making decisions about who represents their movement and their community. They considered which types of stories (and storytellers) would be "palatable"—that would make their movement appear "normal" to mainstream audiences. Selecting "respectable" storytellers has happened across movements from the civil rights movement to the LGBT movement, though it has been thoroughly critiqued as a practice.[58]

NCTE was conscious of the critiques of "respectability politics" and avoided perpetuating a bias toward respectability for two main reasons. For one, contemporary social movements in the United States have largely abandoned the pretense of respectability, as digital media have afforded new routes to visibility for subjects previously marginalized within social movements.[59] NCTE was simply keeping up with activist trends. Perhaps more importantly, though, NCTE was also resistant to the idea of respectability because historically it had been weaponized by the broader LGBT movement as justification for sweeping trans people and their concerns under the rug.[60] And NCTE staff had seen it up close. For example, Family Organizers Debi and DeShanna had both been founding members of the Human Rights Campaign's (HRC) "Parents for Transgender Equality National Council" before joining NCTE as staff, where they had been subjected to the constraints of HRC's focus on respectability. As Debi recounted in interviews, HRC had a small number of families—mostly white, Christian, and with married heterosexual parents—they would promote.[61] When Debi and DeShanna came to NCTE, they latched on to NCTE's stated focus on diverse representations of transgender people and their families. As Debi put it, "there are a same few narratives that are always put out in the media and we want to be able to show different ones and to represent pretty much every facet of the community that we can."[62] For FTE, that meant promoting diversity of "family dynamics," including families with single parents, families with unwed parents, families with same-sex parents, working class families, and (most underrepresented in media) families of color.[63]

Naturally, a focus on family lends itself to respectability politics, as "the family" is considered the fundamental unit of a "respectable" society. NCTE was aware of this dynamic, and FTE was established in no small part because of the importance of family to American culture. VTE storytellers often leaned into the discourse of family by emphasizing their status as grandparents, parents, or children, the love their families had for them, and their participation in family activities on holidays.[64] But from storytellers' perspectives, this framing had more to do with being *relatable* to audiences than being *respectable* to them. As FTE member Jo Ivester, mother of an adult transgender child, put it, "people may not be comfortable or familiar with what it means to be transgender, but people relate to a parent's love for their kid."[65]

Beyond relatability, NCTE emphasized the diversity of their storytellers along lines of gender identity, racial and ethnic identity, age, life experience, and geography. Part of "grounding" the transgender experience involved locating transgender people in *every* social world—across the vast range of communities and subcultures in the United States. As Media Relations Manager Gillian summarized, choosing which storytellers to advance involved trying to "amplify the diversity of the transgender experience."[66] Storytellers provided a way around what Gillian referred to as the "em-dash problem," or the tendency of news stories to report on transgender issues by saying things like, to use her example, "HIV prevention and treatment are difficult to access for transgender people, *em dash*, especially transgender people of color." Such engagements with diversity were shallow and story-telling provided a way to make them substantive.

In sum, the purpose of NCTE's local and community media work was largely to demonstrate to publics that transgender people existed in their social worlds and deserved their concern. As Rebecca amusingly summarized:

> We have talked about the sort of ever-recurring example of, "well if we could get the left-handed trans gardener into *Left-handed Gardening Monthly*." That we have not had any luck with, but we still ask [VTE and FTE members] about hobbies and interests and if, you know, a kink magazine comes up, I have a person to connect them with. And if a hobby piloting magazine comes up, I have a person to connect them with.[67]

The "Placefulness" and "Placelessness" of Local and Community Media

As I have demonstrated in the previous section, NCTE conceived of local and community media as avenues for "grounding" transgender life within specific social contexts. However, how they conceptualized social context differed. NCTE conceived of local media as embedding transgender life in geographic communities and community media as embedding transgender life in imagined communities of individuals with shared identities.[68] These differences reflected respective emphases on "placefulness" and "placelessness" in NCTE's local and community media activism.

The value of local media for NCTE was intimately tied to its placefulness. By that I mean, the strategic value of placing storytellers in local media was the *specificity* of locating trans people within a social world based in geography. The value of placing trans storytellers in local media could be seen in the mobilization surrounding President Trump's announcement of his transgender military ban. To expand on examples from the first chapter, the *Wisconsin State Journal* ran a series of articles focusing on VTE storytellers with histories of military service, whom NCTE connected with the publication. Two of those storytellers were featured as the centerpieces of news articles that clearly articulated the consequences the ban would have on their lives. Significantly, both storytellers were positioned throughout their stories in relation to their Wisconsin geography. Army Master Erika Stoltz, for example, was referred to as a "Sun Prairie resident" and a "LaCrosse native."[69] Likewise, Retired Army Colonel Sheri Swokowski was referred to as "Sheri Swokowski of DeForest" and as a "Manitowoc native" in an article titled "Trump ban on transgender military service hits home for some in Wisconsin."[70] Beyond factors such as religious affiliation, class, and current employment sector—any of which could help an audience identify with the storyteller—*geography* became the basis for members of the public to identify with trans people.

The value of community media, in contrast, was intimately tied to its *placelessness*. That is, the strategic value of placing storytellers in community media was the universality of locating trans people within a social world based in collectively held, but fundamentally imagined identities. Imagined collectivity is clearly seen the in the example of Mateo's interview with *El Tiempo Latino* about the connection between family separation and the detention of transgender migrants at the border from the previous section. Beyond the obvious relevance of the border, the geography of trans people's existence was less significant than the fact that the trans people being discussed belonged to the community the newspaper served. *El Tiempo Latino* was a local community newspaper based in Washington, DC, while the trans people being discussed were at the southern US border after migrating from Central America. But Mateo communicated the importance of these trans people to the readers of the newspaper in terms of their identities as fellow

Latinx people.[71] And a similar placeless dynamic came into play when NCTE pitched storytellers to media focusing on other communities.

The organization's respective emphases on the placefulness and placelessness of local and community media both operated under the same logic of locating trans people within a social world. However, these two concepts seem inherently contradictory. If location within an *imagined* social world were sufficient for the kinds of attitude and opinion change NCTE sought, then storytelling through mass media would be enough. The public could be convinced to identify with trans people through any number of shared identities communicated to them through mass channels. However, storytelling through mass media was *not* enough. That's why NCTE focused on local and community media to place trans people within a *geographic* social world. To repeat VTE member Leslie McMurray's comment from earlier in the chapter, emphasizing her locality in Dallas in her local media work made her more effective at persuading fellow Texans than if she had been trying to persuade people in Chicago, who would view her story as a feature of Texas that did not concern them.[72] On the other hand, if location within a geographic social world were required for attitude and opinion change, then community media work would not be successful. So how did both logics work synergistically?

In essence, both logics worked because the underlying logic of the "local" was *actually* its appeal to an imagined collectivity, not a geographic one.[73] That is to say, the "likeness" established between trans people and the public that learned about them through media was only geographic to the extent that the white, Christian, cisgender, heterosexual mainstream that is the assumed audience for local media only imagine themselves as being "like" people who share their geography. Other individuals who form the target audiences for community media outlets, in contrast, form bonds of "likeness" through difference from the mainstream, regardless of geography. Thus, in targeting local media, NCTE made appeals to cultural similarities assumed to map onto geography, rather than appeals to geography itself. As Director of External Relations Raffi astutely explained in an interview, "local appeal" is fundamentally tied to "the ethnocultural spaces in this country."[74] As one example, she offered, "Southerners need to talk to Southerners in terms of not only language and cadence, but the values, the experiences."[75] Local media carry the discourses of place-based cultures in a manner directly analogous to how community media carry the discourses of the minority communities they serve. The difference is simply that local media carry the discourses of regional mainstreams, rather than supralocal minority communities. Placing storytellers in local media, accordingly, gave them a persuasive resonance by aligning the ways local trans storytellers communicated their experiences with the dominant norms of their regional mainstreams.

Of course, this resonance between storytellers and their regional norms was not the only reason to place storytellers in local media. Increasing the visibility of trans people in local media demonstrated that trans people exist *everywhere* in the country. Spatial presence was important, because it richly illustrated the impact that transgender policy decisions would have on the local community. But for members of the social majority, the locality of storytellers established "likeness" with them though other dimensions of their identities that fell outside of the (white, Christian, cisgender, heterosexual) "mainstream." In one incident in early October 2018, Emily Jones,[76] a transgender student at a middle school in Stafford County, Virginia was placed in potential danger during an active shooter drill. While all other students in her physical education class were instructed to shelter in the gendered locker rooms, Emily was barred from sheltering in either. Instead, she was directed to remain in the bleachers of the gym while the teachers debated where she should shelter. While she was put in no actual danger because the incident occurred during a drill rather than an actual active shooter crisis, her safety from gun violence was clearly considered secondary to her classmates' "safety" from her.

In the aftermath of the incident, NCTE reached out to Emily's mother, Marie, and dialogued with her over the course of the month.[77] Together with Marie and her legal representatives, NCTE crafted messaging around the incident and sought opportunities to use Emily's story to change policy by increasing support for transgender youth.[78] Their efforts focused on local media and local outlets, such as *RVA* magazine in Richmond and the *Free Lance–Star* in Fredericksburg, which thoroughly covered the incident.[79] Although the incident would gain significant national attention,[80] local coverage served a different function and hit a different tone. Local coverage represented the incident as an act of injustice against "one of us" that needed to be addressed, while coverage elsewhere in the country represented the incident as an act of discrimination against a member of a marginalized group. By emphasizing the locality of the incident, local coverage established a "likeness" between Emily and other residents of Stafford County that drove an overwhelming turnout of supporters to a Stafford County school board meeting to urge the superintendent to change the school district's public accommodations policy.[81]

In this sense, local media was an effective tool because of its "placefulness"—its locality drove the political change that followed the incident. At the same time, the logic underlying this "placefulness" was the same as that underlaid the "placelessness" of community media. It caused audiences to imagine a *social* likeness with a trans person, whose issues they then took on as issues of relevance to their own identity. In this case, that identity was one tied to geography—or, perhaps more appropriately, *mapped onto* geography—but it was just as much imagined. It was simply necessary to root the local mainstream's "likeness" with Emily in geography because of their incapacity to imagine "likeness" based on another shared identity category, as was possible for LGBTQ individuals who read her story in queer media outlets.

What is "Local" to the Digital Environment?

Local media matter for activists because they create bonds of imagined likeness between transgender people and regional mainstreams. These bonds rely upon shared geography, as well as the discourses, values, and experiences shared within regional cultures. But in the digital media environment, stories that are produced locally for presumably local audiences do not necessarily *remain* locally distributed. The spread of local to global begs the question of why activists focus on local media in a manner that so clearly and directly emphasizes its locality.

Of course, local media often fail to spread beyond their immediate place-based context in any meaningful way. Even when NCTE tried to count on local news to circulate widely online and become national news, it often didn't. But at a time when transgender issues were a matter of significant cultural and political controversy, it was always possible that local stories would be picked up by larger media outlets or simply shared widely on social media. As Interim Communications Director Dave remarked in an interview, "trans issues are a thing that national reporters want to be talking about," and so they often looked to local media to find stories when nothing of relevance was happening in national politics.[82] Sometimes national reporters' online foraging worked to NCTE's disadvantage, as harmful controversies spread beyond their local origins. Other times it swung in

NCTE's favor, such as in the case of Gavin Grimm, whose experiences of discrimination in the Gloucester Counter school system became a national story, making transgender students a priority on the national political agenda.[83]

Each of these local stories was taken up as a broader instance of the "transgender debate." This was particularly true when these stories were shared over social media, which is how many people encounter new political information.[84] And NCTE was acutely aware of the fact that the spread of news was often interpersonal. In Dave's words, "it's a lot of individual people who, yes, might be sharing stories, but they're the ones who are curating it and putting it in front of me."[85] When those individuals consumed local media and shared stories with their social networks—often with their own commentary on the story added—local issues left their place-based contexts.[86] Once taken out of context, these stories were no longer relevant for their "placefulness" or their connection to a community. Rather, they became relevant instantiations of the national political debate on transgender rights and identity. In such a media environment, each local crisis was also a potential national crisis. Whether a local story would become a national story simply depended on whether it circulated widely enough.

Putting Out Fires as they Spread

The capacity for local news content to circulate beyond its immediate place-based context was both a resource and a challenge for NCTE. Particularly with policy issues, local media coverage could serve a "precedent-setting" function, whereby news of an incident in one local context justified the replication of that incident in another. In the context of transgender nondiscrimination policy, there is significant evidence that successes and failures in implementing policies in nearby states influence whether a state will pursue similar policies.[87] Local media's refractions of the debate over those policies plays an important role in this policy diffusion. For example, the media-fueled public outrage over the passage of North Carolina's "bathroom bill" (HB2) led to the failure of similar proposed laws in Alabama, South Carolina, Tennessee, and Virginia. In such contexts, local media legitimate certain issues as a matter of concern, set the terms of debate for subsequent instance of those issues, and get those issues on the public agenda in new locales.

Managing local media coverage in situations of political crisis was, consequently, necessary work for NCTE. Affecting local coverage could seed positive attitudes toward trans people and opinions of transgender policy or counteract negative ones. At times, this media work was proactive, working to secure support for pro-transgender policies in the pipeline or lay the groundwork for changes NCTE sought to pursue. For example, NCTE engaged in strategic local media work around gender neutral ID policies, which they successfully pursued in numerous states. More often, however, local media work was reactive, either mobilizing opposition to a bad policy (as was the case in North Carolina around HB2) or to do "damage control" on an unexpected crisis—as occurred in Georgia in a case I narrate below. In these cases, NCTE pursued local media work in hopes they could at least set the terms of the debate locally as the story spread from its local context, or ideally "pour water" on the story to prevent a spark from spreading.

In large part, NCTE's epidemiological approach to local media work was based on a belief that it was easier to influence local media than national media. Thus, the effort required to shape or quash a story by affecting local media was much less before it gained national media attention. As Gillian explained, the local journalists she worked with often had lower levels of familiarity with transgender issues because they had never reported on them before, so they had fewer relevant resources locally available to build out their stories.[88] In these instances, Gillian would provide them with background context, data from the US Transgender Survey, and connect them with NCTE's Policy staff or storytellers from the VTE and FTE programs. As she related in an interview, "I've had reporters be thankful because I pretty much just wrote their article for them."[89] If that article was picked up by national outlets, NCTE had successfully influenced the flow of information about and perspective on trans issues.

At the same time, local journalists were often more likely to do the legwork to "get the story right" than national journalists were. This gave NCTE more opportunities to work with them on important stories before (or in hopes of preventing them from) becoming national news. As Gillian explained, local reporters would often call her while working on stories and confess they were "really concerned about doing the right thing."[90] Oftentimes their worries manifested as a fear of misstepping due to their own ignorance, but just as often it manifested as a genuine concern for the impact they would have on the trans people in their community. As was made evident in the previous chapter, national journalists rarely shared that degree of concern. National media tended to "flatten" local transgender issues into mere manifestations of a broader cultural debate and political struggle in a manner akin to horserace election coverage: Who won the most recent battle over transgender rights—trans people or their opponents? Who are the heroes and who are the villains—trans people or their opponents? Local media, in contrast, offered greater depth of analysis, more social and political context, and greater attention to the impact the issues may have on people's daily lives. As such, working with local media to get their deep analysis right, to present the appropriate social and political context, and to emphasize for them the impact issues had or would have on the lives of trans people, NCTE could counteract national media's "flattening" of transgender issues and identities.

The next section details one case from my time in the field that illustrates the dynamics involved in NCTE's local media work. In the fall of 2017, a Decatur, Georgia school was challenged on its transgender-inclusive policies. At a board meeting for the school, Oakhurst Elementary, the Alliance Defending Freedom (ADF)—a conservative Christian legal advocacy organization, designated a hate group by the Southern Poverty Law Center—unexpectedly arrived and demanded the repeal of those policies. NCTE helped organize testimony from local parents of transgender children and their allies, and the school board ignored ADF's demands. One month later—although it would not come to light until the next year—ADF filed a complaint with the school alleging that a five-year-old "gender-fluid" student who was assigned male at birth sexually assaulted a female classmate in the girl's restroom. The school district investigated and determined the allegations were unfounded, and local media refused to run stories on the allegations. The issue resurged and ADF's complaint came to light in October 2018 when the US Department of Education opened an investigation into the Decatur school district's handling of the case at ADF's request. NCTE then found itself working to counteract the spread of the story across the nation. They worked with local and community media outlets to ensure the situation was presented appropriately and in a manner that did not put pro-transgender policies in Decatur and elsewhere at risk. NCTE's management of this crisis illustrates the vital importance of local and community media work to maintaining control over the messages that circulate nationally in the networked public sphere.

The Alliance Defending Freedom Went Down to Georgia

At around 11 a.m. on the morning of October 3, 2018, Director of External Relations Raffi, Education Program Director Rebecca, and I gathered in the small conference room where the weekly Outreach & Education (O&E) team meetings were held. Family Organizers Debi and DeShanna joined over teleconferencing software, as usual, as they were not based in Washington, DC. As everyone settled in, my phone dinged with an email from Media Relations Manager Gillian:

> A reporter just flagged for me that the Department of Education is investigating a complaint filed by ADF [the Alliance Defending Freedom] on behalf of a family in Georgia that believes the trans-inclusive bathroom policy at their five-year-old daughter's public school led to her sexual assault by a trans student. We do not need to respond right away, if at all. Thoughts?[91]

Throughout the O&E team meeting my phone continued to ding as staff responded to Gillian's troubling news.

The first response was from Policy Counsel Ma'ayan Anafi, who noted that the only details available about the situation were provided by ADF's press release and complaint filing. Considering the source of the information, NCTE could not be certain of its veracity. Deputy Executive Director Lisa chimed in, warning, "if this becomes a big story, it has huge terrible potential."[92] She suggested that staff "poke around" to see what they could discover about the underlying facts, and monitor local media to determine "if it is becoming a community conversation."[93] Interim Communications Director Dave replied that NCTE was already receiving calls from journalists about the issue and "it will likely be a big story by the end of the day."[94] He urged everyone to attend the Comms team's weekly messaging meeting that afternoon so NCTE could swiftly coordinate a response. At this point, O&E finally acknowledged the unfolding crisis, as Family Organizer Debi replied to the thread to share that she had recently worked with a parent in the FTE network in Decatur, and that she had emailed the parent to get more information from on the ground. Debi then verbally informed the O&E team that she would attend the messaging meeting and that she hoped to hear from one of the local FTE members by then.

Within half an hour, Debi heard back from some of the FTE network members in Decatur. The parents were unaware ADF had filed a complaint with the Department of Education's Office of Civil Rights (OCR). As they related to her, "The school investigated the incident last year and found no evidence to support it, so they all thought it had been resolved."[95] She added that O&E had conducted messaging training with the parents in Decatur before a big school board meeting that spring and the incident never even came up. Truly, this complaint seemed to be coming out of nowhere.

Shortly after Debi reported her findings over email, Media Relations Manager Gillian let everyone know that an article had been published by *Politico*; the first story on the incident was out in the national press. Worse yet, the story was based exclusively on the information provided by ADF, with no investigation of their claims and no inclusion of information from additional sources. The second paragraph of the article also positioned the incident as yet another manifestation of the Trump administration's "controversial" handling of transgender rights, as just another chapter in the ongoing national political story of the federal government versus trans people. As the article framed it, the issue "signals a major development in Education Secretary Betsy DeVos' controversial policies on transgender bathroom access in schools and her handling of civil rights enforcement for transgender students."[96] The story gave no consideration to the people who lived in the community or what the incident meant for them. After sending the story to NCTE staff, Gillian forwarded it to the Nondiscrimination Communications Working Group—a coalition of communications staff at a number of LGBTQ rights organizations who held a weekly conference call to coordinate on pressing issues—providing them with the full context available to her and imploring them to join the conference call at 3 p.m. to coordinate a response.

The Comms team, Deputy Executive Director Lisa, Policy Counsel Ma'ayan, and Family Organizer Debi gathered in the Comms office at 1:30 p.m. for the weekly messaging meeting, which was now solely focused on the crisis in Decatur. Gillian opened the meeting with a request to simply lay out all the facts. Ma'ayan began to summarize that at some point in past two years, the Decatur school district adopted a set of best-practice trans-inclusive policies, which was met with surprise and dismay by some parents. In accordance with those policies, a gender-fluid student who was assigned male at birth was permitted to use the girl's restroom. This student then allegedly sexually assaulted a cisgender girl in the restroom. The alleged assault was reported to the school, but it is unclear how the school responded beyond launching an investigation (of an unknown kind) that dismissed the report. The school did not change their accommodations policy and, at some point for an unknown reason, the Department of Family and Children's Services (DFCS) investigated the mother of the cisgender student who was allegedly assaulted. It was this mother's belief the school called DFCS in retaliation for filing a complaint.

The major caveat to this summary was that the *only* source of information on this case was ADF, which, in Gillian's words, had "a strong incentive to bend the facts of this case."[97] Lisa suggested that it would be up to NCTE to fulfill the investigative role journalists were failing. The VTE and FTE networks would be a primary resource, as would local media in Georgia. She then turned to Debi for updates on her fact-finding efforts.

Debi informed the group that she had spoken to an FTE parent in Decatur, who had not heard anything about a complaint. Debi followed up her uninformative chat with this parent by calling the Decatur school district, who informed her that they hired an attorney once they heard news of the OCR complaint. But they had thought the issue was "dead and done" because they investigated and found no basis for the allegation.[98] Debi then contacted Vanessa Ford, an FTE parent turned NCTE board member, who had a friend on the board of the Georgia State Schools Coalition. Debi hoped that through this connection she might discover why the investigation dismissed the allegation of assault and why DFCS was brought in. In the meantime, Debi confirmed she was in contact with an impressive four different FTE parents in Decatur—each of whom was shocked to hear of the case—who would report back with any information they could gather. (Interim Communications Director Dave later commented how astounded and impressed he was O&E had four parents in Decatur alone. Truly, it seemed NCTE was able to use VTE and FTE to be *everywhere*.) If NCTE could put together a fuller picture of what happened, they could collaborate with local journalists to get an accurate version of events circulating in public conversation.

The rest of the meeting focused on the joint effort to establish what really happened in Decatur. Debi pulled up documents from her records and sorted through her emails with FTE members. Lisa consulted news coverage of the incident from *Decaturish*, a local news outlet. Rebecca joined the meeting to share emails and her own memories of conducting storyteller training for VTE and FTE members in Decatur. Gillian pulled details from national news stories and the ADF complaint. Together, they pieced together a clearer picture of what happened.[99]

A decade before the alleged incident, the Decatur school district implemented a trans-inclusive policy that gave students access to public facilities that aligned with their gender identities. In the face of the Trump administration rescinding Obama-era guidance on Title IX protections for transgender students, the superintendent circulated a memo in July 2016. The memo reiterated the school policy and affirmed the district's support for transgender students' rights.[100] The superintendent then made a public blog post further circulating the memo in February 2017. That fall, Norcross-based ADF attorney Vernadette Broyles showed up to a school board meeting to protest the policy, although she claimed no affiliation to any actual families with children in Decatur schools. Furthermore, although she presented a petition from a group referring to themselves as a "parents coalition"[101] with over one hundred signatures, not all the signatures were public, and of the public signatories, many were "located in other cities or in some cases other countries."[102] Only two parents—a married couple—spoke out in person, and both denied any affiliation to Broyles.

The result of this September 2017 meeting was a special school board meeting that was scheduled for October 10, during which time the board would accept public input on the policy. To help FTE members and their allies in the local community prepare, Rebecca conducted one of her usual storyteller trainings over video conference. After the school board meeting, the FTE parents informed Rebecca everything had gone well, and the school board released a statement expressing their ongoing support for the policy. Roughly one month later, on either November 14 or 15, the alleged assault occurred. Finally, on December 26, DCFS arrived at the alleged victim's home (which ADF charged was the result of retaliation from the school). The facts uncovered in this Comms meeting didn't line up with the claims made by ADF. Quite possibly, things were not as ADF presented them. Because Family Organizer Debi had already been in contact with several FTE members on the ground, Lisa tasked Debi to "be our primary investigator-detective and continue that role."[103]

At this point, Lisa shifted the group to ask how NCTE would craft a compelling narrative and argument around the facts. "I'm worried that there will be a lot of stories based on the ADF complaint and nothing else," Lisa lamented, and NCTE wanted to preempt those stories.[104] Digital Campaigns Manager Laurel advocated for working with journalists "off the record and on background to get in the story that way."[105] Dave concurred: "The goal is not for us to be in any of these stories . . . We just want to shape what the information is and what the messaging is."[106] Public conversations about the issue would unfold over the next few days, and NCTE would need to be "directly aggressive" in shaping how those conversations unfolded, he said. But letting this conversation come from within the affected community via storytellers, rather than from an outside organization like NCTE, would make their messaging more effective.

Debi then pivoted the focus to the local community, thinking about how to reframe the situation around its local consequences and, only secondarily, its national reverberations. She argued that she should work with the FTE parents in Decatur to prepare them with statements for local media about the benefits of the policy. "Without these policies in place, my child would not be safe using the restrooms because . . ." she rehearsed to herself.[107] She emphasized that these statements would be sympathetic to the concerns of community members. They would reinforce that trans-inclusive policies do not make other children unsafe, and that's why every case of misconduct should be thoroughly investigated on its own merits. Title IX protects all students, regardless of their gender identity, and is a powerful recourse for alleged victims of assault. Dave agreed, saying that the current political framing of the issues centered on how the *policy* led to sexual assault, "but it's not the policy—it's what someone did to someone else."[108] He continued: "If we allow the framing to be that a risk of these policies is more sexual assaults happen," the transgender movement would lose control over the meaning of trans-inclusive policies and play into widely-believed misinformation about transgender people.

Beyond preparing storytellers in Decatur with reactive statements, NCTE needed to decide how to manage the mass media that were fueling this fire. Might the local media extinguish it? The group decided that Gillian would send a reactive press statement from the organization to every journalist that had sent her an inquiry—most of whom were from mass media outlets. Dave then turned to Laurel to ask if any local press had covered the issue yet. Laurel informed him the *Atlanta Journal Constitution* and a few others had run stories, but they hadn't pushed them over social media yet. Dave saw the publishing lag as an opportunity to seize the local conversation before the terms of debate had been established. Gillian added that her media monitoring software covered local outlets, such as *Decaturish*, so she would be able to keep tabs on the on-the-ground conversation.

Everyone across the organization set to their tasks until the 3 p.m. call with the Nondiscrimination Communications Working Group. Then Media

Relations Manager Gillian, Policy Counsel Ma'ayan, and I reconvened in the Comms office. Gillian was leading the meeting and guided legal and advocacy collaborators through discussing the crisis in Decatur.[109] Gillian proceeded by laying out the facts of the case as NCTE understood them. She then added that ADF filed their complaint with the Department of Education in May and the Department's OCR announced they would launch their own investigation into whether the school mishandled the investigation and if policy contributed to a hostile environment that enabled sexual abuse in September. Media pounced on the story, a whole month later, because ADF had issued a press release announcing the Department's decision to investigate. It was issued alongside an eleven-minute documentary they produced about the supposed "dangers" of Decatur's transgender-inclusive policies, featuring families who lived in the area—including the mother of the alleged victim. The video had already been embedded in numerous local news stories and was circulating widely online.[110] Gillian reported that, like many others on the call, she had received several press inquiries throughout the day. However, she wouldn't respond until everyone could meet and "get on the same page" about how to discuss the issue.[111] She then filled everyone in on what decisions NCTE had landed on during their messaging meeting, before opening the call up for questions.

Representatives from ACLU, GLSEN, and Lambda Legal each shared that they were in touch with local affiliates and partners to get more information and would share it as soon as they knew more. In the meantime, they were reliant on ADF and NCTE for the facts. Gillian reiterated that ADF wanted to skew the facts, so there was a need to independently establish them. The national press had picked up the press release from ADF because it was easy to tell, and it fit the ongoing narrative of national clashes over transgender restroom use. However, local media offered space to tell the full story in an impactful way as soon as the activists could craft an appropriate narrative.

Gillian then asked if anyone on the call had received any press inquiries of note. Lambda Legal's representative reported fielding calls from the *Associated Press* (*AP*) and another from *Politico*, received by a colleague in Dallas. Gillian informed the group that NCTE would not be issuing a "proactive" press release. Instead, their talking points would guide how to respond when questions were directly posed. The hope would be to avoid engaging in the national discussion, which would hopefully blow over quickly. Instead, they wanted to focus their energy on controlling the on-the-ground conversations in Decatur to resolve the issue as quickly as possible. Part of that effort, Gillian said, would involve leaning on NCTE's talking points before the *AP* story on the issue hit and it became news everywhere. The rest of the strategy would come from telling stories of support and success with the Decatur policies and working to "elevate those above water."[112]

As the meeting drew to a close, Lambda Legal's representative thanked Gillian for NCTE's strategic leadership, but expressed concern about the impact this would have on young trans people and their rights. Gillian shared their concerns: "Obviously the community concerns are great."[113] But she also tried to assure them NCTE would be able to avert crisis: "I know through our own storyteller programs we're taking steps to make sure that parents are aware of the talking points." Together with the rest of the work the team was doing locally, they would regain control. That evening, Gillian circulated the finalized talking points to the members of the Working Group and sent NCTE's statement to the journalists who had contacted her.

The next morning, Deputy Communications Director Jay, Digital Campaigns Manager Laurel, Director of External Relations Raffi, Gillian, and I gathered in the Comms office for the Comms morning check-in. Laurel kicked the meeting off by informing everyone that, unsurprisingly, the Decatur issue "blew up last night."[114] At least half a dozen major outlets had run articles on it, although some of them had been sufficiently influenced by NCTE to not be catastrophic. *Politico*, for example, issued a new article in their "Morning Education" section, which (1) centered transgender activists' concerns the Department would "inject politics and ideology" into the investigation; (2) appropriately contextualized ADF's long history of specifically targeting transgender-inclusive laws and policies across the country; (3) emphasized anti-sexual violence and anti-domestic violence groups' support for transgender-inclusive policies; and (4) directly quoted NCTE's statement.[115] However, most of the stories, as Gillian noted in the meeting, were from the *Associated Press*. *AP* journalist David Curry had reached out to Gillian, and she gave him NCTE's statement, thinking it would then appear in the *AP* story.[116] Unfortunately, Curry ended up not writing the story that was run; a national education reporter Gillian was not in contact with did. Even if the *AP* were to update their story with NCTE's information, that wouldn't fix the stories that had already been published through the wire.

As a partial remedy, Gillian suggested shifting focus to LGBTQ media. Jay and Laurel both agreed with Gillian's suggestion, and Laurel noted that the LGBTQ press offered NCTE's best change to "get a framing that is not taken directly from ADF."[117] Gillian said she would send out their materials to her LGBTQ press list. Jay suggested instead she should "pick handful of good reporters you know aren't going to fuck it up at a couple of targeted publications."[118] From those outlets, other LGBTQ media would run stories with NCTE's perspective. From that critical mass, so would other media (as happened with the passport crisis in Chapter 3).

Later that day, Debi emailed everyone who had been working on the Decatur issue to tell them that *Decaturish* had run a new story. It built on the information and messaging NCTE had prepared the previous day but, through new investigative work, added two crucial details.[119] First, the Decatur Police Department responded to the sexual assault complaint. They—not the school—referred the families of *both* involved students to DFCS. Second, the alleged assailant was a cisgender boy and did not identify as either transgender *or* gender-fluid. The story further referred to ADF appropriately as a SPLC-designated hate group, aligning with ADF's perspective. The *Decaturish* story was then picked up by national press outlets, including the *Washington Post*, which cited *Dacaturish*'s investigative findings.[120]

During the next week's O&E team meeting, Debi again raised Decatur to update the team on how events had unfolded since the media storm. There was going to be another school board meeting, not to consider repealing the policy, but to discuss the community's concerns. This time they were "making a point to limit who gets to speak . . . so outsiders cannot come in and have a say."[121] This seemed to be a direct response to ADF's prior tactics. Debi promised to follow up with the FTE parents in Decatur about how the meeting went. Rebecca seemed reassured: "It sounds like—knock on wood—ADF overplayed their hand."[122]

Another week later, on October 15, Debi emailed the Comms and O&E teams: "Over the weekend, I became aware of efforts ADF is making within conservative religious networks to find stories they can submit to the OCR around trans-affirming school policies and the case from Decatur, GA," the email began.[123] Executive Director Mara characterized it in her reply as ADF was running their own storyteller program focused on litigation, rather than media attention. Media were only a means to the end of overturning policies, but nonetheless, they were operating a similar strategy to NCTE. They were just on opposite sides of the issue. For example, ADF had successfully placed the story of the alleged victim, who was Black, in the local Black community media outlet *Atlanta Black Star*.[124] The story was built entirely around ADF's framing and included video of the alleged victim's mother, grounding the issue as relevant to the local Black community. Local media became a battleground on which each side used storytelling to fight back the other.

A few days later, *Decaturish* ran an op-ed from a transgender man who was a storyteller in Decatur. In it, Charlie James Cote discussed his experience growing up as a high schooler in Decatur. He explained the concerns and fears transgender people have when accessing public restrooms. He derided opponents of Decatur's transgender-inclusive policies as zealots who wanted to punish openly trans students for busting their closet doors open. He appealed to the collective ethos of Decatur as a community. Powerfully, in closing, he made clear both the local impact of the issue at hand and its significance for the nation as a whole:

> Transgender people live in this town. I'm one of them. . . . Citizens of Decatur must not succumb to the fear mongering of The Alliance Defending "Freedom." We cannot let discriminatory rhetoric replace understanding and information. Our county is watching. There are potentially national consequences of this situation. We are better than this, smarter, kinder, more loving people than this. We must be steadfast and vocal in our conviction that a hate group . . . has no place in governing our community or our schools.[125]

No further articles were published about the issue and the school district did not overturn the policy.

How Fast Can You Fiddle?

NCTE's efforts to manage the unexpected crisis in Decatur and prevent the national spread of panic over schools' transgender restroom access policies exemplify the power and precarity of local and community media for national activists. NCTE again found itself embroiled in hyperlocal politics because the networked nature of the contemporary communication system meant local issues rarely stayed local. If NCTE hadn't gotten involved locally, they risked a domino effect of similar crises elsewhere across the nation. Local and community media became vital resources to manage this conflict. The VTE and FTE storyteller programs were how the organization managed those media. These programs gave NCTE the necessary reach and presence in locales across the country. By working locally, they gained the ability to expediently shape local and community media from the inside, rather than as outsiders parachuting in.

The Decatur case also demonstrates how NCTE used local and community media to "ground" transgender experiences in the social worlds of Americans across the country. NCTE mobilized the stories of trans individuals and their family members within the crisis-affected community to ensure on-the-ground conversations about transgender rights included their sympathetic perspectives, rather than the stigmatizing political opinions of opponents. Through working with the local media outlet *Decaturish* and connecting their journalists with VTE and FTE members, NCTE influenced the local coverage of the crisis. In doing so, they could seed positive opinions and sympathetic attitudes within the community that reverberated in local political discourse. This coverage, in turn, influenced the growing national media attention, shifting the broader conversation on transgender rights.

NCTE capitalized on both "placeful" local media and "placeless" community media to influence the distributed flow of messages within the political information environment. NCTE worked with local media in the Decatur area to influence both the information and the narratives about trans-inclusive school policies, while working with LGBTQ community media across the nation. Through influencing LGBTQ community media, which was naturally more sympathetic to transgender issues, NCTE was able to produce a counterweight to the stories based on ADF's information. Influencing these stories ensured more attention to NCTE's messaging, because of the complex intermedia agenda-setting dynamics of local, community, and national media seen in the previous chapter. Furthermore, both local and community media, from a narrative perspective, were more likely to discuss policy in terms of its impact on the daily lives of people in the affected locale. By contrast, national media were more likely to discuss the issue as a single battle in an ongoing political war. NCTE assisting the publication of more local and community media ensured greater attention to the real-world impacts of trans-inclusive policies.

Ultimately, NCTE found themselves fighting against their own tactics. That is, ADF's approach to local and community media work closely paralleled NCTE's own. It similarly relied on recruiting and training storytellers, and "grounding" those storytellers' experiences in local and community media. In this way, they capitalized on the power of local media to spread stories nationally to drive broader conversations about transgender rights. NCTE was, consequently, in the unexpected position of needing to engage in an on-the-ground battle for control over the flows of social and political information about transgender rights with their opponents. This shift demanded an "all out" approach to countering the transphobic messages circulating in local and community media that drew on all the resources available to NCTE and its partner organizations.

As I noted at the outset of this chapter, national activists' emphasis on local and community media is novel and provides different political benefits than national media work. The takeaway from this chapter is that local and community media work made transgender experiences "real." That realness influenced political opinions and discourse within geographically collocated and dispersed communities. Simultaneously, because of digital technologies, local and community media existed within a broader, "placeless" flow of political information, opinions, and perspectives. Placelessness made the discourses of local and community media significant at *multiple* levels within the communication system. Local and community media inform national coverage and help shape the political information environment on the ground. While NCTE's VTE and FTE networks were important resources for shaping on-the-ground conversations through local and community media, they also served to shape those conversations through other means. Specifically, combining the VTE and FTE networks with NCTE's other social network-based communications transformed the personal political information networks of individuals nationwide by saturating their interpersonal networks with messages in support of transgender rights. The following chapter builds on this discussion of the VTE and FTE networks to consider how national organizations make change in social networks in new and unexpected ways.

5

Making Politics (Inter)Personal

Early on Wednesday, July 12, 2017, I walked up to the large glass doors of 1111 19th Street NW, where Ogilvy, the multinational advertising and public relations behemoth, had its DC offices. I was there to attend an event held by the Public Relations Society of America's (PRSA) National Capital Chapter. Director of Communications Eric Dyson had asked me to attend on behalf of the National Center for Transgender Equality (NCTE).[1] The event was called "Brand-Building Selfies: Using Instagram and Snapchat Stories to Unleash Results," and Eric thought it would be a good learning opportunity for the organization. NCTE had just launched its Instagram account, so I was there to take good notes and report back with insights NCTE could implement.

I made my way up to Ogilvy's suite on the third floor of the building, where I checked in for the event, and was ushered into a glass-encased conference room that was already buzzing with activity. Huddled groups of congressional staffers, lobbying firm executives, advocacy organization interns, and aspiring "young professionals" excitedly rambled to one another about the transformative political potential of social media while downing coffee and pastries from a nearby Au Bon Pain. I sat in the back corner, trying to avoid talking to anyone because I didn't know how to explain why I was there. I suspected the truthful answer of "I'm a researcher studying a small activist organization that needs my detailed note-taking abilities to learn how to use Instagram" would hardly strike up the kind of networking-focused conversations people in the room were looking for.

Shortly after 8 a.m., a woman from the PRSA took to the front of the room to call everyone to order. She introduced the presenters for the day, Sara Tuman and Anthony Shop of Social Driver, a DC-based digital strategy agency specializing in social media-focused brand management. With evangelical fervor, the duo described how the attendees could reach audiences through Instagram and Snapchat. I dutifully jotted down their many points, even picking up a useful trick or two along the way. Then the presenters put up a photo of a lightning bolt striking the earth. Effective communication is like lightning, they said. Although it may look like it from on the ground,

Voices for Transgender Equality. Thomas J Billard, Oxford University Press. © Thomas J Billard 2024.
DOI: 10.1093/oso/9780197695425.003.0005

lightning doesn't descend from the heavens. In reality, negative charges descend from the clouds while positive charges rise from the ground to meet in a brilliant flash. Brand management on social media is like that, they said. A brand might often look from the outside like they are projecting a coherent image on social media. But in reality, much of the brand's image is being built and carried out by the social media activities of the brand's followers and supporters. In that moment, I was struck, like lightning (or not, I guess), by a realization.

Although lightning was a clever metaphor to illustrate their point, the concept they were conveying was hardly original. Theories of brand co-construction—emphasizing the active role consumers and brand community members play in creating brand meaning and the valuation of brand equity—are dominant in the academic literature.[2] Brand co-construction practices are common in most corporate industries. In fact, my colleague Rachel Moran and I have proposed our own theory of "networked branding" to account for how technological change has transformed processes of meaning-making in consumer culture. We had noticed that brands now operate less as *entities* and more as *spaces* in which consumers form social networks that sustain the brand and set its cultural meanings.[3] While the idea of networked branding presented by the Social Driver team was far from new to me, hearing it in this context made me relate the idea to NCTE's work. I realized how it manifested in their approach to *activism*—just not for the purposes of advancing their "brand."

It could often look, from the outside, like NCTE's communications work focused only on mass media (Chapter 3) and on local and community media (Chapter 4). You could see Executive Director Mara Keisling's name following a quote in a news article. Journalists frequently referenced NCTE's 2015 US Transgender Survey, even when they didn't contact NCTE directly. You could see Director of External Relations Raffi Freedman-Gurspan interviewed on broadcast television. NCTE's logo might be on a sign floating in the background of a photo from a protest on the cover of a magazine. But much of NCTE's communications work wasn't carried out by them. It was carried out by people in communities across the country and in social networks (both mediated and unmediated) that NCTE couldn't or shouldn't participate in.

The previous chapter demonstrated how vital local and community media advocacy were to NCTE's political "ground game." An essential component of this advocacy were the Voices for Trans Equality (VTE) and Families for Trans Equality (FTE) projects. VTE and FTE capitalized on the media trainings NCTE provided to create a "deployable" network of storyteller-advocates to engage with local political crises on NCTE's behalf. They would also appear in local and community media (without a publicly declared connection to NCTE) to shape political discussion on transgender issues and identities. But the training NCTE provided to VTE and FTE members was not only useful for engaging with media. Rather, VTE and FTE members' training shaped how they engaged in *all* their communications about transgender issues and identities, from conversations with friends and family to advocating for themselves and others at doctors' offices and parent–teacher associations to managing their social media communications. In fact, the training provided by NCTE was even *more* helpful for these everyday communications, considering that engaging with media was rarer for VTE and FTE members than engaging in discussions within their own social networks.

This chapter investigates how NCTE's training influenced the communicative activities of VTE and FTE members in interpersonal contexts, from their engagements with community institutions and discussions with in-person interlocutors to their participation in digital dialogues. Additionally, this chapter considers the ongoing role NCTE played within individuals' social networks beyond these initial trainings, as well as how they capitalized on the power of social networks to influence the broader communication system, including mass media and local and community media. Taken together, NCTE's social network-focused approach to activism created a "centralized decentralization" that saturated the communication system with voices in support of transgender equality and transformed the conversations circulating through the networked public sphere.

Laying the Groundwork for the Ground War

Jo Ivester was a sixty-one-year-old, white, Jewish woman living in Texas, and mother to a twenty-nine-year-old trans man named Jeremy. At the time I interviewed her, she had cropped dark hair that fell short of her expressive eyes. She had an undeniable warmth and kindness, and absolutely beamed whenever she mentioned her son. It was clear after the first few minutes of talking just how much her love for Jeremy motivated everything she said and did. Toward the end of our conversation, Jo told me about a time when she was speaking with a stranger on an airplane about her son. The man seated next to her was "very conservative" and pressed her on the importance of transgender issues, asking "why should the rest of us have to change the way we do things for such a tiny part of the population?"[4] She was hesitant to engage with him because, clearly, he was not keen on trans people, and she could tell that he held rigid views on masculinity. But she was trapped next to him until the end of the flight, so Jo had to say something. She "figured that talking football would work."[5] As she recounted:

> I talked about Jeremy playing football as a middle schooler and how, at first, we were really proud because we thought we had the only girl in the history of the school that had played football as both a seventh and eighth grader. And then we realized that our kid was saying, "That's not why I'm playing football. I'm not making a statement for women's rights. This is where I belong. I like playing football. These are my buddies. This is what I want to be doing with my time."[6]

The first time Jo had told this story was in a VTE/FTE storyteller training session run by NCTE's Education Program Director Rebecca Kling in Dallas. By her own admission, "it didn't work."[7] But by the end of the session, after workshopping the story with Rebecca and the other participants, she finally had a sufficiently "polished" version that could be a back pocket resource. So, when faced with the man sat next to her on the plane, she whipped it out. Maybe the story worked, maybe it didn't. Jo felt she "never really reached him."[8] But, she thought, "a year from now, he may find out that one of his friends has a trans nephew and he can say 'oh, that weird lady on that plane was talking about this,' and he'll be a bit more understanding and care a bit more."[9] Without the training NCTE provided, Jo said, she never would have had that conversation. The training helped her build a repertoire of polished stories and, as she explained, "having a half-dozen three-minute stories that you can pick from really increases the comfort level and willingness to share with a stranger."[10] That's exactly what NCTE wanted: to give storytellers the comfort and competency that would make them natural advocates. By seeding the country with enough storytellers, they could strive for groundswell social change.[11]

NCTE's VTE and FTE programs were a form of what political communication scholar Rasmus Kleis Nielsen has called "personalized political communication"—"premeditated practices that use *people* as media for political communication."[12] Although Nielsen was writing about the important role canvassers, phone bankers, and other such volunteers play in election campaigns, his concept applies here as well. Just like election campaigns, NCTE employed "a tightly scripted, controlled, and professionalized set of practices" largely aimed at winning the "air war" waged over media.[13] Also just like election campaigns, NCTE provided a material and symbolic infrastructure that allowed storytellers to function as media in the "ground wars" waged in people's social networks.

The previous chapter briefly described the trainings NCTE provided to VTE and FTE network members. These "storytelling" trainings covered the basics of effective narrative communication, with a focus on media interviews. Supplementary trainings covered more specialized content, often focusing on the intricacies of specific policy issues and how to effectively communicate about them. At their core, these trainings prepared VTE and FTE members for "deployment" to serve as sources for mass, local, and community media journalists. But to characterize these trainings as merely "media training" would be wrong. These trainings also prepared VTE and FTE members to serve as expert communicators in other situations.

NCTE designed trainings to prepare storytellers to communicate in their local communities and interpersonal interactions. Indeed, the idea that NCTE's trainings provided transferrable communication "skills" was repeated across nearly every interview I conducted. For example, FTE member Rachel Gonzales, a thirty-five-year-old mother of a transgender daughter in Dallas, explained that the skills needed for media work and advocating for her daughter interpersonally in her community were identical. "You can't separate the two," she said.[14] Of course, certain skills NCTE emphasized were media-specific, but, at their core, the "skills to be an effective media advocate" were the same skills needed to speak before your local legislators or to the school principal or with your parents-in-law.[15] VTE member Leslie McMurray, a sixty-year-old transgender woman living in Coppell, Texas, expressed similar sentiments. Although trainings conveniently provided statistics and policy information in one place, these resources could be gathered independently through one's own research. "They're commodities," Leslie explained, "but the skills training that we're getting from [Education Program Director Rebecca] can't be duplicated elsewhere."[16] And these skills translated far beyond the realm of interviewing.

One of the crucial elements of NCTE's trainings was teaching VTE and FTE members how to assess their audiences to determine whether and how to talk with them. As FTE member Rachel succinctly summarized it, Rebecca's trainings centered on "figuring out who you're talking to, what your point is, [and] making sure you're catering your story to the audience and to your point."[17] Beneath this apparently simplicity, however, lay a more nuanced point about assessing target audiences that was novel for first-time advocates being trained by NCTE. For example, VTE member Paula Sophia Schonauer, a fifty-two-year-old transgender woman from Oklahoma City, explained in an interview how NCTE's training helped her. It made her realize how much she could affect individuals in her conservative community if she was clever in her communications. "There is a lot of intolerance," she explained, but learning how to identify which individuals might be "movable," even though they might not appear so at first, "helped me articulate where effort is worth extending."[18] She continued:

> There's a lot of people who are predisposed to be non-supporting, no matter what we say . . . But then there's those who really don't know how they feel about things. They're the best opportunity and I found that [this group] in Oklahoma is a lot bigger than I realized. . . . All they hear is the negative things, and they will at least publicly support those things because they don't know anything else. But when they have the opportunity to learn better and especially identify with people through story—which is the remarkable thing about the storytelling project—they change their minds.[19]

Without training transgender individuals and their family members in how to identify those "movable" individuals and engage them in dialogue that helps them identify with transgender people, these impactful conversations would be much less likely to occur.

Of course, each storyteller faced different experiences pertaining to transgender issues and identities and, therefore, their communication needed to be customized. NCTE addressed this need by offering a wide array of issue-specific trainings. These trainings, which VTE and FTE members opted into, provided specialized information, statistics, talking points, and storytelling feedback for their specific issues. VTE and FTE members were not expected to be general experts on testifying to "the transgender experience." Rather, they were empowered to testify to their own experiences. VTE member Leslie expressed that this approach ultimately helped make storytellers more effective communicators because they were able to focus on those issues that "resonated" with their life experiences.[20] In her words:

If I'm telling something that I'm not passionate about, it's not going to be as effective. So, if [a new training] pops up from NCTE that I go, "Wow! I experienced that," or "That's happened to me," or "Gee I can see that happening to me or someone that I care about," I will absolutely [participate in the training] and incorporate that.[21]

These trainings taught storytellers how to translate personal experience into persuasive conversation. VTE and FTE members were trained in which stories to tell, when they were effective, and how they could best be communicated. For family members of transgender people, trainings often focused on how to speak with personal authority on transgender issues without speaking for or over transgender people.[22] For example, Leslie described her experiences participating in two different trainings during the 2017 Texas legislative session, when the Texas legislature was contemplating so-called bathroom bills. She explained how Rebecca trained storytellers not to simply talk about how such legislation would "be mean" or how evidence showed that they were "trying to solve a problem that doesn't exist." Rather, Rebecca trained them in "telling your story . . . and making it personal for people."[23] Through the storytelling practice and feedback portions of NCTE trainings, VTE and FTE members acquired the tools needed to tell their story to engage in persuasive conversations at a moment's notice. As Leslie summarized her delivery:

Here's my story. Here's how it would affect me. Here's why I'm afraid if one of these things passes—because these things could happen to me and they're very real. And if you care about me as a human being, you won't do that.[24]

Training VTE and FTE members would not make them experts in policy or champion debaters but it would prepare them to engage in quotidian conversation in ways that could lead to political influence.

Trainings like the ones Leslie participated in around the 2017 Texas legislative session were common. In fact, FTE member Rachel participated in the same trainings when Rebecca traveled to Austin.[25] NCTE invested in these trainings not only to deploy network members in local media work around the "bathroom bills," as described in the previous chapter, but to prepare them to testify before the Texas legislature. Even trainings not tied to specific political crises addressed how to navigate journalist interviews and public testimony because NCTE often deployed storytellers to participate in political meetings as well as media appearances. For example, Rebecca contacted veterans in VTE to arrange their participation in meetings with veteran service organizations. In another instance, she set up a closed-door meeting for an FTE parent, their trans child, and another trans teenager with Secretary of Education Betsy DeVos to "look her in the eye and talk about their experiences."[26]

But beyond public communications centered directly on NCTE's strategic goals, NCTE understood that their trainings served important personal functions in VTE and FTE members' everyday lives. For instance, Rebecca commented that she often heard from VTE and FTE members after training sessions, when they would report that they had used the language they learned in training to talk with their HR department after coming out at work, or to advocate for the care they needed with a reluctant doctor.[27] These small steps of progress in network members' daily lives were just as crucial to the broader strategic objectives of the VTE and FTE programs. Indeed, NCTE viewed the VTE and FTE programs as a means of propagating beneficial conversations, no matter how small or remote. As Family Organizer Debi explained in an interview, "We're looking for the ripple effects. . . . We want people to build on our training and go out and keep doing the work and getting the stories further and further out there."[28] NCTE wanted storytellers to go into the world and carry out the organization's ground game unsupervised.

Making Community Pillars

Throughout the summer and early fall of 2018, NCTE collaborated with the progressive coalition to try to block the confirmation of Brett Kavanaugh to the Supreme Court. In addition to allegedly sexually assaulting Dr. Christine Blasey Ford and at least two other women, Kavanaugh had one of the most conservative ruling records among judges in the United States. NCTE, among other organizations, reasonably feared what he might do to transgender rights if he sat on the highest court in the land.

NCTE joined a rally held outside the Supreme Court building on the afternoon of September 17, a few weeks before the Senate voted to confirm Kavanaugh's appointment. NCTE's Policy Director Harper Jean Tobin was set to speak, but the organization wanted to center the voice of personal experience, not policy. NCTE called in Nicola van Kuilenburg, a forty-seven-year-old mother to a college-aged transgender man living in Frederick, Maryland. Because Frederick is only an hour outside of DC, Nicola drove in to speak at the rally alongside a slate of advocates representing progressive movements, including a woman named Melissa, who was part of the National Network of Abortion Funds' We Testify program, an analogue of the VTE and FTE programs in the reproductive rights movement.[29] Although she was an experienced speaker, Nicola was worried, partly because the last-minute invitation left her little time to prepare, and the rally would take place in torrential rain. NCTE provided her with a structured set of comments, around which she told the story of her transgender son James' experiences of discrimination in school. She argued that Kavanaugh would legalize trans discrimination as a Supreme Court Justice.[30] Nicola delivered her speech in front of the approximately one hundred gathered protesters and camerapersons from media outlets including DC's local ABC affiliate, shortly before the rain drove the protestors home.

Almost a year to the date before Nicola spoke at this rally, FTE member Sarah Watson, a fifty-three-year-old mother to a thirteen-year-old nonbinary child, spoke at a rally against Jeff Mateer, President Trump's nominee for a lifetime judgeship in Texas. Mateer was on record referring to transgender children as evidence that "Satan's plan is working."[31] Sarah wrote a speech to deliver at the rally about the fear her transgender child had coming out because of men like Mateer. This rally was to be her first public speaking experience and so she shared her speech with Rebecca and Family Organizer Debi, who provided feedback and helped her prepare her delivery. Her speech, like many rally speeches, was recorded and the video of it "went viral," racking up three million views.[32]

In both cases, these storytellers were participating in local political activities in their communities. But they didn't have to do so on their own. NCTE provided the resources to enable their participation and make it more effective, thereby extending NCTE's reach into those communities. As an added benefit, both speeches circulated beyond the original time and place they were delivered, either through local media coverage (in Nicola's case) or through digital media circulation (in Sarah's case). Employing storytelling skills helped them become agents for change.

NCTE's trainings and resources gave storytellers the skills and confidence to become more visible, vocal, and active advocates within their communities—their local publics. Even when VTE and FTE members perceived the purpose of trainings and resources as preparing them for media appearances, they found the lessons learned useful for everyday communicative needs within their communities. For NCTE, this was a crucial component of the VTE and FTE programs. Community storytellers increased NCTE's capacity to affect the social and political standing of transgender people across the country, far beyond their reach in Washington, DC. Because NCTE could not actually be in those communities and local and community media were effective, but only to a point and in certain contexts, it was important to cultivate community pillars who could advance NCTE's mission.

One of the key domains in which VTE and FTE members advocated within their communities was local government, including both elected officials and local institutions of the state, such as police departments and local school boards. For instance, VTE member Leslie provided trainings on how to interact with transgender community members for police officers at the Caruth Police Institute. In 2016 and 2017, she also worked with the city of Dallas to provide city employees with healthcare that covered transition-related care. Although the City Attorney and City Manager "fought us tooth and nail on it," Leslie and her collaborators ultimately won, securing transgender-affirming healthcare for the city's fourteen thousand employees.[33] As Leslie explained, NCTE's trainings made her a more effective advocate. They enabled her to influence local government to secure rights and protections for trans people throughout her community.

For many VTE and FTE members, the trainings and resources they received through NCTE were most vital for their community work. They had no intention or desire to engage with media, which was fine with NCTE. FTE member Sarah, for example, had done no media work through NCTE and avoided media whenever possible. She preferred to speak at community events and offer trainings at conferences and within her community.[34]

NCTE's trainings and resources also provided storytellers with the means to organize other advocates in their community, thereby extending the training they received to new participants. FTE member Nicola, for example, organized a sustained campaign to pressure the Frederick County Board of Education to adopt a policy on how public schools in the county treated transgender students like her son James. As she informed me, "We used some resources from NCTE, and every single time that we asked [for more resources], we were provided them."[35] For instance, when they held their first rally in Frederick, which 250 people attended, Nicola got NCTE to share their designs for protest signs. In a different example, drawing more on NCTE's trainings than its resources, FTE member Sarah trained five parents of transgender children in her community on how to deliver a two-minute persuasive story. She led them through a meeting in which they delivered their stories to five Montgomery County Board of Education members, the superintendent, and the assistant superintendent.[36] In each case, storytellers extended the skills and resources NCTE provided them to have a broader, collective impact in their communities.

Outside of explicitly political contexts, VTE and FTE members drew on the skills developed through NCTE trainings to advocate for themselves, their children, and trans people in local community institutions and businesses. Often this meant advocating for trans-affirming care at hospitals or for one's own care in a doctor's office. FTE member Leslie, for example, had to train her own doctor to provide her with trans-competent care. As she told me in an interview, "I've spent four years training my doctor so that I can get decent healthcare out of him because he's so fascinated with the fact that I'm transgender that he misses things that he shouldn't miss."[37] Because of that personal experience, Leslie worked with a number of other healthcare providers, as well as medical schools, to offer trainings.

FTE member Benjamin Kennedy, a twenty-four-year-old, white, transgender man living in Burlington, Vermont, likewise worked extensively with healthcare providers. He conducted trainings and participated on panels at the University of Vermont (UVM) Medical Center—the largest hospital in the state. Like Leslie, his advocacy on behalf of other trans people's needs was inspired by his own experiences. As he recounted:

> They were just so painfully ignorant or unaware when I started my transition as an undergraduate at UVM, and I had to go there a few times. That's what really pushed me into getting more involved locally in education and health care—it was my experiences there and the ability to get involved.[38]

In some respects, the advocacy around healthcare provision is particular (although certainly not unique) to transgender individuals because of the extent to which medical practitioners serve as gatekeepers over so many of trans people's social and political rights, as well as because of the very specific forms of healthcare many trans people require but that most doctors are ignorant of, if not hostile to.[39] At a more general level, though, this kind of advocacy by VTE and FTE members is emblematic of the ways NCTE's trainings made storytellers more effective agents for interpersonal change in their communities.

Another local institution that community storytellers could influence was schools. As Benjamin mentioned in the above quote, his negative experiences transitioning while a student at UVM led him to engage in advocacy in educational institutions. He further explained in our interview that he conducted trainings and consulted with colleges in Vermont. He eventually went on to work with local school districts to help make their policies more "trans-competent."[40] Advocacy in school settings was even more central to the everyday activism of FTE members who were parents of school-aged transgender children. For example, Rachel, whose daughter was eight years old, expended considerable effort educating the parents of other children in her daughter's school, which had effects Rachel wasn't immediately aware of. In one instance, the mother of one of her daughter's classmates approached her in the school parking lot "in tears" apologizing for her former ignorance.[41] As Rachel recalled, the woman confessed to her, "I would totally be on the wrong side of this if I didn't know you personally and watch your kid go through this."[42] The woman then went on to write a guest post for a Republican political blog about why she was "on the right side of this battle," defending transgender students' rights.[43] As Rachel explained, "one of the biggest reasons why we decided to be active and visible is because we could see firsthand what an impact it makes having a personal relationship like this or a personal insight into what this looks like."[44] Through well-trained interpersonal engagement with community members and institutions, storytellers achieved real change that benefited their entire communities—all without the direct involvement of NCTE.

For many storytellers, the trainings NCTE provided helped them serve as opinion leaders in their social networks.[45] They could step into being the authority on transgender issues and identities because they had the skills to lean back on in difficult situations. VTE member Benjamin, for example, explained how he relied on what he learned in trainings to confront his less-understanding family members: "As a person who generally would tend to avoid conflict at all costs, I sometimes find myself being able to push myself to engage" by drawing on techniques developed in NCTE's training.[46] He recounted a conversation in which his grandmother referred to another transgender man as a "she" who "doesn't want to be a 'her' anymore."[47] "I was inclined to just pretend that I was going through a tunnel or that I was sick, or I need to take the dog out—any excuse to not engage in that conversation," he said, but he leaned on his training to engage with her.[48] In his words:

> Something I learned in one of the trainings was about how to do like "Trans 101" without making somebody feel like they're in "Trans 101," because attacking them for not knowing something is not exactly going to appeal to them wanting to listen to me. And so, trying to break things down in a way that makes sense and is accessible to them but doesn't let them know that this is as simple as I could possibly get . . . and that has come in handy with a lot of people in my family. So, instead of screaming at them to like, "How do you not know this? This is so simple! You're so dumb!" which I feel I often want to do in my daily life, turning it into a conversation and a learning opportunity for them because if I just yell at them or more often—actually all the time—just choose not to engage because it's not worth it, it's just going to happen again.[49]

Community storytellers could have profound impacts on individuals in mundane social settings and one-on-one interactions. Interpersonally, they could invisibly improve the acceptance of transgender individuals in their immediate social networks and communities.

This kind of person-to-person and person-to-community-institution change was at the heart of NCTE's work. As Family Organizer Debi described her aims in working with FTE network members:

> I think strength in numbers and being able to have 3,000 people sign a petition is great, but I think having 3,000 people going into their school boards and getting trans inclusive policies passed is better . . . I want us to have this little army of families going out there making changes community by community by community and making all of those kids safe . . . and I want the growth to be kind of organic like that. I want one family to inspire the next and the next and the next, and I want everyone to be empowered that they have an organization behind them.[50]

An "army of families" logic underpinned NCTE's work with VTE, as well. By training storytellers in how to engage with media and to communicate about their issues, NCTE provided them with the resources to effectively reshape conversations about their sociopolitical issues in their more immediate social surroundings. Whether in their families or their places of work, worship,

or learning, they transformed the conversations happening in publics far beyond NCTE's immediate reach.

Making Keyboard Warriors

While engagement with community members and social network contacts
in face-to-face contexts made NCTE's VTE and FTE programs effective at
producing groundswell social change, storytellers' social networks were not
limited to their offline contacts. Most scholarship on social networks and
activism overemphasizes the significance of digital media connections and
underemphasizes far more common but often more significant interpersonal
connections.[51] A myopic focus on digital media in academia was partly what
made NCTE's focus on interpersonal networks so striking. But the trainings
NCTE provided storytellers were useful beyond engaging with media and
interpersonal contacts. They shaped how storytellers engaged in public and
private communications over digital media.

Public communication, such as over Twitter, allowed VTE and FTE
members to establish relationships with people who might be affected by the
perspectives and opinions they shared. Other communications were more
private. On Facebook, storytellers were able to control who saw their content and in what contexts. For example, they might post to their timeline
where only their "friends" could see their commentary or they might post
and comment within private groups they belong to. They might comment
on public posts from organizations, public figures, and news outlets, where
strangers could engage with them. Across these contexts and types of media,
storytellers again found themselves drawing on their training to strategically
engage.

Digital media also afforded storytellers the ability to engage in types of social networking that increased their capacity to make change. Digital media
created spaces for people to share advocacy resources and organize community action beyond NCTE. FTE member Sarah ran her own secret Facebook
group consisting of over 125 other parents of transgender children in her
area.[52] In that group, she shared knowledge, experience, and resources, and
provided members with a space to coordinate advocacy efforts. Beyond
drawing on her own FTE training in guiding these parents as advocates, she
also brokered communication with NCTE by passing along NCTE resources
and calls to action. In one such instance, in the wake of Trump administration

plans to narrow the legal definition of gender as being either male or female and immutable from birth, Family Organizer Debi and I worked with Media Relations Manager Gillian. Together we drafted an open letter to the Trump administration that was signed by over 2,450 parents and family members of transgender people, which we eventually got placed in *Teen Vogue*.[53] We drew on the FTE network to recruit signatories and Sarah, as a member of that network, both signed the letter and recruited the parents in her private Facebook group to sign. Social networking on the part of VTE and FTE members extended NCTE's influence far beyond their immediate reach without disclosing an affiliation with the organization.

NCTE also involved themselves more directly in VTE and FTE members' digital communications by providing them with resources designed for viral dissemination and spaces to engage with a community of NCTE-affiliated advocates. The most significant of these efforts was an NCTE-run secret Facebook group for FTE members. (No such group existed for VTE members.) This group allowed FTE members to "connect with us," as Debi explained, "and for us to share information with them."[54] Debi and fellow Family Organizer DeShanna administered the group, and they could control what information was shared, when, and how. By directly administering the Facebook group, they could keep tabs on FTE members' evolving needs, and reach out to NCTE's Comms, Outreach & Education (O&E), and Policy teams with requests for new information and resources. For example, when FTE members became concerned by a string of incidents in which community members called Child Protective Services (CPS) on families with transgender children alleging abuse,[55] DeShanna worked with Policy Counsel Ma'ayan to put together a video tutorial on so-called safe folders.[56] These folders, which NCTE urged families to keep multiple copies of in different locations, contained a set of documents attesting to the child's sincerely held gender identity. The folder included personal letters (such as from psychiatrists, physicians, friends, family members, and neighbors), legal documents, home studies documenting family stability, and educational resources on transgender identity in children. The folder could be furnished if CPS were to open an investigation. Through providing these resources and answering FTE members' questions, NCTE was able to quell the growing panic and provide information for them to share with their wider networks.

NCTE was also generally able to provide information about ongoing social and political issues facing transgender people, and to provide sample language and talking points for engaging in online conversations. Additionally,

NCTE shared all their Facebook and Twitter graphics with storytellers to share on their own social media profiles. In doing so, NCTE subsidized public online communication for FTE members, enabling them to more easily and actively engage in digital advocacy as part of their everyday social media routines.

As has been illustrated throughout this book, social media conversations play an important role in the broader political information environment. They serve as a direct means of conveying information, perspectives, and opinions to large numbers of people, while driving journalists' attention to news stories and shaping how they represent public opinion on trans issues. Moreover, social media conversations often refract news stories, reframing and contesting official news perspectives when circulating stories through individuals' social networks.[57] NCTE saw VTE and FTE members as a means of affecting social media discourse.

For instance, in crisis situations in which "bad" news stories were circulating through important social media networks, NCTE would mobilize VTE and FTE members to post or comment, extending NCTE's influence over the emerging discussions beyond their own organizational social media communications. Debi explained in an interview that the O&E team mobilized VTE and FTE participants to engage in news comment sections. As she described:

> If there is a really horrible story that's out and comment sections are filled with a lot of ignorance, some of the people who have the emotional capacity to do it and have their social media settings locked down enough, we will ask them to jump into the comments a little bit and try to provide some helpful [resources for them to know what to comment].[58]

Improving the tone of comments could have a significant effect on how news stories were being reframed for social media consumption, improving public perceptions by counteracting negative opinions.

Of course, NCTE acknowledged that VTE and FTE members alone were of limited use in the digital domain. The flow of communications on transgender subjects consisted of the posts and comments of an immeasurably large network of individuals. Of that network, VTE and FTE formed a small (albeit highly vocal) subset. However, VTE and FTE members could be leveraged to mobilize larger networks of social media users to communicate in accordance with NCTE's strategic goals and messaging. For example, FTE members often participated in additional Facebook support groups for parents of transgender children not run by NCTE, which ranged in size up to seven thousand members. The members of these groups were thoroughly vetted by administrators because these groups were often the only safe space parents had and security was a concern. These groups were vital spaces for parents to discuss their transgender children and transgender issues for these families. However, unlike the vetting NCTE conducted prior to training FTE members, the members of these large parent groups were not vetted for their dedication to transgender rights or their acceptance of transgender people beyond their children.

As Debi commented in an interview, many members of these groups would make comments such as, "[Although I support my own child,] I do think some teens are doing this to be trendy," which showed that they "clearly aren't on board yet."[59] If these parents were engaging in public discourse as authorities on transgender issues, they presented a danger to the goals of NCTE and the transgender movement. However, because FTE members usually participated in these large parent groups in addition to NCTE's program, they could influence how non-FTE parents thought and spoke about transgender issues. Sharing NCTE resources in the group and challenging other parents who were not "on board yet" served a purpose. FTE members could cultivate a shared parental discourse that resulted in significantly larger numbers of parents participating in broader social media conversations in productive ways.

Although VTE had no equivalent networks of support for NCTE to tap into except for the advocacy conferences and social events at which NCTE already had an institutional presence, NCTE found other ways to promote VTE visibility in the digital sphere. Transilient was a multimedia project modeled after Brandon Stanton's Humans of New York, a social media-based project presenting humanizing man-on-the-street portraits of and short interviews with people in New York City. Unlike Humans of New York, however, Transilient operated on the road, traveling to towns and cities across the country, photographing and interviewing a diverse array of transgender people. Throughout the summer of 2017, I worked under then-Communications Director Eric's direction to schedule interviews and photo sessions with VTE storytellers along the Transilient team's route. These photos and stories were then shared across Transilient's digital presence, including Facebook, Instagram, Twitter, and their website and blog. When Transilient arrived in Texas, which coincided with a special legislative session in which the Texas legislature was considering an anti-transgender "bathroom bill," we matched Transilient with as many storytellers as possible. The Transilient team was being shadowed by digital media outlets *Buzzfeed* and *Vice* at the time, which increased the presence and visibility of transgender people armed with NCTE's skills, knowledge, and resources. Engaging with programs like Transilient deployed VTE and FTE members to influence digital conversations about transgender issues and identities. In this way, NCTE exponentially increased the reach of their messaging into a domain with significant impact on the broader political information system.

My Best Friend, NCTE

"It's a community," Family Organizer DeShanna said to me, speaking about the FTE members' Facebook group that NCTE managed. "We *have to be* a community. We have to because things are going to get far darker soon and community is going to be very important."[60] It was important to her "not to just call FTE a network"[61] because NCTE was doing more than just "connecting" people. NCTE was a central node within the digital social networks of transgender people and their allies. Beyond sharing resources to help them navigate in-person conversations and social media debates, and beyond mobilizing people to steer conversations of strategic significance, NCTE built meaningful social ties for people.

The FTE members' Facebook group was just one key example of this work. Within the group, parents developed a supportive sense of community and took on a collective capacity-building role, drawing on their own experiences to teach one another advocacy techniques. This was particularly important for keeping FTE members engaged. As FTE member Rachel commented in an interview:

> I think the main reason that I have been involved so much is not only the visibility of changing hearts and minds but also because other parents need to see that this is happening and you're not the only one. That really was the catalyst for me getting involved in all these things. It was that I don't want other people, especially in small towns that super feel alone, [thinking] that they are the only ones going through this.[62]

Through providing a community space, NCTE kept FTE members involved and active, even when simply walking away from advocacy would be easier and completely understandable.

Even outside the group, NCTE connected transgender people and allies through lobby days, conference sessions, and training events. These spaces of in-person connection brought strangers from across the country together and bound them to one another through friendship and a shared mission that persisted and grew digitally. FTE member Jo, for example, recounted meeting a transgender man at an NCTE training in Dallas whom she kept connected with over Facebook. Although they didn't speak frequently, and they rarely saw each other, they were able to connect on issues they were both working on in Dallas when Jo did advocacy work there. "Were it not for NCTE training," she said, "I would have no idea who he was. So, as a community-builder, I think the training is very important."[63] In turn, that community, beyond offering emotional support and camaraderie, translated into advocative support as network contacts "leverage[d] each other" in their activism—all thanks to the connective power of NCTE.[64]

Outside of Facebook groups and VTE/FTE trainings, NCTE's social media feeds provided posts that educated and informed. When crafted to maximize the likelihood of being shared, stories spread through their followers' social networks to individuals beyond NCTE's immediate reach. As I noted in Chapter 3, Facebook Live broadcasts served to share important pseudo-press-conferences in some instances, and broadcast actual press conferences and rallies in others. In still other instances they served to dialogue with NCTE's followers. As Digital Campaigns Manager Laurel, who organized the Facebook Live broadcasts, explained, the original intention was for them to be a weekly live broadcast that ran through the key issues of the week and included a question-and-answer session with viewers.[65] NCTE quickly discovered that a live Q&A wouldn't work, as too few people watched them to synchronously participate. Thus, Facebook Live broadcasts were restructured to cover individual topics each week while staying responsive to community needs. At the beginning of each week, the Comms staff would take stock of the topics circulating on social media and the policy issues on the horizon and. From them, they would set a theme for the week's broadcast.[66] In certain instances, a policy issue (such as a pending court decision) would have an advanced date associated with it, and NCTE would plan ahead for a broadcast, even conducting the Facebook live "on-site" at a relevant location. In others, the theme would emerge as a reactive response to an emergent issue. Other Facebook Live broadcasts covered "evergreen" subjects, which were put on the back burner until there was a week when no pressing issues demanded attention.[67] These themes usually included more quotidian concerns that addressed trans people's everyday lives.

NCTE's Facebook Live broadcasts, like their other posts, served an important educational and informational function. They let transgender people and allies know what was going on in DC and across the country, while helping them talk about important issues and understand which actions they could take to make an impact. FTE member Sarah, for example, remarked in an interview that, in addition to generally using their Facebook page as a "reference," she watched each of the weekly Facebook Live broadcasts to keep up to date with transgender policy issues and with NCTE's talking points.[68] Family Organizer DeShanna's information videos about "safe folders," transgender students' federal civil rights protections (released during the back-to-school season), and other relevant issues likewise served an important educational and information function, while being entertaining. The comedy value she added to the videos, combined with the quality of policy information Policy Counsel Ma'ayan provided, had a wildfire effect.[69] By playing into the logics of what content was more likely to be shared, NCTE used their position in the digital social networks of approximately one hundred thousand people on Facebook to get their content shared, thereby reaching into those individuals' social networks, as well.

Perhaps the most routine social media content that NCTE shared daily, though, was news stories. In fact, sharing news was so central to NCTE's social media activity that the organization's Twitter profile was jokingly referred to as "TNN"—the "Transgender News Network"—around the office. As I've analyzed elsewhere, NCTE served as what communication theorists Kjerstin Thorson and Chris Wells called "curating actors."[70] As a figure within the social networks of their hundreds of thousands of social media connections, NCTE was able to "select, filter, annotate, and frame" the news content that appeared in individuals' feeds, helping shape their individualized political information environments.[71]

NCTE consciously took on a curatorial role because it was rooted in an understanding of just how much they could impact the political information environments of their followers. Most of their followers encountered news stories about transgender subjects incidentally because a news outlet they followed published it. In other instances, stories were shared by their friends, who, like NCTE, curated their news feed. However, NCTE's capacity to curate the political information environments of their followers often exceeded that of individuals' personal social connections. NCTE shared content more frequently, held more authority, and were more likely to be featured prominently on social media platform algorithms because of the volume of engagement their posts typically received.

Thus, NCTE had the capacity to shape much of the information individuals received about transgender issues. By selecting news content that suited their own strategic aims, NCTE cultivated a stream of shared political opinions and perspectives about transgender issues among their social network connections. The combination of social media and NCTE's calls to action, resources, and trainings produced an informed network of transgender advocates that NCTE could depend on to make change in their own social networks.

Turning Personal Politics into Digital News Events

We know that social media conversations provide mass visibility for the marginalized. Social media afford the opportunity for otherwise disregarded or disenfranchised peoples to make themselves, and their social and political issues, visible to the general public.[72] Sometimes these campaigns for visibility circulate exclusively online, but more often they also translate into physical space, where the mass visibility of social media becomes focused visibility within local communities.[73] Whether because of the noteworthiness of the digital movement for visibility or the newsworthiness of the resulting in-person pseudo-events, these campaigns become fodder for widespread media attention.[74]

NCTE often sought to capitalize on social media's capacity to coordinate social media conversations and thereby produce "digital news events." In using the term digital news events, I mean to convey two related ideas.[75] The first meaning of "digital news event" is a topic that is at the heart of social media discussion about current events. That is, the topic is being discussed widely and frequently, to such a degree that the general public has become aware of it due to social media. Such topics are often identified by social media platforms as "trending topics." Although these topics are not necessarily "news" in the sense that professional news outlets have reported on them, they are "news" in the sense that they provide novel social, political, and cultural information to mass publics. The second meaning of "digital news event" is more obvious and refers to instances in which the digital media discussion about a topic has become a news story for journalists to report on. Importantly, these are not instances in which social media activity raised an issue's visibility and eventually attracted news attention. Rather, they are instances in which the social media activity *is* the news story. Effectively harnessing the mass visibility of social media can draw mass media and local and community media attention to digital discourses that, in turn, become media discourse.

The following case unites the threads of this chapter to show how NCTE capitalized on the power of social networks to produce mass transgender visibility, both within the digital sphere and in physical space. In the process, it drew significant local, national, and international media attention. As such, they used social networks as a tool to affect the rest of the political information system, creating a self-perpetuating cycle of public attention and discussion. The case began on October 21, 2018, when the *New York Times* published a report detailing the contents of a leaked memo from the Trump administration's Department of Health and Human Services. The memo was, per the *Times'* reporting, part of "an effort to establish a legal definition of sex under Title IX."[76] According to the article:

> The department argued in its memo that key government agencies needed to adopt an explicit and uniform definition of gender as determined "on a biological basis that is clear, grounded in science, objective and administrable." The agency's proposed definition would define sex as either male or female, unchangeable, and determined by the genitals that a person is born with, according to a draft reviewed by *The Times*. Any dispute about one's sex would have to be clarified using genetic testing.[77]

Were such a memo to become policy, transgender people would, as put in the article's original headline, "be defined out of existence."

Following the publication of the *Times'* article, NCTE fell into its typical pattern of media relations. In addition to that more routine work, it also launched a social media hashtag campaign, #WontBeErased, posting selfies to Twitter with the hashtag and inspiring others to do the same. By the end of the next day, the hashtag had been used over 112,000 times on Twitter alone. By the end of the week, that number climbed to over 208,000. The hashtag also became the central organizing feature of NCTE's press releases and a rally outside the White House. Similar rallies using NCTE's hashtag and graphic resources were held in a number of cities and towns across the country. NCTE also created a Facebook profile picture "frame" (see Figure 5.1), like the famous HRC red equal sign profile picture. It became a ubiquitous symbol of transgender people's resilience and allies' support.[78] Within the week, countless news stories had been published covering the Trump administration's leaked plans *and* the viral social media campaign, as well as the numerous in-person rallies and protests held by NCTE's extended network of advocates. Still today, the language of "won't be erased" continues to shape the discourse of transgender politics in the United States and abroad.

Figure 5.1. Photograph of the author and transgender politician Alexandra Chandler outside the US Capitol building with NCTE's #WontBeErased profile picture "frame."

Transgender People #WontBeErased

Early on the morning of Sunday, October 21, 2018, Media Relations Manager Gillian emailed the Comms and Policy teams, as well as NCTE's executive leadership. She included a link to a *New York Times* article describing the Trump administration's plan to legally define gender as determined by the genitalia with which one was born and thus immutable from birth. "We need to have a statement out ASAP," she wrote.[79] Digital Campaigns Manager Laurel agreed, offering to "take a stab" at drafting a social media statement for immediate release—"like we did on passports" (see Chapter 3)—and then put out a full press release the following day.[80] Gillian pushed an immediate social media release and full press release, and informed the group she was already drafting a statement for both. At that point Executive Director Mara chimed in, asking Gillian to call her to talk about "an angle" for the release.[81] While Gillian and Mara spoke offline, the discussion turned to how to mobilize other organizations around transgender rights. Once her call with Gillian ended, Mara emailed the group again. She was adamant that once the statement was out, NCTE needed to develop "a big strategy" that would mobilize widespread opposition and "lead on messaging for the whole movement."[82] She said it was crucial that NCTE lead individual transgender people to respond to this crisis, and Comms Director Jay agreed.

Shortly after 10:30 a.m., Gillian sent out the finalized press release, which included a statement attributed to Mara. Like most press releases, it began with a comment deriding the cruelty and political ineptitude of the leaked memo—the kind of comment news articles would quote as the oppositional perspective. However, it shifted after introducing the language of erasure: "no rule—no administration—can erase the experiences of transgender people and our families."[83] The release was no longer speaking to the media or in response to the Trump administration; it spoke directly to the trans community:

> To transgender people: I know you are frightened. I know you are horrified to see your existence treated in such an inhumane and flippant manner. What this administration is trying to do is an abomination, a reckless attack on your life and mine. But this administration is also staffed by inexperienced amateurs overplaying their hand by taking extreme positions that ignore law, medicine, and basic human decency.

With each awful headline like this, remember that you are far from alone. NCTE and other organizations are continuing to fight against this bigotry. Remember that there is an entire human rights community that not only stands with us but will always fight back—and fight hard. Thousands of us have devoted our lives to protecting you and your families, and our ability to do so is nothing short of a privilege. And we will not lay down now. . . .

At the heart of our work at NCTE is the belief that no one should have to suffer just to be true to themselves. And yet transgender people are still often forced from their homes, fired from their jobs, harassed at their schools, and denied the most basic level of dignity by a broken system. Knowing this, millions of transgender people wake up every day and step into an uncertain world. This is the most common trait shared by transgender people: A strength and resilience for hard and difficult times. If this administration is hoping to demoralize us, they will be disappointed. If they are hoping we will give up, they should reconsider the power of our persistence and our fury.[84]

State Policy Director Arli, Policy Counsel Luc, and Director of External Relations Raffi all expressed their admiration of the statement. Half an hour later, it was adapted and posted to Twitter, where it was retweeted almost three thousand times without the #WontBeErased hashtag.[85]

Between the time the statement was released to journalists and when it was posted to Twitter, Policy Director Harper Jean forwarded it to a coalition of LGBTQ advocacy groups, asking them to put out their own statements mirroring NCTE's language. Jay followed that up by sharing out a messaging guidance document through Google Docs, which included NCTE's statement and top-line messages. By the end of the day, the document included the #WontBeErased hashtag, a stock social media graphic for organizations to apply their own brand colors and add their own logos to before sharing it (see Figure 5.2), and a guide for individuals to hold their own in-person #WontBeErased rallies.

After drafting and distributing the press release, Mara convened staff for a call to plan steps for a sustained campaign in the wake of Trump administration's leaked plans. It was decided that the end goal of this campaign was to "give trans people something to do, make a big noise, [and] create a sense of momentum that allies can easily roll into."[86] To that end, the Comms staff decided a hashtag would promote a sense of collectivity and publicize public awareness about the mounting resistance. Drawing on the

Figure 5.2. NCTE's stock organizational social media graphic for the #WontBeErased campaign, with placeholder colors.

language from the statement Gillian and Mara had drafted, Laurel suggested #WontBeErased as the hashtag. The social media portion of the campaign would center on the message of "I'm trans, I'm here, and you can't redefine me out of existence"—a sentiment aptly captured by #WontBeErased.[87] NCTE would encourage trans people to post selfies using the hashtag as a symbolic act of counter-invisibility. It would also provide social media-sharable graphics for people who wanted to make their solidarity visible but who didn't want to share images of themselves. It was also decided that NCTE would send out an email to its entire list—including all VTE and FTE members—with the mobilizing portions of the statement, as well as the hashtag and sharable graphics (see Figures 5.3, 5.4, and 5.5).

The other main portion of the campaign would consist of a protest rally outside the White House. The Human Rights Campaign (HRC) was already planning a press conference for the next morning, which Mara would be speaking at. The rally, hosted by NCTE, would be held right afterward and include a processional march from HRC's offices to the White House. Jay was tasked with designing and printing protest signage, Laurel would create a Facebook event and share the event over NCTE's social media accounts, and Gillian took on working with HRC to issue a media advisory about the press conference and rally. After the rally, Mara would conduct a Facebook Live broadcast and, if deemed necessary, a Twitter chat.

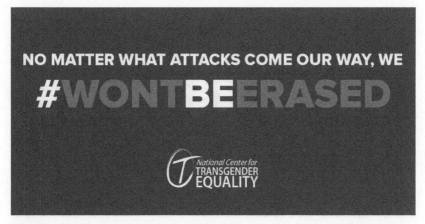

Figure 5.3. First of three sharable social media graphics for individuals to participate in the #WontBeErased campaign, with NCTE branding.

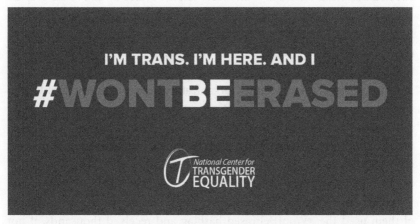

Figure 5.4. Second of three sharable social media graphics for individuals to participate in the #WontBeErased campaign, with NCTE branding.

After the call was concluded and they had time to design the graphics, Jay sent an email out to all staff directing them to attend the protest rally the next day and, as soon as possible, post a selfie or NCTE-created graphic with the hashtag. Within a few hours, several staff had complied. Each of their selfies received hundreds of likes, dozens of retweets, and inspired responses from other transgender people and allies posting their own selfies, setting off the first wave of the #WontBeErased social media campaign.[88] Laurel also

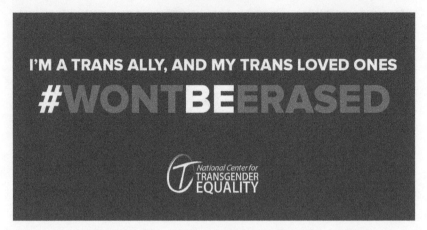

Figure 5.5. Third of three sharable social media graphics for individuals to participate in the #WontBeErased campaign, with NCTE branding.

tweeted out a call for trans individuals to post selfies or an NCTE graphic with the hashtag, and a separate call for allies to post their support with an NCTE graphic and the hashtag from NCTE's account—each of which received almost 600 retweets.[89] Over the course of the day, thousands of individuals shared their own selfies and posts using NCTE's graphics.

By the end of the day, allied organizations, including The Leadership Conference on Civil and Human Rights and GLSEN, a LGBTQ K–12 education advocacy organization, had followed NCTE's messaging guidance to release their own statements and share them over social media.[90] Other organizations, such as the American Civil Liberties Union, Netroots Nation, the Center for American Progress, Lambda Legal, GLAAD, and the Planned Parenthood Action Fund, released statements solely over social media. Most of them used the #WontBeErased hashtag and received thousands, if not tens of thousands, of retweets.[91] By that point, news articles had also been written about NCTE's fight against the Trump administration. Several were, as Executive Director Mara put it, "basically promoting our rally."[92] After a few more logistical emails about tomorrow's rally, the day's flood of emails and phone calls stopped.

The next morning, I walked into an office in a state of excited chaos. Equipment for the rally—large speakers, podiums, a dolly, and a generator—blocked my desk. Doors were opening and closing rapidly as people ran between impromptu meetings. Laurel informed me I would be handling the Facebook Live broadcast. She gave me instructions for installing the app and told me I would be added as an administrator to the page. While I fiddled with my phone, I overheard then-Deputy Communications Director Jay and Policy Counsel Luc Athayde-Rizzaro talking about the newest *New York Times* article on the Trump administration's memo and transgender people's response.[93] Jay was excited NCTE was credited with the launch of the #WontBeErased campaign and having the hashtag included in the headline. Jay and Luc also celebrated that the *Times* was "not doing the whole both-sides nonsense" and there were no quotes from hate groups like the Alliance Defending Freedom.[94] Jay wondered aloud if the story was front page above the fold. I joked that there is no fold on a computer screen, and Jay responded that Deputy Executive Director Lisa was grabbing a physical copy of the paper; indeed, it was above the fold.

Despite the awful circumstances and disarray, NCTE's messaging was circulating widely. I scrolled through my Facebook as we sat there, noticing how many friends had changed their profile pictures to use the NCTE filter. I mentioned to Jay that I was glad that they left the NCTE logo off the filter, because I always hated how HRC and GLAAD would make these profile picture campaigns that were so clearly about advancing their own brand over the issue at hand. Jay smirked. "I agree, which is I left it off. But it's funny you say that because Mara reamed me for doing that."[95]

A short while later, I received an unprompted Facebook message from a woman who was in my friend circle during my undergraduate studies at the George Washington University. She explained that she was now the communications manager at UltraViolet, a digital-forward women's advocacy organization, and that she would "like to make sure we're uplifting everything Trans Equality is doing to stop this Trump policy on social."[96] She asked for any toolkits the organization had or materials for allies in advance of the rally. I got her email address and sent her the toolkit Jay had prepared, cc-ing Jay to connect them for coordination and potential collaboration. Rebecca then asked for the messaging document because she was preparing a template for VTE and FTE members to write op-eds on the issue for their local papers. I sent her the toolkit and she thanked me.

A few minutes into quietly typing and scrolling, Jay exclaimed, "Raffi looks so good!"[97] They were looking at an image of her interview on *MSNBC*. I asked if the interview was airing now, and they answered that it had already finished. Laurel realized she could pull up the interview on the streaming service Hulu and began to do so. In the meantime, Jay mentioned that Mara was currently on a phone interview with *Rolling Stone* and got up to answer

Gillian's phone, which had hardly stopped ringing. Racial and Economic Justice Policy Advocate Mateo entered the Comms office and all of us gathered around Laurel's phone to watch Raffi's interview. Raffi, right out of the gate, called the decision "an abomination." Everyone laughed and Jay fist-pumped, exclaiming, "Coming out strong!" She also plugged the rally, which excited everyone. Calming down everyone's excitement with a moment of earnestness, Jay reminded everyone we would need to leave in fifteen minutes to set up for the rally. At 11:15 a.m. we began heading down with our boxes and equipment. While Jay, Luc, and Rebecca packed up in Rebecca's car and drove over together, Mateo, Laurel, and I grabbed a cab in front of the office. In the car, Laurel talked logistics for social media: Policy Director Harper Jean (rather than Mara) would be hosting the 3 p.m. Facebook Live Q&A about the leaked memo, but she would need to stick to time closely because she had a 4 p.m. interview with *Huffpost* afterward.

When we arrived outside the White House, no one had yet arrived apart from other NCTE staff. We began unpacking the cars and setting up the equipment when we were approached by a woman and a young girl. The woman explained that she was there with her trans daughter, and they had come in from the DC suburb of Bethesda, Maryland. She excitedly told us she had held her daughter out of school for the day so they could come. The team started setting up and dealing with the audio system, then a Secret Service member approached Jay to ask questions about permits. While they spoke, the crowd started growing, people began taking photos, and the first journalists—from *The Advocate* and *Media Matters*—arrived. The air began to buzz.

As we continued to set up, people continued to arrive and received signs, stickers, and other protest materials. Harper Jean was on the phone being interviewed while pacing through the crowd. Raffi was being interviewed by *Media Matters*. After a little while, Development Director Jami Westerhold suggested I hand out stickers NCTE had designed to people in the crowd. The designs included a sticker saying, "I'm a Parent of a Transgender Child," a sticker with artwork turning the NCTE Action Fund logo into the shape of a fist, and a sticker with the NCTE logo. So many parents were eager to get stickers that showed support for their trans kids that I had to make a trip back to the large supply box to get more.

Then I wandered through the crowd handing out the NCTE logo and Action Fund stickers to random people. As I did, I ran into FTE member Nicola, who had come in from Fredericksburg, Virginia for the rally. She showed me five pages of letter paper on which she had written "#WONTBEERASED" at the top. Each page was filled with first names followed by commas and state abbreviations. Nicola explained that she had posted online asking parents to send her the names of their trans children and she covered these pages with them. There were more than 650 kids' names listed and these pages were her protest signage.

A distant noise became louder, overwhelming everything else going on—the sound of chanting coming through Lafayette Park. The delegation of activists was marching over from the HRC press conference, flags waved high. Media Relations Manager Gillian was at the front, screaming the chants at the top of her lungs, alongside Mara. Their group swelled our ranks and brought most of the speakers to the rally. At this cue, I took my place among the crowd, directly in front of the podium, to begin the Facebook Live broadcast—which was ultimately viewed over two hundred thousand times and shared over twenty-five hundred times. After the rally ended, everyone started breaking down the setup, so we didn't get harassed by the Secret Service. Mara asked Jay about the logistics of her interview with *MSNBC*, while Mateo was interviewed by *Telesur*. The rest of the staff thanked people for coming, took photos, and packed up the rally materials.

Over the day, prominent organizations issued supportive press releases, including the American Psychological Association, the National Alliance to End Sexual Violence, the National Association of School Psychologists, and the National Network to End Domestic Violence.[98] NCTE thanked each of them for their support over Twitter. Late that night, Family Organizer Debi emailed staff to share some news. While everyone based in NCTE's main office had been busy dealing with the rally, media, and other pressing issues in DC, she had been working from home in Kansas City (with my help via email) to coordinate an open letter from parents. She drafted the letter (with support from Gillian) and had already secured two thousand signatures. Dave suggested that at the next morning's Comms meeting the team discuss which media outlet they could get the letter placed in.

The next morning as I walked toward my desk, I saw Gillian sitting in the Comms office, which surprised me because she normally came in around 10 a.m. I popped my head in and joked, "Please tell me you went home."[99] She nodded, while struggling to finish chewing a sandwich. She said she had to get a shovel. Again jokingly, I asked who she was going to kill. She said she had a lot in her inbox to trudge through. She had to write op-eds for *Scientific American* and *Ms.* magazine, arrange radio show interviews, "and work to keep this in the news."[100] I told her if she needed anything to just ask, and went back to my desk. There I saw an email from Gillian recapping the media attention the memo crisis had received in the last forty-eight hours. NCTE alone had been featured in almost six hundred news articles around the world, not including broadcast media. Highlights included the *New York Times* article from the preceding day, Raffi and Mara's respective appearances on *MSNBC*, a *New York Magazine* feature that included the Twitter posts by Jay and Laurel that created #WontBeErased, *Associated Press* and *Reuters* news wire stories, and a *Slate* article that featured a nineteen-year-old non-binary teen who had attended the preceding day's rally. The coverage also included hundreds of local news outlets across the country, many of which reported on the actions—inspired by NCTE—being taken by transgender people in their local community.

A couple minutes later, Gillian came out to my desk. She excitedly told me that one of the great things about this news event was that "we're being seen as a group. . . . The headlines aren't saying 'LGBT,' they're saying 'trans-gender.'"[101] We chatted a bit about the similarities and differences between this news cycle and the Trump military ban day, and then she returned to her office. At 10 a.m. I entered the Comms office for the morning meeting, which turned out to be a full-blown meeting rather than the usual fifteen-minute check-in. Interim Communications Director Dave focused everyone's atten-tion on the question: "How do keep this momentum going? What do we do? The news of this starts to fade pretty quickly." Specifically, Dave wanted to focus on "things we can get done this week."[102] Anything else that took longer would risk missing the wave of attention NCTE and #WontBeErased were receiving in the news cycle.

Jay brought up an idea Dave had floated by email the previous eve-ning: having people organize local rallies at state capitols and other impor-tant political landmarks in their communities. They noted that people were already inspired by NCTE's actions to organize their own actions in their communities, and it would be a good idea to offer them a "rally kit." Dave said he loved the idea, as did Gillian. Dave continued that NCTE should share news of these local rallies over social media because "it will spark other people to think 'oh, how can I do this in my city, too?,'" at which point they would be directed to NCTE's rally kit.[103] Gillian then pivoted to television opportunities in the works. She was in conversation with the producers of *The Ellen DeGeneres Show*, for example, and working to pitch shows like *The Late Show with Stephen Colbert* and *Jimmy Kimmel Live!* She was also pushing to get the issue—if not NCTE—featured on the cover of a national weekly magazine, even though everyone agreed that it was unlikely given the upcoming election.

The team excitedly brainstormed how to convert their brush with social media fame into long-term opportunities for change. Gillian seemed struck by inspiration: "Celebrity videos to trans children, standing up in support of them."[104] She suggested having them send selfie-mode videos to NCTE for the organization to share. Jay countered that it would be better for them to share them on their own feeds but tagging NCTE and/or using the #WontBeErased hashtag, as that would increase the message's reach. Dave brought everyone back to the idea of a big visual display, suggesting an action on the National Mall or some other notable landmark, which could be video recorded and shared over social media. Gillian suggested finding ways to bring giant transgender pride flags into public spaces, such as draping one over the Lincoln Memorial Reflecting Pool. Jay had a similar idea of doing "an AIDS quilt-style thing."[105] The collective worry was that one idea might take too long to coordinate. Jay pivoted the meeting to prioritize actions that could be taken as soon as possible. It was decided Gillian should draft a "what you can do" post to be shared over social media so that transgender people and allies could take direct action in their communities. To support that effort, it was decided Jay should prepare the materials for the rally kit, including graphics, signs, and talking points. Laurel would handle outreach to celebrities and influencers to solicit supportive videos, and I was tasked with monitoring social media for local rallies and celebrities tweeting using the #WontBeErased hashtag. The meeting ended and everyone set to their assigned tasks.

Around midafternoon, Gillian emerged from the Comms office exuberant. She fist-pumped the air and screeched down the hallway that comedian-actors Amy Poehler and Amy Schumer would both being doing videos for #WontBeErased. Rebecca shouted out "What?!" from the O&E office and several people could be heard laughing or cheering at Gillian's proclamation.[106] Gillian mentioned while walking back into the Comms office that there probably would be an op-ed from NCTE in the *New York Times* within a week, too. She entered the Comms office and closed the door behind her. Her and Jay began repeatedly and loudly, in disbelief, chanting "Amy Fucking Poehler." Laughs were heard throughout the office because everyone could still hear them, and someone joked loudly, "I wonder what she'd think of her new middle name."[107]

Later, Gillian emerged again and was walking toward the kitchen area when she passed Laurel, telling her the good news. Laurel exclaimed, "Why didn't you text me!" and came speeding down the hallway into the Comms office.[108] I followed her in and took a seat at the table by the door as the team sorted through the celebrities who had agreed to make videos so far. Laurel said actors Sara Ramirez and Piper Perabo agreed, and Jay said actors Amber Tamblyn and Lena Dunham had as well. Gillian then began explaining an ask from a journalist at *NowThis*, but Jay had already seen Laurel's screen as she went to cover it, and their face lit up. "Alyssa Milano!" Laurel erupted.[109] Gillian and I let out noises of excited disbelief that someone so instrumental in converting #MeToo into a national hashtag movement was going to lend their platform to the campaign. Once the excitement subsided, Gillian conveyed that a journalist at *NowThis*, a social media-focused video news outlet, wanted a multi-person interview with NCTE staff, asking specifically for Gillian, Laurel, and Jay to be interviewed—although Gillian would insist on Mara, and possibly Raffi, too.

With a number of celebrities signed on to amplify NCTE's messaging, the team considered how best to capture the energy their involvement would bring. Jay mentioned, "Amy Poehler's not on any social media, so she will send us the video to post on our own accounts." Gillian suggested that NCTE "post her video as the launch of this next phase of the campaign." These celebrity videos can "make their own news event" that would drive continued coverage on the issue.[110] Shortly thereafter Dave came by, and Laurel filled him in on the celebrities who had agreed to make videos and how they would tweet them out. A short while later Jay got a phone call. "Hey, Amber," they sheepishly answered.[111] Jay began packing up their bag to leave for their Big Table meeting while talking to actress Amber Tamblyn about the videos. Jay mentioned that while there wasn't any specific time request, the goal would be ASAP to "keep afloat" the issue because "8,000 other things are happening" that might drive this down the news agenda. They clarified that she should post to her own social media, but "we will share out" and share with the other civil rights groups to boost, too.[112] After the call ended, Jay recounted that apparently several of the celebrities were planning to do a compilation video; Amy Schumer was paying a professional company to edit a video together and would have it done tomorrow.

Once Jay left, Gillian enlisted me to help record video of her and Laurel answering interview questions for *NowThis*. The questions focused on eliciting their reflections and feelings about launching the #WontBeErased campaign in a more personal way. Combined with the first-person perspective of the selfie-mode video, the questions would make for a much more intimate, conversational style of news clip. Considering it was being shared into *NowThis* followers' social media feeds, it would offer viewers a short parasocial interaction with Gillian and Laurel. Gillian and Laurel, for their part, each took proper credit for what NCTE had achieved around the launch of the campaign. They also redirected attention to the transgender people who had taken up the hashtag for their own activism and to organize their own community-based political action.

Over the next ninety minutes, Gillian, Laurel, and I worked in the Comms office, as Gillian took phone calls from news outlets, including *ABC News*. Around closing time, the first celebrity video was posted by Amber Tamblyn. As we arranged, the post tagged NCTE and featured the hashtag #WontBeErased.[113] Next came videos from actor Bitsie Tulloch and another from transgender beauty influencer Gigi Gorgeous.[114] Then NCTE received two videos they had been expecting but would need to post themselves: one from Amy Poehler—unexpectedly featuring comedian-actors Ilana Glazer and Abbi Jacobson—and another from Amy Schumer. NCTE posted the videos that evening.[115]

Over the next few days, good news continued to roll in. On the morning of October 24, *Teen Vogue* agreed to run the open letter Debi had drafted that, in the meantime, had grown to 2,450 signatures.[116] The next day, the *NowThis* video featuring Gillian, Laurel, and Jay, among others, was posted to Facebook, where it received over four hundred thousand views and was shared over three thousand times. Transgender actor Jen Richard posted a video to Twitter alongside actor Laura Linney, speaking in support of transgender people across the country, and the post tagged NCTE and included the #WontBeErased hashtag.[117] Voice actor Tara Strong likewise posted a video, as did actor Sara Ramirez, who included a number of transgender actors alongside her, including Indiya Moore.[118] Still another day later musician Tegan Quin of the twin sister duo band Tegan and Sara posted a video—with the wrong hashtag but tagged NCTE—as did actor Piper Perabo, who both used the correct hashtag and tagged NCTE.[119]

On October 29, NCTE wrapped up the #WontBeErased campaign with their direct action, unfurling a series of 150-foot plastic tablecloths (blue, pink, and white) along the steps of the Lincoln memorial to form a giant transgender pride flag (Chapter 3). The video and photographs of the unfurling were posted to social media, where it was picked up by news media, forming a nice endcap to NCTE's active promotion of the campaign and of the hashtag that organized it. Over the course of the remainder of my field-work, the language of "won't be erased" persisted in the broader transgender movement—a testament to the power of NCTE's social network-focused activism.

"Centralized Decentralization": Here Comes Everybody

I opened this chapter with an anecdote from my visit to Ogilvy's DC offices, where the digital strategy agency Social Driver argued that successful or-ganizational communication is like lightning: not a top-down process, but a meet-in-the-middle one. Their clever metaphor drew my attention to how organizations like NCTE capitalized on social networks to circulate their messages in ways that often go undetected or seem, from the outside, to only center their own public communications. A meet-in-the-middle dy-namic was evident in the case of the #WontBeErased campaign, in which NCTE combined more traditional media relations tactics with social media-focused communications and the interpersonal networks of VTE and FTE storytellers. These strategies became a regular part of NCTE's social networked approach to activism.

Admittedly, "social networks" is a broad category. They include the close-knit networks of family and friends that people form as the core of their so-cial support. It also refers to the slightly wider networks of acquaintances and strangers that people are connected to in their local communities. People might share membership in a group, frequent the same businesses, interact within community institutions, or just live near each other. "Social networks" also include the still wider network of strangers that people find themselves communicating with over their whole lives. Due to the emergence of digital technologies—and particularly social media—the term accommodates vast masses across the world with which people find themselves empowered to communicate. NCTE's approach to activism sought to systematically satu-rate *each* of these kinds of social networks with messages in support of trans-gender equality.

Importantly, their social networking strategy wasn't centralized in the ways that the organization's mass media work was, but it also resisted being decentralized in the ways scholars have typically thought of networked movements and social media-based activism.[120] NCTE's work could best be characterized as "centralized decentralization." It was centralized to the extent that NCTE was responsible for providing the knowledge, skills, and resources required for storytellers to navigate their own interpersonal publics in ways that advanced the movement's aims. NCTE coordinated community storytelling for strategic reasons, while remaining invisible. But it was decentralized to the extent that NCTE had no control over what FTE member Jo Ivester said to the conservative man seated next to her on the plane—nor did they want that kind of control. NCTE created a self-mobilizing network that gave them reach into interpersonal publics across the nation in a way that appeared organic, rather than coordinated.

Most importantly, centralized decentralization happened with the VTE and FTE networks. The media and communications training NCTE provided helped VTE and FTE members develop the skills needed to occasionally work with journalists and continuously engage in effective pro-transgender communication within their social networks. VTE and FTE members drew on their training, as well as resources provided by NCTE, (1) to serve as opinion leaders for their family, friends, colleagues, and others in their immediate social worlds; (2) to advocate for themselves and others in local business, community institutions, and political contexts; (3) to share their experiences with the strangers they encountered in everyday life; and (4) to engage in both public and private conversations about transgender issues online. NCTE also served as a crucial node in VTE and FTE members' social networks, capitalizing on the affordances of networked communication technologies to keep in constant contact with storytellers and use them as a means of reaching wider audiences through their personal social networks.

Beyond the VTE and FTE projects, NCTE used their organizational social media presence to shape the political information environments of transgender people and their allies. It reached hundreds of thousands of people with their strategically curated content—much of which was crafted to maximize sharing to reach still wider audiences. Through this strategic social media communication, NCTE, in turn, shaped wider conversations on social media. Succeeding in that, they produced digital news events that transformed those conversations to local, community, and national media discourse, while inspiring on-the-ground action within people's social networks across the country. Here, the relationships among the components of the communication system start to become clear, demonstrating what the final chapter calls a *politics of flows*.

6

A Politics of Flows

On March 12, 2019, news broke that Emmy Award-winning actress Felicity Huffman, *Full House* star Lori Loughlin, and dozens of other famous and wealthy individuals had been charged by federal prosecutors with perpetrating a nationwide fraud in elite college admissions. The criminal investigation, named "Operation Varsity Blues" after the 1999 film about a small-town high school football team, uncovered a vast conspiracy. Wealthy parents had allegedly bribed exam proctors to fake or otherwise alter their children's test scores, paid off coaches and college administrators to falsely identify their children as elite athletes targeted for recruitment, and used a fake charity to cover their tracks in laundering their bribery payments. Their ultimate goal was to secure spots for their children at top universities like Yale, Harvard, Stanford, Georgetown, the University of California Los Angeles, and the University of Southern California. The internet's reaction was, predictably, to joke about it.

Huffman and Loughlin, the most publicly recognizable individuals involved, received the lion's share of the mockery. Loughlin had bribed her daughters' way into USC, where I was completing my graduate studies, and Huffman had played a trans woman in the 2005 dramedy film *Transamerica*. As a result, my personal social media feeds were flooded with jokes referencing the scandal. One of the posts on my feed was by Katelyn Burns, a trans journalist then working at *Rewire News Group*. She had quote-retweeted a "March Madness"-style bracket originally posted by user @happygoingrid. In the graphic, famous actresses were pitted against one another in a single-elimination tournament to play Huffman in a hypothetical future film about the scandal.[1] Burns noted that all the actresses were cisgender women, writing, "A trans woman should play Felicity Huffman imo [in my opinion]."[2] The implied joke was that because Huffman (a cisgender woman) had played a trans woman, a trans woman should get the reciprocal chance to play her.

Without giving it any thought, I replied to Burns' tweet: "I vote Trace Lysette," a transgender actress then best known for playing Shea on the Amazon original show *Transparent*. "But they need to give her terrible

Voices for Transgender Equality. Thomas J Billard, Oxford University Press. © Thomas J Billard 2024.
DOI: 10.1093/oso/9780197695425.003.0006

prostheses so she looks like a bad Cro-Magnon exhibit at a natural history museum."[3] My tweet referenced Huffman's offensive facial prostheses in *Transamerica*, which attempted to "masculinize" her forehead and jaw to make her "look transgender." But in my assessment, the prosthetics made her look more like the figure of an Early European modern human I had seen in the Smithsonian National Museum of Natural History. By my own admission, it was a bad joke and it received only five "likes." Within minutes of tweeting the joke, I had entirely forgotten about it.

Imagine my surprise, then, when I received a Google Alert notification for my name that evening during dinner. I had been mentioned in a news article published in *The Advocate*, the oldest and largest LGBTQ publication in the United States. The article was titled "College Scam Movie About Felicity Huffman Should Star a Trans Woman, Says Twitter." It contained a scant five paragraphs that explained the admissions scandal, and embedded in the story were a half-dozen tweets listing suggestions for who should play Huffman—including mine.[4] A ridiculous tweet I put zero thought into, tweeted to an acquaintance talking about a tabloid news story, was now in a news article read by the public. That news article was, in turn, shared on *The Advocate*'s Facebook page, where it was reacted to by hundreds of people, shared by forty-one people, and commented on by forty-six people. Who knows how many people shared the news article on their own pages or on other social media sites.

As inconsequential as this example is, it demonstrates the porousness of the contemporary communication system. Information and ideas flow freely from news media into social media, from social media back into news media, from news media into interpersonal conversations (both online and offline), and from interpersonal conversations back into social media. This flow is continuous, amorphous, and wildly unpredictable, and in contexts more serious than the one I experienced, the dynamics of communicative flow can empower or stymie sociopolitical change efforts. In contexts like the ones described in this book, the politics of flows can determine the social and political equality of transgender people.

I opened this book with a story of the fateful day President Donald Trump tweeted his dismissal of the over fifteen thousand transgender service members in the US armed forces. In response, the National Center for Transgender Equality (NCTE) mobilized their resources and their expertise. Executive Director Mara Keisling made numerous mass media appearances, ranging from newspapers to broadcast to magazines. Other media principals at the organization did the same. NCTE connected members of their Voices for Trans Equality (VTE) project who had histories of military service with mass media organizations and local media outlets where they lived. The organization also provided VTE and Families for Trans Equality (FTE) members with information and resources to communicate about the issue in media and their social networks. NCTE also used its own social media profiles to try to steer the public conversation about transgender military service online.

The case that closed the preceding chapter unfolded similarly. As on the day of the military ban, NCTE sprang into action when faced with an un-anticipated attack from the Trump administration.[5] When the news hit that President Trump's Department of Health and Human Services intended to change the legal definition of sex in a manner that would, to paraphrase the *New York Times*, "define transgender people out of existence," NCTE enacted a similar course of action. Mara and other media principals appeared in mass media outlets, again including newspapers, broadcast, and magazines. VTE and FTE network members were mobilized to make media appearances and engage in local, in-person protests. The organization provided local advocates across the country with "rally kits" to stage their own protests. NCTE also launched a viral social media campaign that recruited hundreds of thousands of participants (including numerous celebrities) who used NCTE's #WontBeErased hashtag and graphic resources to reach millions of Americans with messages in support of transgender equality.

These two cases neatly encapsulate this book's core argument: that social movements must craft their strategies around the demands of the networked public sphere. That is, movements must expand their focus far beyond "mass media," which have been decentered as the primary avenue for the flow of political information, perspectives, and opinions. Successful media strategies now involve local and community media and tap interpersonal networks, both digital and face-to-face. Moreover, activists must contend with how these domains of the broader communication system intersect and interpenetrate, which makes the concurrent management of every domain necessary to maintain influence over the public sphere and, in doing so, im-prove the sociopolitical standing of transgender people in the country. In all the cases discussed in this book, the primary domain of interest—whether mass media, local and community media, or social networks—could not be affected in isolation. Managing one domain of interest required managing each other domain, as well. In short, making change in the networked public sphere requires that activists master the politics of flows.

Understanding the Politics of Flows

I live in Chicago, Illinois, where every year the Plumber's Union Local 130 pumps a mysterious orange powder into the Chicago River to magically dye it a brilliant green in celebration of St. Patrick's Day. Over the course of a couple days, the green color fades as new water from Lake Michigan enters the river and as the green water flows down into the blue Des Plaines River. The process is safe and clean, giving the city a short burst of unnatural color to mark an otherwise unremarkable holiday. It may sound strange, but this image of the river being dyed and the green slowly fading as flows of water dilute the color into nothingness almost perfectly matches how I envision the process of activism in the networked public sphere.

If we revisit Figure 1.1 from the first chapter, we can see the three domains—mass media, local and community media, and social networks— that comprise the contemporary communication system. They are connected and conjoined by streams of communicative flow. If we imagine the messages that flow in this system as water, we can think of activism as depositing dye. When activists attempt to shape one domain of the communication system, they drop dye in it. That dye colors the water pooled in that domain and, as water flows from one domain into the others, the water carries some of that color with it. But if activists only drop dye in *one* domain, then as that water circulates the color becomes diluted enough that it ceases to be visible. If, however, activists drop dye in *all three* domains, then the color doesn't dilute—at least, not nearly as quickly. Instead, the colored water circulates from domain to domain where it can be seen by all. And, if they adequately understand the currents that flow through the system, activists can be strategic about when and where in each domain they drop dye to maximize its circulation.

This approach to activism represents what I call "a politics of flows." In a politics of flows, activists must understand and manage the constantly evolving movement of political information that characterizes our communication system if they are to hope to effect sociopolitical change. A politics of flows approach is a far cry from the media work traditionally undertaken by social movement organizations, and it represents a different understanding of the logics of media power. In a bygone era, activists sought to affect the messages and information conveyed in mass media by working to make mass media more sympathetic to their experiences and perspectives.[6] Activists worked under the assumption that mass media convey the narratives, discourses, and values that inform society. If they could improve their representation in mass media, they could improve society. These activists were correct, in that mass media *did* convey the narratives, discourses, and values that informed society. Their activism consequently had a profound social impact. Nowhere is the influence of earlier generations of activists clearer than in the media activism of the gay and lesbian movement, which used media to achieve unprecedented social change in the past half-century.[7] However, in the contemporary communication system, mass media no longer hold a monopoly on the narratives, discourses, and values that inform society— especially in the domain of politics.

The dominance of networked communication technologies has transformed the political information environment and redistributed power within the communication system as we've transitioned into what I referred to as a chimaeric media system in the opening chapter. For instance, local and community media now distribute to widely dispersed audiences over digital networks alongside mass media, impacting not only publics outside their intended ones but also mass media. Additionally, networked communication technologies have empowered individuals to communicate outside their immediate social environments to mass publics. Individuals and the digital social networks they participate in also influence mass media as journalists turn to their public communications as sources of novel information and public opinion. Within such a system, to only affect mass media would let opposing streams of communication dilute a message as it circulates. Thus, contemporary activism must affect *all* domains of the communication system if it is to effectively influence the attitudes and opinions of the general public. That said, contemporary activism does not and cannot transform the multiple domains of the communication system *individually*—even if it does so simultaneously. Communicative activism must effectively manage the flows of information, opinion, and perspectives *between and among* those multiple domains. Activists must change which domains they work in—and how they work in them—in flexible, adaptive, and quick-moving ways as the flows of communication shift vis-à-vis the incompressible quantity of other messages flowing in unpredictable ways through the system. This is the politics of flows.

The first case presented in Chapter 3—the panic over transgender passports in the summer of 2018—demonstrated NCTE's evolving forms of mass media relations. Indeed, the case challenged NCTE to learn how to navigate the new tensions that drive interactions between activists and the press. NCTE adjusted their activities to maximize their control over the political information environment as new actors sought to displace them as the primary sources of transgender political information. However, the relationships between NCTE and mass media outlets had already been disrupted by the new relationships between mass media and digital social networks. Conversations happening over social media became the primary source of information for an LGBTQ community media outlet, which was in turn picked up as the source for a flood of mass media coverage. To reestablish control over the narratives in mass media, NCTE needed to gain control over messages circulating over social media that mass and community media indexed and influence the content of the community media outlets that mass media sourced their stories from. Only once NCTE had effectively managed the flow of information in community media and social networks did they regain control over mass media.

In Chapter 4, I presented a case in which the Alliance Defending Freedom, a conservative Christian legal advocacy organization and Southern Poverty Law Center-designated hate group, stirred up controversy in an attempt to repeal the transgender-inclusive policies of the Decatur, Georgia school district. The case showed NCTE's (perhaps unexpected) focus on local media. NCTE mobilized the resources of VTE and FTE, which provided them with an on-the-ground presence in locales across the country, enabling the organization to rapidly solve crises as they began to spread. The case also demonstrated the powerful place local and community media occupy within the broader contemporary communication system. Local and community media are now an early battleground on which political information is established and from which it then spreads both "downward" into local social networks and "upward" into mass media. To put out the fire of the crisis in Decatur, NCTE leveraged local community members who could use their position within local social networks to combat the effects that local media coverage was having on their community. With the messages circulating in local social networks and local media under control, NCTE was able to redirect mass media attention to the crisis.

The final case of the #WontBeErased campaign, presented in the previous chapter, showed how NCTE capitalized on the power of social networks. The organization effected social change by empowering transgender individuals and allies to impactfully communicate their subjectivities online and in their local communities. Beyond affecting the discourses of social media or influencing the attitudes and opinions of the individuals and institutions they interacted with in daily life, NCTE used social networks to create digital news events. These digital news events secured sympathetic coverage of transgender social and political issues in local, community, and mass media. By coordinating the #WontBeErased campaign in such a way that social networks, local and community media, and mass media *all* carried their messages about transgender equality, NCTE seized control over the political information environment, setting the terms of debate on transgender rights in ways that are still seen today.

In each case, NCTE mastered the politics of flows, capitalizing on the powers and fighting the limitations of the networked public sphere.

What Does the Politics of Flows Mean for the Networked Public Sphere?

Voices for Transgender Equality offers a new way to look at the networked public sphere. Thus far, scholarly analyses of the networked public sphere have mostly been conceptual or metaphorical.[8] Scholars have argued that the advent and proliferation of digital technologies have led us to a networked public sphere because individual participation in public conversations is now easier than it was in the era of mass media dominance. They invoke "networked" in a metaphorical manner; individuals are "networked" together by technology, and therefore the public sphere is likewise "networked." In recent years, this conceptual evolution has involved shifting the scholarly frame of reference from focusing on mass media institutions to focusing on social media platforms. But beyond the occasional network analysis of social media conversations on issues of public concern, there has been a dearth of empirical research that considers what the networked public sphere *actually is*.[9] As a corrective, this book offers a map of what the networked public sphere looks like in practice and how its constituent parts (which extend far beyond social media) are stitched together into a coherent system of communicative flows.

This book also deeply considers how the structure of the networked public sphere shapes efforts at sociopolitical change at two levels. The first level is the macro level of media system dynamics. Most of the scholarly debate on the networked public sphere has made normative claims that networking the public sphere has democratized political speech or transformed the practices of newsmaking within the "fourth estate" of journalism.[10] This book sets aside the normative questions about deliberative democracy by considering how the networked public sphere has become a system of power to be navigated, rather than evaluating it against expectations that it is a tool to actualize an ideal politics. In so doing, it mobilizes the concept of the chimaeric media system to address questions about the changing nature of journalism in the networked public sphere and the capacity for activists to affect change in the context of shifting power distributions.[11] In other words, this book answers the question: what does it take to make system-level change in our rapidly evolving communication system?

The second level that this book considers how the networked public sphere shapes sociopolitical change efforts is the micro level of activists' everyday activities. This book demonstrates what the abstract structural changes in the public sphere mean *in practice* for people trying to use the public sphere for its ostensible purpose, which is reaching consensual public opinion to, in turn, influence the public institutions of political power. This is not the abstract process scholars have typically regarded it as. The structure of the system shapes and constrains what is possible in daily life. People assemble their quotidian practices with the intention of maximizing the benefits and minimizing the limitations of the media system. This book demonstrates in rich detail how activists develop (re)new(ed) daily practices to navigate the networked public sphere and make clear how and why those practices are necessary to make change.

What Does the Politics of Flows Mean for Social Movements?

Voices for Transgender Equality also reorients how we think about social movements in the digital age. The proliferation of digital technologies has unquestionably enabled movements to emerge with decentralized structures and develop new, individual-centered repertoires of contention through which to engage in activism.[12] But while scholarly attention has narrowed in on these "networked movements," traditional social movement organizations remain the most central and significant sources of progress. This book recenters social movement organizations by analyzing their structured practices within the new communication system.[13] As this book shows, decentralized networks of activists are often not as decentralized as they first appear; oftentimes they have undisclosed and invisible relationships to the organizations that enable their activism. Moreover, decentralized activists often capitalize on the political opportunities created by organizations when they contribute their individual efforts to movement activity. Without organizations to create these opportunities, individual actors would struggle to attract the attention needed to make sustained impacts in the public sphere.[14]

At the same time, social movement organizations have been unquestionably impacted by the changes in social organization wrought by digital media. As I argued across the first two chapters of this book, the transgender movement is a prime example of a movement that was forged by the digital environment. By that I mean that it didn't adjust to the networked public sphere (as many movements have), but rather was *born* within it. Being born in the digital environment had a profound impact on how organizations within the movement, like NCTE, functioned. I offered the concept of "media imprinting" to describe the particular ways that organizations take on persistent characteristics reflective of the media environment they operated in at their founding and in their early years.[15] As scholars consider the diverse array of social movement practices in the digital media environment, media imprinting offers a conceptual resource for explaining differences among organizations of different ages. As the chapters of this book have shown, NCTE engaged in innovative forms of activism that were markedly different from those of organizations in the broader LGBT movement, such as those founded in the era of mass media dominance.

Finally, this book augments the sanguine view that the networked public sphere has enabled movements to mobilize supporter bases, bypass news gatekeepers, set public agendas, and increase visibility for their causes. While these statements are sometimes true, the demands of the networked public sphere are often more costly for movements than they are beneficial. Media can be understood as a strategic resource for social movements, but they're also a resource that strains organizations' time, attention, and money.[16] The need to simultaneously contend with every domain of the communication system represents a significant cost to movements as organizations are required to redirect their finite resources away from other movement activities.[17] At the same time, failing to do so comes at a significant cost to organizations' ability to effectively influence the political system as they lose control over the messages circulating in the public sphere. In short, the networked public sphere has created more resource-intensive communications work for social movement organizations. As such, the networked public sphere has had under-considered consequences not only for public discourse, but also more broadly for the change-making abilities of movement organizations.

What Does the Politics of Flows Mean for the Transgender Community?

Finally, *Voices for Transgender Equality* offers new insight into the US transgender movement, and transgender media visibility and politics more broadly. It provides an insider's view into not only how the hypervisibility of transgender people in the United States has occurred, but also how that hypervisibility has been strategically managed by the transgender movement. The transgender movement did not seek out the degree of public attention it has received, but rather received it largely because of conservative opposition. Nonetheless, it has channeled that attention deftly using the strategies analyzed in these chapters, parlaying mass visibility into political salience to further advance the cause of transgender equality. Of course, my vantage point for the internal machinations of the transgender movement was NCTE. This organization was unique among transgender movement organizations and, for a long time, was the movement's most central player. As such, this book offered a glimpse into the leading organization for the transgender movement at a time of historical importance. Under the presidency of Donald J. Trump, the trans movement faced momentous battles over transgender equality, and this book documents how those battles were fought.

Voices for Transgender Equality richly illustrates how the battle for transgender rights is a war of communication. But the rules of engagement for this war are not unique to transgender rights and the innovations I observed at NCTE are not exclusive to the transgender movement. As I observed while at NCTE, other media-focused movement organizations saw the need to transform their activism to suit the new communication system, even while maintaining an emphasis on mass media. For example, driven by the success of NCTE's VTE and FTE programs, LGBT media advocacy organization GLAAD launched their own "Media Institute," which deployed GLAAD

personnel around the country to give LGBTQ people media and communications training. Organizations like Freedom for All Americans, although
not totally dedicated to media and communication-based activism, have
also taken inspiration from these programs to launch their own "Faces of
Freedom" program. This program created a directory of personal stories
from LGBTQ people and allies intended to persuade the public to support
nationwide nondiscrimination protections. Outside of LGBTQ identity, organizations like the National Network of Abortion Funds have launched similar programs, such as "We Testify," an abortion storytelling program akin to
VTE and FTE. But it's not just progressive movements doing this; conservative and reactionary movements have made similar innovations in strategy.[18]

As I discussed in Chapter 4, the Alliance Defending Freedom employed
a similar set of tactics. It relied on recruiting and training storytellers,
"grounding" those storytellers' experiences in local and community media
and capitalizing on the power of local media to spread stories nationally. Even
though NCTE was at the forefront of such practices, they were surprised to
find themselves up against an opponent who used the same weapons, and
they were initially unprepared to handle it. This approach to activism in
the networked public sphere is widespread and quickly becoming the new
standard.

As I look out at the landscape of transgender media representation and
politics, I see where future battles will be waged. Although I loathe to make
predictions for fear of being wrong, I feel confident in asserting that the dynamics of flow in the networked public sphere will be crucial in the fight for
transgender equality. We can see already where the transgender movement
is losing ground. We can look at the Save Adolescents from Experimentation
(or SAFE) act that was passed and signed into law in Arkansas in 2021. The
law not only bans the provision of transition-related care for trans people
under eighteen years of age and prohibits doctors from referring patients to
other providers for such treatments, but it also bans the use of public funds
for and prohibits insurance from covering transition-related care for anyone,
regardless of age. A coordinated communication campaign succeeded in
getting this legislation passed, but it did several other things as well. In essentially outlawing transition-related care, it made it impossible to receive the
care necessary to receive legal name and gender-marker changes (including
on federal documents); it increased the risk of exposure to discrimination in
housing, employment, education, and public accommodations; and it laid
the groundwork for further legislation targeting trans people both within

Arkansas and in other states. The campaign to pass the law also introduced misinformation into mass media discourse and into public opinion, likely increasing prejudicial attitudes and creating a more hostile environment for transgender people seeking to live daily life. As anti-trans advocates pump out misinformation about transgender people and the policies that would support them,[19] the transgender movement will need to innovate further. Our lives hang in the balance.

Ethnographic Research in the Face of Social Injustice

In this Appendix, I reflect on my experience conducting the research that informed this book. In doing so, I build on some of my prior writing on the importance of "public scholarship" and how scholars involved in social justice research can do public good with their work.[1] I narrate how I came to study the National Center for Transgender Equality (NCTE), what I did while there, and how I balanced my scholarly obligations with my political investments in the process. I also consider the methodological complexities of studying organizational practices in a highly (digitally) mediated work environment and discuss how I navigated multiple streams of concurrent data collection. Finally, I reflect on how I moved from grounded ethnographic research on everyday practices to a macrostructural argument about the nature of the contemporary communication system.

Extending the Extended Case Method

Woven throughout this discussion are the ideas of eminent sociologist and ethnographer Michael Burawoy. While I draw on both his notion of public sociology and his extended case method approach to ethnographic research, it is especially useful to preview the extended case method in advance of my reflections to frame them adequately.

Summarized briefly, the extended case method encourages reflexive, theory-driven fieldwork in which research sites are not simply viewed as sites from which to induct general rules to describe a population of cases of which the site is one example (as is the case in conventional grounded theory approaches to ethnographic research). Rather, research sites are viewed as specific cases shaped and constrained by larger social, cultural, or institutional forces such that the particular dynamics of a research site can illuminate the structural forces of "the world in which it is embedded."[2] The aim is thus not the generation of novel "grounded" theories of a middle range, but rather the development of "reconstructed" theory, built on extant theory, "extending from microprocesses to macroforces."[3] Like Burawoy, I sought to extend from the microprocesses of my field site to the macrostructural forces that shaped and constrained them. And like many of Burawoy's students, I augmented the extended case method with tools and perspectives repurposed from the grounded theory approach (like the constant comparative method) and from qualitative research in communication studies.[4]

As articulated by Burawoy, the extended case method requires four "extensions" in the research process: *intervention*, which extends the observer to the participant; *process*, which extends observations over space and time; *structuration*, which extends process to force; and *reconstruction*, which extends theory.[5] The first of these, *intervention*, acknowledges that the process of research is not, as per a positivist model of social scientific observation, unobtrusive. Rather, the process of research impinges upon the field site and, in doing so, reveals truths about the social world in which the field site is located as observer and participant mutually react. The second extension, that of *process*, requires researchers to unpack the situational experiences of participants by tracing their conditions over space and time, whether that means directly observing their participants over extended periods or analyzing historical data against which to compare contemporary observations. The third, *structuration*, acknowledges that field sites exist within "wider field of relations [that] cannot be bracketed or suspended," and yet are beyond the scope of direct observation.[6] As such, the social processes observed within a field site become the lens through which that wider field of relations can be seen. The researcher must then "move beyond social processes to delineate the social forces that impress themselves on the ethnographic locale."[7] Finally, *reconstruction* bridges observation with theory, as data from fieldwork inform neither the confirmation of extant theory nor the construction of new theory, but rather the extension of existing theories that can be improved through reconstruction in light of anomalous cases.

As I show throughout this Appendix, my research attended to each of these four reconstructions. In articulating my positionality in the field, I address the extension of *intervention*, reflecting on the truths revealed by my involvement with my research participants. In describing my access to the field site, I address the extension of *process*, reflecting on my over-time observations of NCTE at a time of rapid change, as well as my (unexpected) historical research while in the field. And in reflecting on how I moved from grounded ethnographic research on everyday practices to a theoretical argument about the structure of the networked public sphere, I address the extensions of *structuration* and *reconstruction*.

Access to the Field Site

Ethnographers typically select field sites for one of two reasons. Either (1) they make the theoretically driven decision to study a site because it provides a good testing ground for their pet theories or (2) they make the empirically driven decision to study a phenomenon that interests, amuses, or intrigues them. Although Burawoy advocates the selection of theoretically driven field sites rather than empirically driven ones, I endeavored to do both simultaneously.[8] The empirical "object" of this book—and indeed my career—is the US transgender movement, and so I wanted to select a field site at the forefront of the movement. At the same time, the theoretical object of this book is movement–media relations, and I therefore wanted to select a field site within the transgender movement that posed specific challenges to extant theories of media-centered activism in the digital age. These criteria led me to select the National Center for Transgender Equality as my site of study.

Once I settled on NCTE as my ideal research site, I had to secure access to the organization. I secured my initial three-month round of fieldwork at the organization in the summer of 2017 through a mixture of external funding, prior movement experience, and serendipitous connections. I applied for a fellowship with the Consortium on Media Policy Studies (COMPASS), which places PhD students in summer fellowships at DC-based media activist and public policy organizations. The program helps students establish meaningful long-term relationships with civil society institutions and teaches them how to translate academic skills and theoretical knowledge into professional practice outside the academy.[9] Winning this fellowship provided me with a living stipend and meant I could approach NCTE with the promise of free labor. For a movement organization short on money but with a lot of work to be done, it was an attractive proposition. I was formally hired as an unpaid general intern.

Of course, my access to NCTE was further aided by my deep connections within the trans community, my history of activism in the movement, and the relevance of my research. And as a testament to either how deep my connections were or how small the world is, I already knew two NCTE staff members before beginning my fieldwork: Communications Manager Jay Wu and Research Director Sandy James. My connection to Sandy was somewhat unsurprising. He was a PhD student in American government at Georgetown University studying transgender politics. We had been to the same conferences and had significant overlap in our professional contacts, although we had never met in person before. My connection to Jay was more serendipitous, though. They went to Swarthmore College with my best friend from secondary school in the Czech Republic, Daniela Kucz, who introduced us via social media because of our overlapping "interests" (those interests, of course, being transgender rights). By the time I arrived at NCTE, Jay and I had been somewhat passively connected for a couple of years. In short, I was able to get access to NCTE in part because I approached the organization as an "insider" who wanted to work with them, rather than as an outsider who wanted to observe them.

In my capacity as COMPASS-Fellow-*cum*-general-intern, I worked closely with the Communications (Comms) and Outreach & Education (O&E) departments, which together coordinate all NCTE's communicative activities. As part of my work, I contributed to these activities by drafting official statements from Executive Director Mara Keisling, ghostwriting editorials as Mara (one of which was picked up by the *Washington Post*, although ultimately not run), pitching stories to reporters, coordinating activities for NCTE's 2017 lobby day on Capitol Hill, writing blog posts, and recruiting members for the growing Voices for Trans Equality and Families for Trans Equality projects, among other responsibilities.

Before my departure from this first round of fieldwork in August 2017, I discussed how I might return for the next phase of my research. Each of the staff members with whom I discussed these plans expressed excitement at the prospect of my return, although they were uncertain under what auspices I might work with them. In my debriefing with Deputy Director Lisa Mottet, she suggested that one auspice could be the creation of an historical archive of the policy wing of the US transgender movement at NCTE. As she told me, the organization had myriad uncatalogued documents sitting in boxes both in the office and in (present and former) staff member's homes that they were worried would be damaged or lost over time. She also expressed interest in collecting oral histories from some of the organization's departed founders and key staff while they were still alive. Although the development of a historical archive was somewhat outside my domain of expertise and would require me to develop new skills, it was an important project for the organization (and the movement), and one they lacked both the capacity and the skill set to do. And despite being outside my primary area of focus, it would benefit my research, too. In accordance with Burawoy's concept of *process* extension in the extended case method, these historical materials allowed me to analyze the evolution of the organization's communication practices over time in a way that could not be achieved with observation alone. Per Lisa's suggestion, I prepared a formal proposal for such an archive, which was approved by NCTE leadership.

I then returned to Los Angeles, where I was completing my doctoral studies at the University of Southern California's Annenberg School for Communication. For the next nine months I was away from the field, but I remained connected to the field site (or at least the people in it) by the personal relationships I maintained with many staff members. Indeed, many staff members evolved from incidental acquaintances prior to entering the field site to genuine friends of mine. I was also "friends" on Facebook with every staff member who has a Facebook account, and we kept in touch with relative frequency. On October 24, 2017, Mara and Development Director Jami Westerhold hosted a fundraising reception for the NCTE Action Fund in Los Angeles, which they happily invited me to (and from which they sent me home with excesses of leftover catering). While at the event, despite my unofficial affiliation, I fell into old habits and helped Jami work the registration desk and, during Mara's passionate plea for donations, circulated the room handing out pens and donor cards—much to the relief of the overwhelmed duo. Such connections were cultivated for personal gratification, but also served to maintain open exchange that permitted a return to the field site in the summer of 2018.

When I returned to the field in June 2018, it was to a much-changed organization, and one in which I was still an active participant, but more of an observer than I had been before. (I discuss these shifts more in the next section.) At the same time, it was now an organization in which I was more deeply personally embedded, as I came to work with (and to research) people I considered friends. It was also under different institutional auspices, as I was appointed to NCTE as an Archival Fellow, responsible not only for my own field research with the Comms and O&E teams, but also for the creation (and eventual placement) of an archive.[10] This appointment structure and division in responsibility meant that, beyond being a "researcher" in the field, I was a true member of the NCTE team. This member status brought with it a particular positionality as I experienced direct supervision from Deputy Director Lisa and developed colleague relationships with the nonmanagerial staff.

Positionality in the Field

I did not simply *study* NCTE; I participated in the organization's work. But what does that mean for my scholarship? What does my active participation in the field site mean for the "scientific-ness" of my research findings and for the politics of my knowledge production? To answer these questions, it is necessary to take a step back and think about the idea of "public scholarship."

Perhaps the most widely held understanding of public scholarship is actually of public intellectualism. That is, when most people—including most academics—think of public scholarship, they think of the media-centered careers of well-known academics like Manuel Castells, Noam Chomsky, Jürgen Habermas, Paul Krugman, Steven Pinker, and other (usually white, cisgender, straight, and male) scholar-celebrities from elite universities. And public intellectualism is certainly a form of public scholarship, particularly as practiced by some. Some public intellectuals focus(ed) their media-based work on public education, such as Stuart Hall, who among other feats of incredible media visibility presented the television series *Redemption Song* on BBC2, and Melissa Harris-Perry, who hosted the *Melissa Harris-Perry* show on MSNBC from 2012 to 2016. Other public intellectuals provide(d) cultural criticism, such as Susan Sontag, who wrote essays on art and culture in many popular publications, and Slavoj Žižek, whose opinions on everything from cinema to politics seem unavoidable no matter how hard one tries. But public intellectualism is not the totality—nor even the majority—of public scholarship. As Michael Burawoy argued in his now-classic work on public scholarship in sociology:

> we should not simply think of writing op-ed pieces for *The New York Times* with its invisible, thin, passive, and national public, but of carrying sociology into the trenches of civil society, where publics are more visible, thick, active, and local, or where indeed publics have yet to be constituted.[11]

At the core of Burawoy's model of public scholarship is a distinction between public sociology and three other "types" of sociology: professional sociology, policy sociology, and critical sociology. Drawing on Bourdieusian field theory, Burawoy envisions two axes generating a two-by-two matrix. On the one axis is audience—either academic or "extra-academic."[12] On the other axis is forms of knowledge—either instrumental or reflexive. Whereas public sociology sits at the intersection of reflexive knowledge and extra-academic audiences, professional sociology sits at the intersection of instrumental knowledge and academic audiences, while policy sociology sits at the intersection of instrumental knowledge and extra-academic audiences, and critical sociology sits at the intersection of reflexive knowledge and academic audiences.

As with all typologies, this four-fold model is necessarily flawed. What it offers, though, is a way of thinking through how public scholarship distinguishes itself from other forms of scholarship. Rather than being accountable to professional peers or to clients or patrons, as other forms of scholarship are, public scholarship is accountable to designated publics. Rather than legitimating itself through scientific norms, administrative effectiveness, or ideological purity, public scholarship is legitimated by its public relevance. And, most importantly, it dispenses with the (impossible) academic fetish for "objective" research.

For my purposes, Burawoy's distinctions *within* public sociology are where he is most helpful.[13] Specifically, Burawoy distinguishes between what he calls "traditional" public sociology and "organic" or "grassroots" public sociology. (I will retain his terminology here for the sake of fidelity, although I find his choice in labels somewhat distracting and inaccurate.) "Traditional" public sociology is much like the publicity-centered public scholarship within communication that I have already critiqued in other writing, although it is somewhat broader, including columns in national newspapers, blogging, and social media presence, as well as academic books that reach large nonacademic audiences. While these forms of scholarship are public in that they speak to, if not form, common publics, they also do so "at arm's length."[14] "Organic" or "grassroots" public sociology, on the other hand, "engages the particularistic interests of more circumscribed publics—neighborhood groups, communities of faith, labor organizations, and so on" through "an unmediated face-to-face relation of sociologists with publics."[15] As Burawoy argues, "This subterranean form of public sociology is often more effective and longer lasting," particularly because it speaks to more active publics, both mainstream and counter.[16]

Drawing on Burawoy's ideas, as well as work on participatory action research, I have—both alone and together with the brilliant Silvio Waisbord—articulated my own vision of what public scholarship should look like.[17] Public scholarship needs to be more than just engagement with nonacademic publics. It needs to be engagement rooted unambiguously in the public good. Public scholarship demands that researchers use their personal skills and competencies to do good with and for others, to bolster the organs of civil society, and to defend the interests of humanity, ultimately making societies more humane, egalitarian, democratic, tolerant, rational, other-oriented, and empathetic.[18] The essence of public scholarship is contributing one's specialized skills and knowledge toward the mitigation of the social problems facing relevant publics. If a scholar publicly engages in issues of social justice *without* orienting their public work toward alleviating injustice, then they are actively sustaining the systems of oppression they benefit from researching.

Ethnographic fieldwork, I find, is naturally suited to this kind of research because at the heart of fieldwork sits participant observation, which necessarily entails a certain degree of participatory work. Of course, there are certain dynamics to ethnographic fieldwork that do not automatically translate. For example, ethnographic fieldwork rarely involves members of relevant publics engaging in the research process in as obvious a way as one might find in, for example, a community health promotion campaign. In ethnographic fieldwork, the engagement of relevant publics in the research process often occurs more subtly in interaction—although this will vary widely by field site and by research situation.

One key tension involved here is the extent to which ethnographic fieldwork can be described as participant observation versus observant participation. We can conceive of these two as end poles on a spectrum with few, if any, studies occupying the absolute ends of, on one side, completely inactive observation as if through a two-way mirror and, on the other, completely inattentive participation in every activity at the field site. Most studies will fall somewhere in between, with the majority falling further toward participant observation than toward observant participation. However, public scholarship necessitates being closer to the observant participation side than most scholars are likely comfortable with, as orienting one's work toward alleviating social problems necessarily means engaging in a higher degree of participation in one's public's actions.

At NCTE, my dedication to a public scholarship approach to fieldwork meant I vacillated between the poles of this participant-observation–observant-participation spectrum. My participation in my first round of fieldwork in the summer of 2017 fell cleanly on the observant participation side of the spectrum. Following sociologist Josh Seim's distinction, my ethnography was, at that point, one of incarnation rather than inscription; I learned by taking notes with my body rather than with a pen (although I certainly took plenty of notes by pen, as well).[19] On the day of Trump's announcement of the transgender military ban, for example, I became just as immersed in the flurry of activity as every NCTE staff member. As I described in Chapter 1, it was all-hands-on-deck, and I spent a ten-hour day involved in every form of communications activity there was. By the end of the day, I had no energy to turn jottings into fieldnotes in the full narrative style, as I would have done on a slow day that consisted only of meetings. Instead, I had frenzied jottings, sketchings and diagrams, email threads, and my own embodied memories of the day; days like that don't leave your memory.

For NCTE, the benefits of having me around were clear: They were used to undergraduate (and occasionally high school) interns, as well as legal fellows, but PhDs were a new class of unpaid help for them. In fact, within the first day of my arrival I was already recruited as a strategy advisor for Communications Director Eric Dyson, who was somewhat new to the job and eager to implement new strategic practices. He felt my expertise in the field could help him direct his energies. But my own understanding of my role was still uncertain. At times I struggled with the tension between the fact that sometimes what NCTE needed was just another body (not an expert), whereas at other times my expertise was in high demand.[20] I was more comfortable acting under their direction, but I didn't want to introduce "bias" into my data by sharing my own expertise. That is, I worried that if I offered my expert opinions and NCTE acted based on them, I would not really be studying *their* practices. By the end of my first round of fieldwork, I realized that this concern arose out of my own misunderstanding of the participatory research process. My role as a participatory researcher was to work to the benefit of their mission, and theirs was to inform my research through inviting my participation in the areas they deemed most helpful.

Out of this first phase of research at NCTE, I gained two important things that helped my participatory fieldwork move forward appropriately. First, I learned through action what NCTE needed. I gained intimate familiarity with the work they did, how they did it, why they did it, and what my skill sets could contribute to it. Perhaps more importantly, though, my time at NCTE established "flattened" relationships between myself and organization staff; I was an equal participant, rather than an outside intervener or consultant—and this was a perception shared on both sides. Not only did they come to view my research as integral to their own working, but I came to view their active participation in my research as more integral to my academic objectives.

For the nine months I was away from the field from September 2017 to May 2018, the research process became "mine" again; there was little to no participation from NCTE, except for the occasional feedback from Lisa on archive proposal drafts. I worked my embodied observations into a tentative theory that informed the development of research questions for my next round of fieldwork. I also found theoretical ideas that I could weave together to explain (and find absences of explanation) for my experiences in the field. But in that time, I also forgot, to a certain extent, what I had learned about participatory fieldwork; I began thinking of my role as an observer again, and not as a participant. The participatory aspect of my research, I began thinking, was the archive (which, of course, it also was).

When I returned to the field in June 2018, it was to a much-changed organization. (Social justice organizations move fast.) NCTE had hired several more staff members, and a few had left. The communications team had lost its director and digital media specialist but gained two new staff members plus an interim director. And those were only the changes to the department I worked most closely with. It was, in a few ways, a resetting for me; I still had flattened relationships within the organization, but I also had several new relationships, which took time to settle into. Also having a new role as Archival Fellow, rather than working on the Comms team, changed the nature of my participation and shifted it much further toward the participant observation side of the spectrum. In this new position, I participated in Comms (and, to a somewhat lesser extent, Outreach & Education) work, but I also had my own discrete set of participatory research obligations to the archive. Most of my time with the Comms team was in the daily morning check-ins, the weekly operations meetings, the weekly messaging meetings, standing meetings for various campaigns and special projects, general staff meetings, and ad hoc strategy meetings. In these meetings, I was an active participant (eventually), but more of an observer than I had been before. (In other settings, I was a more active participant, such as in trainings, rallies, press conferences, and various other relevant events.)

Finding my footing with, and remembering the importance of, actively participating in NCTE work took time and took the encouragement of my new collaborators. In my first week back in the field, I observed a messaging meeting on education issues. I sat toward the end of the table with my notebook out and took notes quietly as everyone discussed and debated. We broke for lunch, and I went back to my desk, resuming work on the archive project. A couple of hours later, the team reconvened in the large conference room for a follow-up messaging meeting on criminal justice issues. I resumed my place at the end of the table, notebook out, and waited for everyone to arrive so the meeting could begin. Policy Director Harper Jean Tobin walked in and seemed a bit surprised to see me. "Were you at the previous meeting?" she asked. I replied that I was, but I was just in the corner. She commented that I had been so quiet she hadn't realized. Rapid Response Communications Manager Laurel Powell, who was new to me, as she had joined staff while I was away from the field, quipped that I needed to speak up—I was no good if I just sat quietly. I joked back that I wasn't there to speak, but to listen. She looked at me in a mockingly stern way over her glasses, and we began the meeting. Over the next few days, her words echoed in my head, and I slowly started remembering the importance of conducting my fieldwork as participatory research.

Over the next couple of weeks, especially as I grew comfortable around and working with the new staff members, I leaned into my participatory obligations more. I spoke up more in meetings; I offered my critical, research-based perspective on issues; and I often found—somewhat to my surprise—Interim Communication Director Dave Noble and Media Relations Manager Gillian Branstetter turning to me in meetings as ideas were being discussed, asking me if I knew what research had to say about certain things. But because, despite my research prowess, I am sometimes slow to learn, I still didn't make myself as valuable to the team as I could have until the Comms team realized I had conducted research on things of significance to their work that I hadn't mentioned to them. When it was announced in July 2018 that Nicole Maines, a transgender actor and longtime friend of the organization, would be joining the cast of the CW's *Supergirl* as the first transgender superhero on network television, I mentioned excitedly to Gillian that I had written a book chapter about transgender superheroes in comic books early in my career, and so to see one finally on television was incredibly gratifying.[21] She screeched at me: "How did I not know this before! Why didn't you mention it?" She mused that she could pitch me to journalists as an expert commenter. (She ended up not doing so because her media relations energies were better served working on stories about more pressing issues.)

When Dave walked by, Gillian shouted out to him, asking if he knew I had done research on transgender superheroes. He expressed surprise and said no. He then turned to me and asked why I hadn't shared it with them and what else I had researched that I was "holding out on" sharing. I muttered uncomfortably that I didn't think my work would interest any of them, that people usually wanted me to talk about my research less and not more. Dave gave me a look that told me I was being daft.

After that, Gillian went to my website to download and read my papers and to find out more about my work. She began asking me questions about the work I had published, and some of the work I was still doing, but that hadn't come out yet. When I had another paper accepted for publication on transgender news coverage, I shared it with her, and we had extensive conversations about its implications for her work.[22] We eventually set up a number of meetings to talk about NCTE's communications strategy and what my research might be able to contribute. In one meeting, she asked for my feedback on the current draft of the style guide that NCTE used in-house and that she often shared with journalists; I had published about how journalists should write about trans people, and she thought I could help improve the style guide.[23] I was most uncomfortable here because I felt like I was stepping over the participant–researcher boundary. I worried that I was finally breaching the role of the researcher and was now acting more as a "professional expert."

My worries were unfounded, though, and I realized later that they stemmed from the fetish academics have for the "neutral" scientific observer, who in actuality does not exist.

And I realized that, in line with the vision of public scholarship I articulated earlier, as well as the extended case method's extension of *intervention*, I could improve that which I studied while also gaining valuable research insight from the process. In discussing the style guide and what improvements or alterations were possible with Gillian, I learned far more about why the style guide took the form it currently did and the logics underpinning it than I had in all my other interactions and conversations about it. From then on, I was more steadfast in my participatory research approach, often bringing my research and expertise to bear and learning immense amounts about NCTE's communicative strategies in doing so that I otherwise would never have discovered.

Through my fieldwork (and the archive, in its own way), I was able to make my research process truly public scholarship to the extent that I oriented my work, via participatory methods, toward improving the social justice work at NCTE. While I would not claim to have made a large influence or even to have been unambiguously helpful—those claims would need to be made by NCTE—I can claim with certainty that the work I did added to NCTE's capacities, bringing my own unique skills and expertise to bear on their work, all without placing increased demands on their material (and relatively few demands on their temporal) resources.

Data Collection Across Media

In the appendix to her brilliant ethnographic study on the meaning of algorithms in digital newsrooms, critical data theorist Angèle Christin discussed the challenges that digital mediation pose for ethnographers.[24] When the people we study are constantly looking at screens, communicating and interacting non-verbally, and participating in activities across several platforms concurrently, how do we, as participant observers, observe everything? At NCTE, for example, any given staff member was doing important work over email, in Google Docs, on Twitter, all in rapid succession. And because I wasn't sitting directly behind them, watching their screens like an over-concerned parent, I couldn't possibly take notes on everything they were doing. Instead, I had to rely on a robust and taxing set of notetaking practices that merged my observations with documentary evidence from different media sources into a cohesive and coherent set of fieldnotes. In essence, I developed my own form of what science and technology scholars R. Stuart Geiger and David Ribes called "trace ethnography."[25]

Most of my ethnographic research practices were standard. I approached my participant observation guided by social theorist Richard Swedberg's conception of the research process, dividing the project into two phases.[26] The first phase, the "prestudy," consists of early field observations during which the researcher identifies an interesting or surprising phenomenon inadequately explained by existing theory. This initial fieldwork further informs the development of new conceptual categories, theoretical constructs, analogies, typologies, etc., which are sketched into a tentative theory explained by the field observations. The prestudy for the dissertation was conducted as a COMPASS Fellow in the summer of 2017 working with the Comms and O&E teams. This pilot study indicated striking disjunctures between the forms of media work practiced by social movement organizations described in past literature and the emerging models of activism suited to an evolving communication system with new organizing logics as practiced by NCTE and its partner organizations.

The second phase of Swedberg's research process, the "main study," consists of a more focused research design oriented toward answering the research questions raised by the tentative theory developed out of the prestudy. This research then informs the refinement of the tentative theory into a final research report. My main study consisted of seven months of participant observation at NCTE from June 2018 to December 2018 during my stint as Archival Fellow. Throughout these seven months, I was in the office as a participant observer at least eight hours per day, five days per week (and often many more). My observations again focused primarily on the Comms and O&E teams, although I was present at many meetings with and of Policy team members, as well. Among the meetings I observed were the daily Comms team morning check-ins, the weekly Comms operations meetings, the weekly messaging meetings, the weekly O&E team meetings, standing meetings for various campaigns and special projects, general staff meetings, and ad hoc strategy meetings. I took field jottings during meetings, trainings, rallies, staff interviews with journalists, and various other relevant events, and later expanded those jottings into complete fieldnotes.[27]

Per political ethnographer Paul Lichterman's approach to theory-driven fieldwork, I analyzed fieldnotes via the constant-comparative method as they were collected, memoing emerging theoretical insights to inform subsequent observation decisions.[28] This process also informed the generation of interview protocols, which were individualized for each interview subject. Each Comms staff member was formally interviewed twice (with the exception of the Interim Communications Director), as was each O&E staff member except the Director of External Relations, who was interviewed once due to scheduling constraints. These interviewees included Media Relations Manager Gillian Branstetter, Digital Campaigns Manager Laurel Powell, Communications Director Jay Wu, Interim Communication Director Dave Noble, Education Program Director Rebecca Kling, Family Organizer Debi Jackson, Family Organizer DeShanna Neal, and Director of External Relations Raffi Freedman-Gurspan. Additionally, two policy staff members were interviewed: State Policy Director Arli Christian and Racial and Economic Justice Policy Advocate Mateo De La Torre.

Beyond staff, I conducted interviews with nine members of NCTE's Voices for Transgender Equality (VTE) and Families for Transgender Equality (FTE) projects, which together establish a national network of nearly one thousand "community storytellers" who have received media and communication training from NCTE to make them effective spokespersons. These storytellers consist of both transgender individuals (VTE) and the parents or other family members of transgender children (FTE). Five of these interviewees were transgender members of VTE (Ray Gibson, Benjamin Kennedy, Chloé LaCasse, Leslie McMurray, and Paula Sophia Schonauer), while four were cisgender parents of transgender children (Rachel Gonzales, Jo Ivester, Nicola van Kuilenburg, and Sarah Watson). Interviews lasted between sixty and ninety minutes and were transcribed and then analyzed via the constant-comparative method alongside fieldnotes.

Beyond these standard research practices, I also collected documentation of as many digital activities as I could. Sometimes this was easily done. For example, I copied and pasted portions of relevant emails into my fieldnotes. However, I wavered on whether to put them in my fieldnotes when I saw them, so that my fieldnotes reflected my personal experience of the field, or to put them in my fieldnotes at the time when they were sent, so that my fieldnotes reflected the chronology of the day. Ultimately, I decided to take the latter approach, which greatly eased the data analysis process.

At other times, I felt overwhelmed by my need to document digital happenings. I struggled to know when something was significant enough to document. For example, I kept NCTE's official social media platforms and the Twitter profiles of all NCTE's staff up in tabs on my laptop, so I could trace their communications throughout the day. When something work-related happened, I would screenshot the post, embed the image into my fieldnotes document, and paste in the post's hyperlink so that I could find the original again later. This criteria of "work-related" was clear on days like those when the #WontBeErased campaign launched. However, on most days, it was hard to tell when something was significant. This meant I often would have to go back days later when a subsequent event *made* a previous post relevant. And this most often happened with NCTE's official platforms, which posted too frequently in any given day to document every post (although certain kinds of posts, like press releases, I always documented).

I also needed to consider the propriety of what I documented and how. When it came to social media posts, the ethics were clear: these posts were public information, and thus fair game as data to be stored and kept. But when it came to things like email, direct messages, Google Docs, and other working documents, I felt unable to store that data in ways that let me "take" it with me. Just as making an audio recording of a meeting without the group's consent would be unethical—you must make your notes and anything you didn't remember or write down you don't get to have—saving these documents to my laptop and leaving the field with them felt wrong. (I believe NCTE staff would have agreed with those feelings.) Thus, I needed to make conscious decisions at the time about what warranted copying and pasting into my fieldnotes and how to keep track of where I originally observed those things.

Of course, relying only on digital data that I encountered or had access to while in the field necessarily means I missed vast quantities of data that wasn't shared with me by virtue of the fact I didn't have access to staff members' private communications or personal working documents. But even without that data, the amount of documentary data I *did* collect was overwhelming to analyze. At a certain point, I simply needed to trust that the theoretical saturation I achieved when coding my data meant I probably had enough pieces of the puzzle that I wasn't missing anything that would profoundly change my argument.

From Right Here to Everywhere, Part 2

As I noted toward the beginning of this Appendix, the extended case method aims to "extend" existing theory by illuminating how social macroforces manifest in the microprocesses of daily life in the field site, which in turn "reconstructs" our understanding of those macroforces. This is, in brief, how I moved from my very grounded and material observations of everyday life in the field to a more general theoretical argument about the structure of the networked public sphere. In my case, "generalization" was not achieved by selecting a research site that was perfectly exemplary of what every other organization in its category is like. Rather, generalization was achieved by showing how the forces that constrained my research site operate in ways that apply more broadly.

When discussing this approach to theorizing with students and colleagues, I often use the metaphor of a cinematic jewel heist. It is now a well-worn trope in American film to have a thief try to steal a jewel or some other precious object by breaking into a secure establishment at night. The precious object is stored in the middle of what appears to be an empty hall, but the cunning thief knows that there is actually a security system—it's just invisible. So, the thief fills the room with smoke, which reveals an intricate web of laser sensors cutting across the hall through which the thief must maneuver. If someone were watching the thief through a security camera, they might just see the thief making a strange, fragmented set of movements and fail to understand their bizarre behavior. But knowing where the laser sensors are placed would make clear what is going on. As Burawoy noted in discussing the extended case method's extension of *structuration*, social forces are, like the web of lasers navigated by the thief, beyond the scope of direct observation. But they are there! By observing people's behaviors within the relevant settings, the unobservable becomes visible. The ethnographer must simply fill the hall with smoke.

Of course, Burawoy's idea of "structure" was "social structure." That is quite a limiting perspective, especially for research on communication, where "structure" works differently. To arrive at a structural understanding of communication, we must begin with a structural understanding of culture. Cultural sociologists Nina Eliasoph and Paul Lichterman aid us with their extension of the extended case method.[29] As they observed, Burawoy presents an implicit understanding of culture as separate from, and often subordinate to, the social structure. For Burawoy, culture comprises the social processes of the field site, which merely reflect the social structure in which the field site is embedded. Eliasoph and Lichterman offered three interrelated correctives to Burawoy's limited conception of culture. First, "culture and social structure interpenetrate," such that neither is subordinate to the other but rather both are mutually constitutive.[30] Second, social structure is only comprehensible in the form of cultural patterns, and it is through cultural patterns that individuals interpret their social conditions. Finally, and most importantly, culture is, *unto itself*, a structure. That is, as "a set of publicly shared codes or repertoires," culture forms the "building blocks that structure people's ability to think and to share ideas," and, indeed, to act.[31] Accordingly, they argued, the extended case method can (and should) be applied to the study of culture, reconstructing cultural theories in the same manner as Burawoy advocated the reconstruction of theories of social forces.

Importantly, Eliasoph and Lichterman maintained that culture is inherently communicative. They argued that the structure of culture is formed through communicative interaction. This then offers an entry point for thinking through structure as it relates to communication, because to employ the extended case method as a means of theorizing communication requires thinking of communication *as a structure*. But structure in communication is not the same as structure in the sense that Burawoy uses it—because it can't be. For Burawoy, structure is analogous to what Habermas calls the "system"; it is the forces of power that organize social domination (e.g., capitalism).[32] Communication does not operate at that level. At the same time, Eliasoph and Lichterman's conception of culture as both structured *by* and structuring *of* communication, while a useful starting point, does not go so far as to theorize the structure of communication.[33] By that I mean it considers the content of communications and the settings in which (mostly interpersonal) communication occurs. But it does not consider the mediums through which communications are exchanged. Thus, thinking of structure in communication requires yet another reconstruction of the extended case method.

In communication, structure is both material and cultural, infrastructural and interactional. Communication occurs through technological media that are themselves informed by culture, but which simultaneously serve as platforms for culture. These technologies form a literal, material structure in communication as the media through which communications flow. But communications, per Eliasoph and Lichterman, are also structured (in the sense of ordered) by cultural norms, which are also themselves constructed via communication.[34] These communicative norms and styles form an immaterial structure that necessarily interfaces and interacts with the material structure of technology. As such, technology and culture are mutually implicated in the structuring of communication in a manner perhaps best envisioned as double helical. The (infra) structure of communication technologies form one helix which is inextricably linked to a second helix of the structure of patterned communication norms. The theory elaborated in the first chapter of this book represents such a structural theory of communication to the extent that it considers, simultaneously and interdependently, the technological structure of the contemporary communication system that activists work to influence *and* the communicative norms that activists enact vis-à-vis that system.

I did not observe the networked public sphere. I observed an organization's attempts to navigate it. But through careful observation and the rich layering of analysis documented in the chapters of this book, I was able to move beyond the social processes I observed to trace the structural forces that impressed themselves upon NCTE. In doing so, I *reconstructed* our extent theoretical understanding of the networked public sphere, as well as of movement–media relations, in a manner that attended to the structuring forces of the contemporary communication system. Future research in other anomalous cases may extend my theorizations in still further ways that map out areas of the networked public sphere I did not chart, as different behaviors reveal new invisible forces.

Conclusion: Research in the Spirit of Michael Burawoy

This Appendix, like this book, sought to do several things at once. I reflected on the various converging inspirations and obligations that shaped my approach to ethnographic fieldwork at the National Center for Transgender Equality. In line with my political and theoretical investments, I treated my fieldwork as a form of public scholarship, and I believe that doing so did not just "impact" my research findings but enhanced them. At the same time, doing so made my work "matter" in a way that reaches beyond the traditional significance of academic work. I also approached my research informed by the extended case method, as I hoped to use my grounded ethnographic fieldwork to make general theoretical claims about the nature and consequences of the contemporary communication system. The fingerprints of Michael Burawoy are clearly evident in my particular blend of public scholarship and the extended case method. In both regards, Burawoy has inspired me to make my work grander than what I once hoped it could be. I hope my reflections here similarly inspire others.

Notes

Chapter 1

1. Jay, like many trans people, uses the singular pronoun "they." Throughout this book, "they" will be used both to refer to individuals for whom it is the appropriate personal pronoun and to indicate generic personhood in the same manner some writers use "he or she," "s/he," etc.
2. These storytellers consist of both transgender individuals (VTE) and the parents or other family members of transgender individuals (FTE).
3. Mattie Kahn, "A Trans Air Force Veteran Responds to Trump's Ban," *Elle*, July 26, 2017, http://www.elle.com/culture/career-politics/news/a46960/trans-veteran-trump-military-ban-responds/.
4. Steven Verburg, "Sun Prairie Soldier Fears Trump Transgender Ban Will Force Her from Army," *Wisconsin State Journal*, July 27, 2017, http://host.madison.com/wsj/news/local/govt-and-politics/sun-prairie-soldier-fears-trump-transgender-ban-will-force-her/article_2f543bac-bac0-57fa-82c2-896a8dd2b143.html.
5. Steven Verburg, "Trump Ban on Transgender Military Service Hits Home for Some in Wisconsin," *Wisconsin State Journal*, July 27, 2017, http://host.madison.com/wsj/news/local/govt-and-politics/trump-ban-on-transgender-military-service-hits-home-for-some/article_7d47e877-0d54-57f1-99d8-0ed2d4443b86.html.
6. W. Neil Eggleston and Amanda Elbogen, "The Trump Administration and the Breakdown of Intra-Executive Legal Process," *Yale Law Journal Forum* 127 (2018): 825–847.
7. Thomas J Billard, "Together We Rise: The Role of Communication and Community Connectedness in Transgender Citizens' Civic Engagement in the United States," *Mass Communication and Society* 25, no. 3 (2022): 335–360.
8. Erica L. Green, Katie Benner, and Robert Pear, "'Transgender' Could be Defined Out of Existence Under Trump Administration," *New York Times*, October 21, 2018, https://www.nytimes.com/2018/10/21/us/politics/transgender-trump-administration-sex-definition.html.
9. Thomas J Billard, "Writing in the Margins: Mainstream News Media Representations of Transgenderism," *International Journal of Communication* 10 (2016): 4193–4218; Thomas J Billard, "Setting the Transgender Agenda: Intermedia Agenda-Setting in the Digital News Environment," *Politics, Groups, and Identities* 7, no. 1 (2019): 165–176; Thomas J Billard, "Movement–Media Relations in the Hybrid Media System: A Case Study from the U.S. Transgender Rights Movement," *The International Journal of Press/Politics* 26, no. 2 (2021): 341–361; Thomas J Billard and Larry Gross, "LGBTQ Politics in Media and Culture," in *The Oxford Research Encyclopedia of Politics*, ed.

William R. Thompson (New York: Oxford University Press, 2020); Jami K. Taylor, Daniel C. Lewis, and Donald P. Haider-Markel, *The Remarkable Rise of Transgender Rights* (Ann Arbor: University of Michigan Press, 2018).

10. For example, Billard, "Writing in the Margins"; Jamie C. Capuzza and Leland G. Spencer, "Regressing, Progressing, or Transgressing on the Small Screen? Transgender Characters on U.S. Scripted Television Series," *Communication Studies* 65, no. 2 (2018): 214–230.

11. See, for an introduction, Kjerstin Thorson and Chris Wells, "Curated Flows: A Framework for Mapping Media Exposure in the Digital Age," *Communication Theory* 26, no. 3 (2016): 309–328.

12. See, e.g., Pablo J. Boczkowski and Zizi Papacharissi, eds, *Trump and the Media* (Cambridge, MA: MIT Press, 2018).

13. See Jürgen Habermas, "The Public Sphere: An Encyclopedia Article," *New German Critique* 3 (1974): 49–55; Jürgen Habermas, *The Structural Transformation of the Public Sphere: An Inquiry into a Category of Bourgeois Society* (Cambridge, MA: MIT Press, 1991).

14. E.g., Nancy Fraser, "Rethinking the Public Sphere: A Contribution to the Critique of Actually Existing Democracy," *Social Text* 25/26 (1990): 56–80; Catherine R. Squires, "Rethinking the Black Public Sphere: An Alternative Vocabulary for Multiple Public Sphere," *Communication Theory* 12, no. 4 (2002): 446–468; Michael Warner, "Publics and Counterpublics," *Public Culture* 14, no. 1 (2002): 49–90.

15. See, for example, Noortje Marres, "Issues Spark a Public into Being: A Key but Often Forgotten Point of the Lippmann-Dewey Debate," in *Making Things Public: Atmospheres of Democracy*, ed. Bruno Latour and Peter Weibel (Cambridge, MA: MIT Press, 2005), 208–217.

16. Axel Bruns and Tim Highfield, "Is Habermas on Twitter? Social Media and the Public Sphere," in *Routledge Companion to Social Media and Politics*, ed. Axel Bruns et al. (New York: Routledge, 2015), 56–73.

17. On the changing nature and organization of audiences, see for example, Philip M. Napoli, *Audience Evolution: New Technologies and the Transformation of Media Audiences* (New York: Columbia University Press, 2011); Matthew Hindman, *The Internet Trap: How the Digital Economy Builds Monopolies and Undermines Democracy* (Princeton, NJ: Princeton University Press, 2018). On changes in media revenue streams and funding models, see, for example, Jeff Kaye and Stephen Quinn, *Funding Journalism in the Digital Age: Business Models, Strategies, Issues and Trends* (New York: Peter Lang, 2010). On changes in media distribution, see, for example, W. Lance Bennett and Shanto Iyengar, "A New Era of Minimal Effects? The Changing Foundations of Political Communication," *Journal of Communication* 58, no. 4 (2008): 707–731; Bregtje van der Haak, Michael Parks, and Manuel Castells, "The Future of Journalism: Networked Journalism," *International Journal of Communication* 6 (2012): 2923–2938. On the mass spread of individual communications see, for example, Manuel Castells, "Communication, Power and Counter-power in the Network Society," *International Journal of Communication* 1 (2007): 238–266.

18. For a more robust definition (and defense) of the concept of the "networked public sphere," see Yochai Benkler, *The Wealth of Networks: How Social Production Transforms Markets and Freedom* (New Haven, CT: Yale University Press, 2006); Lewis Friedland, Thomas Hove, and Hernando Rojas, "The Networked Public Sphere," *Javnost—The Public* 13, no. 4 (2006): 5–26; Stephen D. Reese and Pamela J. Shoemaker, "A Media Sociology for the Networked Public Sphere: The Hierarchy of Influences Model," *Mass Communication and Society* 19, no. 4 (2015): 389–410; among others.

19. Bennett and Iyengar, "A New Era"; Bruns and Highfield, "Is Habermas on Twitter"; Marres, "Issues Spark a Public."

20. Bruns and Highfield, "Is Habermas on Twitter," 62; see also Craig Calhoun, "Introduction," in *Habermas and the Public Sphere*, ed. Craig Calhoun (Cambridge, MA: MIT Press, 1992), 1–48; Lincoln Dahlberg, "The Habermasian Public Sphere: Taking Difference Seriously?" *Theory and Society* 34, no. 2 (2005): 111–136; Iris Marion Young, "De-centering Deliberative Democracy," *Kettering Review* 24, no. 3 (2006): 43–53.

21. On understandings of "media" see Kurt Lang and Gladys Engel Lang, "Mass Society Mass Culture, and Mass Communication: The Meaning of Mass," *International Journal of Communication* 3 (2009): 999. As they wrote, "when people speak of the media, they usually have in mind corporate bodies or government agencies whose access to modern technology enables them to disseminate the same uniform content to a geographically dispersed multitude." On understandings of news, see, for example, W. Lance Bennett, *News: The Politics of Illusion*, 10th ed. (Chicago: University of Chicago Press, 2016); Matt Carlson, "Journalistic Epistemology and Digital News Circulation: Infrastructure, Circulation Practices, and Epistemic Contests," *New Media & Society* 22, no. 2 (2020): 206–246.

22. On the concept of mediatization, see Nick Couldry and Andreas Hepp, "Conceptualizing Mediatization: Contexts, Traditions, Arguments," *Communication Theory* 23, no. 3 (2013): 191–202; Andreas Hepp, Stig Hjarvard, and Knut Lundby, "Mediatization: Theorizing the Interplay Between Media, Culture and Society," *Media, Culture & Society* 37, no. 2 (2015): 314–324; Jesper Strömbäck, "Four Phases of Mediatization: An Analysis of the Mediatization of Politics," *The International Journal of Press/Politics* 13, no. 3 (2008): 228–246; among others. On reconceptualizing news, see, for example, Andrew Chadwick, *The Hybrid Media System: Politics and Power*, 2nd ed. (New York: Oxford University Press, 2017); Ulrike Klinger and Jakob Svensson, "The Emergence of Network Media Logic in Political Communication: A Theoretical Approach," *New Media & Society* 17, no. 8 (2015): 1241–1257.

23. Chris Wells, *The Civic Organization and the Digital Citizen Communicating Engagement in a Networked Age* (New York: Oxford University Press, 2015), 7.

24. Wells, *Civic Organization*, 7; see also Chadwick, *The Hybrid Media System*; Patrícia Rossini et al., "Dysfunctional Information Sharing on WhatsApp and Facebook: The Role of Political Talk, Cross-cutting Exposure and Social Corrections," *New Media & Society* 23, no. 8 (2021): 2430–2451; Chris Wells et al., "Trump, Twitter, and News

Media Responsiveness: A Media Systems Approach," *New Media & Society* 22, no. 4 (2020): 659–682.

25. Chadwick, *The Hybrid Media System*; Andrew Chadwick, "The Political Information Cycle in a Hybrid News System: The British Prime Minister and the 'Bullygate' Affair," *The International Journal of Press/Politics* 16, no. 1 (2011): 3–29; Andreas Jungherr, Oliver Posegga, and Jisun An, "Discursive Power in Contemporary Media Systems: A Comparative Framework," *The International Journal of Press/Politics* 24, no. 4 (2019): 404–425.

26. Chadwick, *The Hybrid Media System*; Chadwick, "The Political Information Cycle."

27. See, for example, Thomas J Billard, "Deciding What's (Sharable) News: Social Movement Organizations as Curating Actors in the Political Information System," *Communication Monographs* 89, no. 3 (2022): 354–375; Billard, "Movement–Media Relations"; David Karpf, "Digital Politics after Trump," *Annals of the International Communication Association* 41, no. 2 (2017): 198–207; Francis LF Lee, "Social Media, Political Information Cycle, and the Evolution of News," *Communication and the Public* 3, no. 1 (2018): 67–76.

28. On the media activism strategies of earlier movements, see Kathryn C. Montgomery, "Gay Activists and the Networks," *Journal of Communication* 31, no. 3 (1981): 49–57; Kathryn C. Montgomery, *Target, Prime Time: Advocacy Groups and the Struggle over Entertainment Television* (New York: Oxford University Press, 1989). On audiences' changing amount of media choice, see Bennett and Iyengar, "A New Era." On changing distributions of communicative power, see Castells, "Communication, Power and Counter-power." On hybridity, see Chadwick, *The Hybrid Media System*.

29. See, for example, W. Lance Bennett and Alexandra Segerberg, "The Logic of Connective Action: Digital Media and Personalization of Contentious Politics," *Information, Communication & Society* 15, no. 5 (2012): 739–768; Manuel Castells, *Networks of Outrage and Hope: Social Movements in the Internet Age* (Medford, MA: Polity, 2015); Sasha Costanza-Chock, *Out of the Shadows, Into the Streets: Transmedia Organizing and the Immigrant Rights Movement* (Cambridge, MA: MIT Press, 2014); Jennifer Earl and Katrina Kimport, *Digitally Enabled Social Change: Activism in the Internet Age* (Cambridge, MA: MIT Press, 2011); Sarah J. Jackson, Moya Bailey, and Brooke Foucault Welles, *#HashtagActivism: Networks of Race and Gender Justice* (Cambridge, MA: MIT Press, 2020); Josep-Lluís Micó and Andreu Casero-Ripollés, "Political Activism Online: Organization and Media Relations in the Case of 15M in Spain," *Information, Communication, & Society* 17, no. 7 (2014): 858–871; Zizi Papacharissi and Maria de Fatima Oliveira, "Affective News and Networked Publics: The Rhythms of News Storytelling on #Egypt," *Journal of Communication* 62, no. 2 (2012): 266–282; Clay Shirky, "The Political Power of Social Media: Technology, the Public Sphere, and Political Change," *Foreign Affairs* 90, no. 1 (2011): 28–41; Zeynep Tufekci, *Twitter and Tear Gas: The Power and Fragility of Networked Protest* (New Haven, CT: Yale University Press, 2017).

30. See, for example, Earl and Kimport, *Digitally Enabled Social Change*; Michael Etter and Oana Brindusa Albu, "Activists in the Dark: Social Media Algorithms and Collective Action in Two Social Movement Organizations," *Organization* 28,

no. 1 (2021): 68–91; Karpf, "Digital Politics after Trump"; Daniel Kreiss, *Taking Our Country Back: The Crafting of Networked Politics from Howard Dean to Barack Obama* (New York: Oxford University Press, 2012); Wells, *Civic Organization*.

31. On the distinction between mass media logic and network media logic, see Klinger and Svensson, "Network Media Logic"; Chadwick, *The Hybrid Media System*.

32. Sandra J. Ball-Rokeach, Yong-Chan Kim, and Sorin Matei, "Storytelling Neighborhood: Paths to Belonging in Diverse Urban Environments," *Communication Research* 28, no. 4 (2001): 392–428; see also Yong-Chan Kim and Sandra J. Ball-Rokeach, "Civic Engagement from a Communication Infrastructure Perspective," *Communication Theory* 16, no. 2 (2006): 173–197. Note, whereas Ball-Rokeach identifies face-to-face networks of family, friends, colleagues, and community members as the interpersonal networks at the heart of communication infrastructure, I conceive of interpersonal networks as potentially more dispersed, consisting both of people who exist within face-to-face social networks *and* people who exist in mediated social networks through digital technologies (while recognizing that those two groups often overlap). Note also that Ball-Rokeach defined the levels of macro as mass media, meso as local media and community resources (which I have adjusted to local and community media), and micro as interpersonal networks (which I have adjusted to social networks), but the definitions of mass media, local and community media, and social networks are my own.

33. Chadwick, *The Hybrid Media System*.

34. See, for example, Daniel C. Hallin, Claudio Mellado, and Paolo Mancini, "The Concept of Hybridity in Journalism Studies," *The International Journal of Press/Politics* 28, no. 1 (2023): 219–237; Tamara Witschge et al., "Dealing With the Mess (We Made): Unraveling Hybridity, Normativity, and Complexity in Journalism Studies," *Journalism* 20, no. 5 (2019): 651–659.

35. This is, in many ways, unsurprising. As Hallin, Mellado, and Mancini write, "forms that emerge initially as hybrids can also become stabilized in reality, as rules and routines develop around them"; Hallin, Mellado, and Mancini, "The Concept of Hybridity," 230.

36. For the sake of metaphorical clarity, I have greatly over-simplified biological definitions of hybrids and chimaeras. For example, hybrids and chimaeras can be animals *or* plants. Additionally, there are various types of hybridity and chimaerism beyond the examples I provided.

37. Bernadette Barker-Plummer, "News as a Political Resource: Media Strategies and Political Identity in the U.S. Women's Movement, 1966–1975," *Critical Studies in Mass Communication* 12, no. 3 (1995): 306–324; Bernadette Barker-Plummer, "Producing Public Voice: Resource Mobilization and Media Access in the National Organization for Women," *Journalism & Mass Communication Quarterly* 79, no. 1 (2002): 188–205.

38. Bruns and Highfield, "Is Habermas on Twitter," 62.

39. See for further discussion Thomas J Billard, "Out of the Tower and Into the Field: Fieldwork as Public Scholarship in the Face of Social Injustice," *International Journal of Communication* 13 (2019): 3512–3528; Thomas J Billard, Avery R. Everhart, and Erique Zhang, "Whither Trans Studies? On Fields, Post-Disciplines, and the Need

for an Applied Transgender Studies," *Bulletin of Applied Transgender Studies* 1, no. 1-2 (2022): 1-18; Thomas J Billard and Silvio Waisbord, "The Promethean Imperative: An Introduction to Public Scholarship in Communication Studies," in *Public Scholarship in Communication Studies*, ed. Thomas J Billard and Silvio Waisbord (Urbana-Champaign: University of Illinois Press, 2024).

40. For more on the general concept of imprinting in the organizational soci-ology and management literatures, see Christopher Marquis and András Tilcsik, "Imprinting: Toward a Multilevel Theory," *Academy of Management Annals* 7, no. 1 (2013): 193-243; Arthur L. Stinchcombe, "Social Structure and Organizations," in *Handbook of Organizations*, ed. James G. March (Chicago: Rand McNally, 1965), 142-193. For further discussion of my novel concept of media imprinting, see Chapter 2.

41. It is important to note here that the transgender movement is not just a social move-ment, but rather a specific kind of social movement—and identity-based social movement. While a number of other non-identity-based movements will share the transgender movement's strategic aims and activities, not all movements will because they have different social, cultural, and political circumstances. For example, identity-based movements often center public education as a key strategic goal; educating the public about what transgender identity is and what issues face people who hold this often-misunderstood identity is necessary for the kinds of sociopolitical change the movement pushes for. While some non-identity-based movements may similarly prize public education—such as health reform movements, which often use story-telling to educate the public on the consequences of for-profit healthcare systems—other movements will not place such a premium on public education—such as movements for gun reform, as public education does little to curb gun violence or promote gun regulation. As such, some of the tactics I describe here will not gener-alize to all social movements.

42. Anthony Nownes, *Organizing for Transgender Rights: Collective Action, Group Development, and the Rise of a New Social Movement* (Albany: State University of New York Press, 2019), 40.

43. NCTE is one of three transgender rights organizations that operates nationally as of the time of writing. The other two are the Transgender Law Center (TLC) in Oakland, California and the Transgender Legal Defense and Education Fund (TLDEF) in New York City. However, both organizations differ from NCTE in focus; TLC and TLDEF both focus primarily on litigation, rather than advocacy, and TLC focuses heavily on California politics, though it operates outside the state occasionally. Moreover, neither TLC nor TLDEF has as extensive connections to broader civil rights movements or as robust public communications programs as NCTE.

44. Many of these staff members held multiple titles during my time in the field. The titles presented here are those they held at the end of my fieldwork. See Table 2.1 for a full breakdown of positions held by each staff member during my time in the field.

45. On criticisms of pseudonymization, see Nancy Scheper-Hughes, "Ire in Ireland," *Ethnography* 1, no. 1 (2000): 117-140; Arlene Stein, "Sex, Truths, and Audiotape: Anonymity and the Ethics of Exposure in Public Ethnography," *Journal of Contemporary Ethnography* 39, no. 5 (2010): 554-568; Will C. van den Hoonaard,

"Is Anonymity an Artifact in Ethnographic Research?" *Journal of Academic Ethics* 1, no. 2 (2003): 141–151.

Chapter 2

1. Thomas J Billard, "Hybrid Social Movements: An Historical Perspective on Social Movement Hybridization in the Case of the US Transgender Movement," Unpublished manuscript, Northwestern University, 2023; see also Billard and Gross, "LGBTQ Politics."
2. Stinchcombe, "Social Structure and Organizations."
3. Marquis and Tilcsik, "Imprinting," 199.
4. For that full history, see Thomas J Billard, "The Origins and Development of the National Transgender Rights Movement in the United States of America," *Journal of Social History*, forthcoming; see also Zein Murib, "Transgender: Examining an Emerging Political Identity Using Three Political Processes," *Politics, Groups, and Identities* 3, no. 3 (2015): 381–397; Susan Stryker, *Transgender History: The Roots of Today's Revolution* (New York: Seal Press, 2017).
5. Many alternate histories of the transgender movement could be, and have been, written. Specifically, a robust body of trans studies work rooted in critical theory and cultural studies argues that the origins of the transgender movement should be traced to transgender street activism of the 1970s in places like New York, Los Angeles, and San Francisco and, later, to the emergence of local and grassroots organizations in the late 1990s and early 2000s that claimed lineage to that tradition, while being highly critical of the "nonprofit industrial complex" in which formal movement organizations like NCTE participate; see, e.g., Morgan Bassichis, Alexander Lee, and Dean Spade, "Building an Abolitionist Trans and Queer Movement with Everything We've Got," in *Captive Genders: Trans Embodiment and the Prison Industrial Complex*, ed. Eric A. Stanley and Nat Smith (Oakland, CA: AK Press, 2011), 15–40; Dan Irving, "Transgender Politics," in *The Wiley Blackwell Encyclopedia of Gender and Sexuality Studies*, ed. Nancy A. Naples (Hoboken, NJ: John Wiley & Sons, 2016); Dean Spade, *Normal Life: Administrative Violence, Critical Trans Politics, and the Limits of Law* (Durham, NC: Duke University Press, 2015); Stryker, *Transgender History*. My history of the transgender movement is markedly different, not because I find the anti-statist and ant-liberal strain of thought that runs through this work irrelevant or incorrect, but because I approach the idea of social movements from a different theoretical perspective—a sociological one that draws a distinction between a *social movement* and *collective action*. Within political sociology, social movements are understood as *multiorganizational fields*—networks of interacting organizations that are engaged in a shared sociopolitical conflict on the basis of a shared collective identity, which carry out the routine work of the movement, ranging from mobilization to coordination to interaction with political elites, using their accumulated resources; see Russell L. Curtis and Louis A. Zurcher, "Stable Resources of Protest Movements: The Multi-Organizational Field," *Social Forces* 52, no. 1 (1973): 53–61; Bert Klandermans,

"The Social Construction of Protest and Multiorganizational Fields," in *Frontiers in Social Movement Theory*, ed. Aldon D. Morris and Carol McClurg Mueller (New Haven: Yale University Press, 1992), 77–103; see also work in the political process tradition, such as Doug McAdam, Sidney Tarrow, and Charles Tilly, *Dynamics of Contention* (New York: Cambridge University Press, 2001); Charles Tilly, "Social Movements and National Politics," in *State-Making and Social Movements: Essays in History and Theory*, ed. Charles Bright and Susan Harding (Ann Arbor: University of Michigan Press, 1984), 297–317. The more colloquial usage of "social movements" taken for granted in much of the trans studies literature describing the work of decentralized activists is more accurately considered *collective action*, which is distinguished from proper social movements by its focus on groups of *individual persons* acting together in pursuit of their perceived shared interests. In short, collective action focuses on informal groups of individuals, while social movements focus on enduring interactions among resourced organizations. For this reason, my history of the transgender movement focuses on the emergence of more formal nonprofit organizations that focused their activism on the state and other institutions of social, cultural, political, and economic power.

6. Pauline Park, "GenderPAC, the Transgender Rights Movement and the Perils of a Post-Identity Politics Paradigm," *Georgetown Journal of Gender and the Law* 4 (2003): 747–766.

7. Importantly, several of these organizations operated according to very different theories of change and thus had very different relationships to the state and other institutions of societal power. For example, the Sylvia Rivera Law Project followed an abolitionist activist framework that focused less on inclusion within the state and more on the dismantling of administrative systems that enact violence on marginalized peoples; see Spade, *Normal Life*. These organizations thus took different organizational forms, employed different strategies of activism, served different populations, and targeted different institutions; see, e.g., Dan Irving, "Against the Grain: Teaching Transgender Human Rights," *Sexualities* 16, no. 3–4 (2013): 319–335; Irving, "Transgender Politics."

8. Nownes, *Organizing for Transgender Rights*, 40. For a more thorough narration of how NCTE emerged at the forefront of this multiorganizational field, see Billard, "Origins and Development."

9. Sean Bugg, "Trans mission: Mara Keisling and the Politics of ENDA," *Metro Weekly*, August 19, 2004; Mara Keisling, Interview, December 5, 2018; Lisa Mottet, Interview, November 28, 2018.

10. Mottet, Interview, November 28, 2018.

11. Keisling, Interview, December 5, 2018.

12. Donna Cartwright, Interview, November 27, 2018; Mottet, Interview, November 28, 2018.

13. Lisa Mottet, Interview, December 12, 2018; Masen Davis, Interview, December 21, 2018.

14. Cartwright, Interview, November 27, 2018.

15. Bugg, "Trans Mission."

16. Mottet, Interview, November 28, 2018.

17. Cartwright, Interview, November 27, 2018.

18. Diego Miguel Sanchez, Interview, December 19, 2018.

19. Communications Program Analysis, June 19, 2012, Box 12, Folder 24, Trans Equality Archive, National Center for Transgender Equality, Washington, DC.

20. Communications Program Analysis.

21. Katy Steinmetz, "The Transgender Tipping Point," *TIME*, May 29, 2014, https://time.com/135480/transgender-tipping-point/.

22. Mottet, Interview, November 28, 2018.

23. Keisling, Interview, December 5, 2018.

24. Jay Wu, Interview, August 22, 2018; Vincent Paolo Villano, Exit Memo, September 2015, Box 12, Folder 31, Trans Equality Archive, National Center for Transgender Equality, Washington, DC.

25. Although such a designation may seem strange for an activist organization, many key civil rights organizations hold 501(c)(3) status, including the majority of LGBTQ rights organizations, such as the National LGBTQ Task Force, GLAAD, and the Equality Federation, and leading organizations in other civil rights movements, such as the National Organization for Women and the NAACP.

26. Keisling, Interview, December 5, 2018.

27. For a brief introduction to the differences between 501(c)(3) and 501(c)(4) and why they matter, see Rosemary E. Fei and Eric K. Gorovitz, "Practitioner Perspectives on Using 501(c)(4) Organizations for Charitable Lobbying," *NYU Journal of Legislation & Public Policy* 21 (2018): 535–582.

28. Andrew R. Flores et al., *How Many Adults Identify as Transgender in the United States?* (Los Angeles: Williams Institute, 2016); Esther L. Meerwijk and Jae Sevelius, "Transgender Population Size in the United States: A Meta-Regression of Population-Based Probability Samples," *American Journal of Public Health* 107, no. 2 (2017): 216; G. Nic, Rider, Barbara J. McMorris, Amy L. Gower, Eli Coleman, and Marla E. Eisenberg, "Health and Care Utilization of Transgender and Gender Nonconforming Youth: A Population-Based Study," *Pediatrics* 141 (2018): e20171683.

29. National Center for Transgender Equality, *2018 Annual Report* (Washington, DC: National Center for Transgender Equality, 2019).

30. Former Staff of NCTE, "This Is Why We Left the National Center for Trans Equality," *Out*, November 15, 2019, https://www.out.com/transgender/2019/11/15/why-we-left-americas-largest-trans-advocacy-organization; Kate Sosin, "National Center for Trans Equality Staff Walks Out Over Union Woes, Racism," *NewNowNext*, August 20, 2019, http://www.newnownext.com/national-center-for-trans-equality-walkout/08/2019/.

31. Sosin, "Staff Walks Out."

32. Former Staff of NCTE, "Why We Left."

33. Former Staff of NCTE, "Why We Left"; Sosin, "Staff Walks Out."

34. Sosin, "Staff Walks Out."

35. Former Staff of NCTE, "Why We Left"; Nonprofit Professional Employees Union (NPEU), "Nonprofit Professional Employees Union Files Unfair Labor Practice

Against National Center for Transgender Equality Leadership For Retaliation Against Staff Organizing," *Nonprofit Professional Employees Union*, November 15, 2019, https://npeu.org/news/2019/11/15/nonprofit-professional-employees-union-files-unfair-labor-practice-against-national-center-for-transgender-equality-leadership-for-retaliation-against-staff-organizing; Kate Sosin, "NCTE's Mara Keisling Talks Next Steps After Calls for Her to Step Down," *NewNowNext*, December 13, 2019, http://www.newnownext.com/mara-keisling-national-center-for-trans-equality-racism-union-busting-allegations/12/2019/; Daniel Villarreal, "Most of the Staffers at One of the Nation's Biggest Trans Organization Just Quit," *LGBTQ Nation*, November 15, 2019, https://www.lgbtqnation.com/2019/11/workers-countrys-biggest-trans-organization-just-quit/.

36. Villarreal, "Most of the Staffers."
37. Kate Sosin, "Harper Jean Tobin to Leave NCTE as Fallout Grows," *NewNowNext*, December 20, 2019, http://www.newnownext.com/harper-jean-tobin-leaving-national-center-for-trans-equality/12/2019.
38. Daniel Trotta, "Staff Exodus Hits Top U.S. Transgender Group on Eve of 2020 Election Campaign," *Reuters*, November 15, 2019, https://www.reuters.com/article/us-usa-lgbt-transgender-idUSKBN1XP2FI.
39. NPEU, "Retaliation Against Staff Organizing."
40. Concerned Transgender Community Leaders, "Over 400 Trans Community Leaders Stand With Former NCTE Staff," *Out*, December 12, 2019, https://www.out.com/activism/2019/12/11/over-400-trans-community-leaders-stand-former-ncte-staff.
41. Chris Johnson, "National Center for Trans Equality Regroups After Mass Staff Departures." *Washington Blade*, December 11, 2019, https://www.washingtonblade.com/2019/12/11/natl-center-for-trans-equality-regroups-after-mass-staff-departures/.
42. William Lafi Youmans, *An Unlikely Audience: Al Jazeera's Struggle in America* (New York: Oxford University Press, 2017).
43. Youmans, *An Unlikely Audience*, 49.
44. Vincent Doyle, *Making Out in the Mainstream: GLAAD and the Politics of Respectability* (Montreal: McGill-Queen's University Press, 2016).
45. For a rich analysis of the social dynamics among DC-based political journalists and how that shapes news-making process, see Nikki Usher and Yee Man Margaret Ng, "Sharing Knowledge and 'Microbubbles': Epistemic Communities and Insularity in US Political Journalism," *Social Media + Society* 6, no. 2 (2020).
46. Nikki Usher, "Putting 'Place' in the Center of Journalism Research: A Way Forward to Understand Challenges to Trust and Knowledge in News," *Journalism & Communication Monographs* 21, no. 2 (2019): 84–146.
47. Carl Abbott, *Political Terrain: Washington, DC, from Tidewater Town to Global Metropolis* (Chapel Hill: University of North Carolina Press, 1999).
48. For a discussion of this dynamic in the realm of management, see Herminia Ibarra and Mark Lee Hunter, "How Leaders Create and Use Networks," *Harvard Business Review* 85 (2007): 40–47. Outside of management, surprisingly little has been written about networking culture, especially in industry towns like DC and Los Angeles; cf.

Elizabeth Currid-Halkett, *Starstruck: The Business of Celebrity* (New York: Faber and Faber, 2010), ch. 5. As such, my analysis of this dynamic in DC social movement politics is built upon ethnographic observation and personal experience extrapolating from Ibarra and Hunter's work.

49. For example, Barbara S. Romzek and Jennifer A. Utter, "Career Dynamics of Congressional Legislative Staff: Preliminary Profile and Research Questions," *Journal of Public Administration Research and Theory* 6, no. 3 (1996): 415–442; William R. Freudenburg, "Sociology in Legis-Land: An Ethnographic Report on Congressional Culture," *The Sociological Quarterly* 27, no. 3 (1986): 313–326.

50. On the evolving nature of participation amicus curiae briefs among social movement organizations, see Janet M. Box-Steffensmeier and Dino P. Christenson, "The Evolution and Formation of Amicus Curiae Networks," *Social Networks* 36 (2014): 82–96.

51. On the revolving door of congressional staff to lobbyist, see Timothy M. LaPira and Herschel F. Thomas III, "Revolving Door Lobbyists and Interest Representation," *Interest Groups & Advocacy* 3, no. 1 (2014): 4–29; Joshua McCrain, "Revolving Door Lobbyists and the Value of Congressional Staff Connections," *Journal of Politics* 80, no. 4 (2018): 1369–1383.

52. Derek Hyra and Sabiyha Prince, eds. *Capital Dilemma: Growth and Inequality in Washington, DC* (New York: Routledge, 2016).

53. For more on the racial divides in trans political activism in DC, see Elijah Adiv Edelman, *Trans Vitalities: Mapping Ethnographies of Trans Social and Political Coalitions* (New York: Routledge, 2020). For a broader discussion of how organizations function as racial structures that perpetuate racial inequality, see Victor Ray, "A Theory of Racialized Organizations," *American Sociological Review* 84, no. 1 (2019): 26–53.

54. Dan Nimmo and James E. Combs, *The Political Pundits* (New York: Praeger, 1992).

55. Green, Benner, and Pear, "Defined Out of Existence."

56. Gordon Evans, "Director of National Transgender Rights Group Says 'The Law Is on Our Side.'" *WMUK*, May 30, 2018, https://www.wmuk.org/post/wsw-director-natio nal-transgender-rights-group-says-law-our-side.

57. Nikki Usher, *News for the Rich, White, and Blue: How Place and Power Distort American Journalism* (New York: Columbia University Press, 2021), 103.

58. Regarding virtual newsrooms, see Mel Bunce, Kate Wright, and Martin Scott, "'Our Newsroom in the Cloud': Slack, Virtual Newsrooms and Journalistic Practice," *New Media & Society* 20, no. 9 (2017): 3381–3399; Rachel E. Moran, "Subscribing to Transparency: Trust-Building Within Virtual Newsrooms on Slack," *Journalism Practice* 15, no. 10 (2021): 1580–1596. Regarding the rise of freelance journalism, see Kathryn Hayes and Henry Silke, "The Networked Freelancer? Digital Labour and Freelance Journalism in the Age of Social Media," *Digital Journalism* 6, no. 8 (2018): 1018–1028; Avery E. Holton, "Intrapreneurial Informants: An Emergent Role of Freelance Journalists," *Journalism Practice* 10, no. 7 (2016): 917–927; Birgit Røe Mathisen, "Entrepreneurs and Idealists: Freelance Journalists at the Intersection of Autonomy and Constraints," *Journalism Practice* 13, no. 8 (2017): 1003–1007.

59. In her pioneering analysis of gay and lesbian activists' relationship with mass media, Kathryn C. Montgomery discussed how gay activists used "agents in place"—gay people who worked *inside* the media institutions they were targeting—as key resources for getting information and exercising influence. In many ways, the queer journalists NCTE worked with in NCTE fulfilled a similar role, providing the organization a route to wider media attention by advocating for sympathetic transgender coverage inside their media companies. See Kathryn C. Montgomery, *Target, Prime Time: Advocacy Groups and the Struggle over Entertainment Television* (New York: Oxford University Press, 1989); see also Larry Gross, *Up from Invisibility: Lesbians, Gay Men, and the Media in America* (New York: Columbia University Press, 2001).

60. See, however, Doyle, *Making Out in the Mainstream*, for a thorough critique of how GLAAD decided what "positive" representation was, as well as how GLAAD serves as a marketing resource for entertainment media companies.

61. Lori Kido Lopez, *Asian American Media Activism: Fighting for Cultural Citizenship* (New York: New York University Press, 2016).

62. Billard, "Origins and Development."

63. For a thorough history of the schism between the gay and lesbian and the transgender movements, see Billard, "Origins and Development."

64. Cartwright, Interview, November 27, 2018; Field notes, July 13, 2018.

65. Keisling, Interview, December 5, 2018.

66. For a deeper exploration of the theoretical concept of hybrid social movements, see Billard, "Hybrid Social Movements."

67. Rebecca Kling, Interview, October 12, 2018.

68. Field Notes, October 22, 2018.

69. Debi Jackson, Interview, August 16, 2018; Debi Jackson, Interview, October 10, 2018; DeShanna Neal, Interview, August 7, 2018.

Chapter 3

1. Credit for this observation is owed to Peter Loge, now an associate professor in the School of Media and Public Affairs at the George Washington University. When I was an undergraduate in the School, Loge was an adjunct professor who used his decades of experience consulting on lobbying and advocacy strategy for a range of issues to teach practice-focused approaches to political communication. He frequently recounted instances in which advocates for local policy initiatives would ask him to secure coverage of their issues on cable news or in national newspapers, despite the ineffectiveness of mass media attention at persuading the usually small number of people who had locally concentrated power over relevant policies.

2. Sarah Sobieraj, *Soundbitten: The Perils of Media-Centered Political Activism* (New York: New York University Press, 2011), 105.

3. Michelle Wolfe, "Putting on the Brakes or Pressing on the Gas? Media Attention and the Speed of Policymaking," *Policy Studies Journal* 40, no. 1 (2012): 109–126; Yanovitzky, "Effects of News Coverage on Policy Attention and Actions: A Closer

Look into the Media–Policy Connection," *Communication Research* 29, no 4 (2002): 422–451.

4. Larry W. Isaac et al., "Striking News: Discursive Power of the Press as Capitalist Resource in Gilded Age Strikes," *American Journal of Sociology* 127, no. 5 (2022): 1602–1663.

5. For example, Sandra J. Ball-Rokeach, "The Legitimation of Violence," in *Collective Violence*, ed. James F. Short, Jr. and Marvin Wolfgang (Chicago: Aldine, 1971), 100–111; Herbert J. Gans, *Deciding What's News: A Study of CBS Evening News, NBC Nightly News, Newsweek, and Time* (New York: Vintage, 1979); Todd Gitlin, *The Whole World Is Watching: Mass Media in the Making & Unmaking of the New Left* (Berkeley: University of California Press, 1980); Larry Gross, "Out of the Mainstream: Sexual Minorities and the Mass Media," *Journal of Homosexuality* 21, no. 1–2 (1991): 19–46; Stuart Hall, "Media Power: The Double Bind," *Journal of Communication* 24, no. 4 (1974): 19–26; Daniel C. Hallin, *The Uncensored War: The Media and Vietnam* (Berkeley: University of California Press, 1989); Pamela J. Shoemaker, "The Perceived Legitimacy of Deviant Political Groups: Two Experiments on Media Effects," *Communication Research* 9, no. 2 (1982): 249–286.

6. Billard, "Writing in the Margins."

7. For example, Sarah J. Jackson and Brooke Foucault Welles, "#Ferguson is Everywhere: Initiators in Emerging Counterpublic Networks," *Information, Communication & Society* 19, no. 3 (2016): 397–418; Sharon Meraz and Zizi Papacharissi, "Networked Gatekeeping and Networked Framing on #Egypt," *The International Journal of Press/Politics* 18, no. 2 (2013): 138–166; Lindsay Erin Young and Paul M. Leonardi, "Social Issue Emergence on the Web: A Dual Structurational Model," *Journal of Computer-Mediated Communication* 17, no. 2 (2012): 231–246.

8. Nikki Usher, *Making News at The New York Times* (Ann Arbor: University of Michigan Press, 2014).

9. Chadwick, *The Hybrid Media System*, 69.

10. Chadwick, *The Hybrid Media System*, 69.

11. At the same time, mass news media remained critical for other reasons, including political economic ones. As Matthew Powers shows, nonprofit organizations often pursue mass news media coverage because achieving that coverage is viewed as a metric of success by funding agencies and individual donors; see Matthew Power, *NGOs as Newsmakers: The Changing Landscape of International News* (New York: Columbia University Press, 2018).

12. Gitlin, *The Whole World Is Watching*.

13. Gitlin, *The Whole World Is Watching*, 15.

14. Gitlin, *The Whole World Is Watching*, 13.

15. Bernadette Barker-Plummer, "The Dialogic of Media and Social Movements," *Peace Review* 8, no. 1 (1996): 27–33; for examples of scholarship in the "strong hegemony" school of thought, see Robert M. Entman, *Democracy Without Citizens: Media and the Decay of American Politics* (New York: Oxford University Press, 1989); William Gamson, "Constructing Social Protest," in *Social Movements and Culture*, ed. Hank Johnston and Bert Klandermans (Minneapolis: University of Minnesota Press, 1995),

85–106; Edward Herman and Noam Chomsky, *Manufacturing Consent: The Political Economy of the Mass Media* (New York: Pantheon Books, 1988).

16. For a sampling of such scholarship, see Kenneth Andrews and Neal Caren, "Making the News: Movement Organizations, Media Attention, and the Public Agenda," *American Sociological Review* 75, no. 6 (2010): 841–866; Barker-Plummer, "News as a Political Resource"; Barker-Plummer, "Media and Social Movements"; Barker-Plummer, "Producing Public Voice"; Robert Benford, "Frame Disputes within the Nuclear Disarmament Movement," *Social Forces* 71, no. 3 (1993): 677–701; William Carroll and R. S. Ratner, "Media Strategies and Political Projects: A Comparative Study of Social Movements," *Canadian Journal of Sociology* 24, no. 1 (1999): 1–34; Deana Rohlinger, *Abortion Politics Mass Media, and Social Movements in America* (New York: Cambridge University Press, 2014); Charlotte Ryan, *Prime Time Activism: Media Strategies for Grassroots Organizing* (Boston: South End Press, 1991); Charlotte Ryan, "It Takes a Movement to Raise an Issue: Media Lessons from the 1997 U.P.S. Strike," *Critical Sociology* 30, no. 2 (2004): 483–511; Charlotte Ryan, Kevin Carragee, and Cassie Schwerner, "Media, Movements, and the Quest for Social Justice," *Journal of Applied Communication Research* 26, no. 2 (1998): 165–181.

17. Barker-Plummer, "News as a Political Resource"; Barker-Plummer, "Media and Social Movements." Similar to Barker-Plummer's dialogic model, Edwin Amenta and colleagues' institutional mediation model identifies several features that interact to affect the quality of news coverage social movements receive, including the standard operating practices of news organizations, the characteristics and strategic actions of movement organizations, and the political contexts in which coverage occurs; see Edwin Amenta and Neal Caren, *Rough Draft of History: A Century of US Social Movements in the News* (Princeton, NJ: Princeton University Press, 2022); Edwin Amenta et al., "Making Good News: What Explains the Quality of Coverage of the Civil Rights Movement," *Mobilization* 24, no. 1 (2019): 19–37.

18. Barker-Plummer, "News as a Political Resource"; Barker-Plummer, "Media and Social Movements"; Robert Benford and David Snow, "Framing Processes and Social Movements: An Overview and Assessment," *Annual Review of Sociology* 26 (2000): 611–639; Gamson and Wolfsfeld, "Movements and Media."

19. William R. Gamson and Gadi Wolfsfeld, "Movements and Media as Interacting Systems," *Annals of the American Academy of Political and Social Science* 528 (1993): 114–125; Powers, *NGOs as Newsmakers*; Sobieraj, *Soundbitten*.

20. See for a critical summary, Christina R. Foust and Kate Drazner Hoyt, "Social Movement 2.0: Integrating and Assessing Scholarship on Social Media and Movement," *Review of Communication* 18, no. 1 (2018): 37–55.

21. Amenta and Caren, *Rough Draft*; Amenta et al., "Making Good News"; Andrews and Caren, "Making the News"; Barker-Plummer, "Producing Public Voice"; Rohlinger, *Abortion Politics*; Ryan, *Prime Time Activism*; Ryan, "It Takes a Movement."

22. Vincent Paolo Villano, Interview, November 20, 2018.

23. Jaime M. Grant et al., *Injustice at Every Turn: A Report of the National Transgender Discrimination Survey* (Washington, DC: National Center for Transgender Equality and National Gay and Lesbian Task Force, 2011).

24. Jay Wu, Interview, August 22, 2018.

25. Dave Noble, Interview, October 17, 2018.

26. Gillian Branstetter, Interview, August 7, 2018.

27. Branstetter, Interview, August 7, 2018.

28. Branstetter, Interview, August 7, 2018.

29. Field Notes, August 6, 2018.

30. See, by way of introduction, Maxwell McCombs and Amy Reynolds, "How the News Shapes our Civic Agenda," in *Media Effects: Advances in Theory and Research*, ed. Jennings Bryant and Mary Beth Oliver (New York: Routledge, 2009), 1–16.

31. Billard, "Setting the Transgender Agenda."

32. On the intermedia agenda-setting power of the *New York Times*, see Allan Mazur, "Putting Radon on the Public Risk Agenda," *Science, Technology and Human Values* 12, no. 3/4 (1987): 86–93. On intermedia agenda-setting in the digital media environment, see Billard, "Setting the Transgender Agenda"; Ramona Vonbun, Katharina Kleinen-von Königslöw, and Klaus Schoenbach, "Intermedia Agenda-Setting in a Multimedia News Environment," *Journalism* 17, no. 8 (2016): 1054–1073.

33. Gillian Branstetter, Interview, August 21, 2018.

34. Evan Urquhart, "Facing Bullies and Court Battles, Transgender Kids Head Back to School," *Slate*, August 24, 2018, https://slate.com/human-interest/2018/08/facing-bullies-and-court-battles-transgender-kids-head-back-to-school.html.

35. On the concept of informational subsidies, see Oscar Gandy, "Information in Health: Subsidized News," *Media, Culture & Society* 2, no. 2 (1980): 103–115. On editorial subsidies, see Daniel Jackson and Kevin Moloney, "Inside Churnalism: PR, Journalism and Power Relationships in Flux," *Journalism Studies* 17, no. 6 (2016): 763–780; see also Christopher A. Bail, "The Fringe Effect: Civil Society Organizations and the Evolution of Media Discourse about Islam since the September 11th Attacks," *American Sociological Review* 77, no. 6 (2012): 855–879.

36. Lisa Mottet, Interview, November 28, 2018.

37. Field Notes, October 26, 2018.

38. Field Notes, August 20, 2018.

39. Field Notes, August 20, 2018.

40. Field Notes, August 20, 2018.

41. Branstetter, Interview, August 7, 2018.

42. Field Notes, August 20, 2018.

43. Branstetter, Interview, August 7, 2018.

44. For criticisms of press releases as ineffectual, see Sobieraj, *Soundbitten*; Dan Berkowitz and Douglas B. Adams, "Information Subsidy and Agenda-Building in Local Television News," *Journalism Quarterly* 67, no. 4 (1990): 723–731. For scholarship demonstrating the effectiveness of press releases, see Jelle Boumans, "Subsidizing the News? Organizational Press Releases' Influence on News Media's Agenda and Content," *Journalism Studies* 19, no. 15 (2018): 2264–2282; Susan Forde and Jane Johnston, "The News Triumvirate: Public Relations, Wire Agencies and Online Copy," *Journalism Studies* 14, no. 1 (2013): 113–129.

45. For estimates of how often news articles are initiated by press releases, see Boumans, "Subsidizing The News." For work on how news outlets adopt rhetoric and language from organizational press releases, see Bail, "The Fringe Effect."

46. Branstetter, Interview, August 7, 2018.

47. For more on the concept of journalistic metanarratives, see Kobie van Krieken and José Sanders, "What Is Narrative Journalism? A Systematic Review and an Empirical Agenda," *Journalism* 22, no. 6 (2021): 1393–1412.

48. Field Notes, June 12, 2018.

49. Field Notes, June 12, 2018.

50. Monika Djerf-Pierre, "The Crowding-Out Effect: Issue Dynamics and Attention to Environmental Issues in Television News Reporting Over 30 Years," *Journalism Studies* 13, no. 4 (2012): 499–516.

51. For the classic study of journalists' newsworthiness criteria in editorial decision-making, see Gans, *Deciding What's News*. For a summary of more recent findings, see Helen Caple, "News Values and Newsworthiness," in *The Oxford Research Encyclopedia of Communication*, ed. Jon Nussbaum (New York: Oxford University Press, 2018).

52. Field Notes, July 26, 2018.

53. Branstetter, Interview, August 7, 2018.

54. Branstetter, Interview, August 7, 2018.

55. Branstetter, Interview, August 7, 2018.

56. For example, Field Notes, June 8, 2018; Field Notes, June 18, 2018; Field Notes, June 22, 2018; Field Notes, June 26, 2018; Field Notes, July 6, 2018.

57. De La Torre, Interview, August 28, 2018.

58. Arli Christian, Interview. September 6, 2018.

59. Branstetter, Interview, August 7, 2018.

60. Field Notes, December 6, 2018.

61. Branstetter, Interview, August 21, 2018.

62. National Center for Transgender Equality (TransEquality), Twitter post, August 13, 2018, 10:19 a.m., https://twitter.com/TransEquality/status/1029100259140689920.

63. See, for example, Emilio Ferrara and Zeyao Yang, "Measuring Emotional Contagion in Social Media," *PLOS ONE* 10 (2015): e0142390; Ariel Hasell, "Shared Emotion: The Social Amplification of Partisan News on Twitter," *Digital Journalism* 9, no. 8 (2021): 1085–1102; Gerard J. Tellis et al., "What Drives Virality(Sharing) of Online Digital Content? The Critical Role of Information, Emotion, and Brand Prominence," *Journal of Marketing* 83, no. 4 (2019): 1–20.

64. Shannon C. McGregor and Logan Molyneux, "Twitter's Influence on News Judgment: An Experiment Among Journalists," *Journalism* 21, no. 5 (2020): 597–613.

65. Noble, Interview, October 17, 2018.

66. On the most significant differences between the traditional logics of mass media and the "network" logics of social media, see Klinger and Svensson, "Network Media Logic"; Chadwick, *The Hybrid Media System*. On differences in the temporality between mass media and social media, see Andreas Jungherr, "The Logic of Political Coverage on Twitter: Temporal Dynamics and Content," *Journal of Communication*

64, no. 2 (2014): 239–259. On the personal nature and emotional charge of so-cial media-based political information, see Papacharissi and Oliveira, "Affective News"; Castells, "Communication, Power and Counter-power." On the heighted significance of non-elite, individual communicators on social media, see W. Lance Bennett, Alexandra Segerberg, and Yunkang Yang, "The Strength of Peripheral Networks: Negotiating Attention and Meaning in Complex Media Ecologies," *Journal of Communication* 68, no. 4 (2018): 659–684; Chadwick, "The Political Information Cycle"; Lauren Guggenheim et al., "The Dynamics of Issue Frame Competition in Traditional and Social Media," *Annals of the American Academy of Political and Social Science* 659 (2015): 207–224; Alfred Hermida, "Twittering the News: The Emergence of Ambient Journalism," *Journalism Practice* 4, no. 3 (2010): 297–308; Alfred Hermida and Neil Thurman, "A Clash of Cultures: The Integration of User-Generated Content within Professional Journalistic Frameworks at British Newspaper Websites," *Journalism Practice* 2, no. 3 (2008): 343–356.

67. Chadwick, *The Hybrid Media System*.

68. For more on the adaptation of activism strategies to suit dominant media technologies, see David Karpf, *Analytic Activism: Digital Listening and the New Political Strategy* (New York: Oxford University Press, 2016).

69. Daniel J. Boorstin, *The Image: A Guide to Pseudo-Events in America* (New York: Vintage Books, 1992).

70. Field Notes, July 17, 2018.

71. Field Notes, July 17, 2018.

72. Field Notes, October 22, 2018.

73. Wu, Interview, November 10, 2018.

74. Branstetter, Interview, August 21, 2018.

75. Branstetter, Interview, August 21, 2018.

76. Wu, Interview, November 10, 2018.

77. Field Notes, October 29, 2018.

78. Emily Birnbaum, ""Transgender Rights Group Unfurls Massive Flag in Front of Lincoln Memorial," *The Hill*, October 29, 2018, https://thehill.com/business-a-lobbying/413706-transgender-rights-group-unfurls-massive-flag-in-front-of-linc oln; Wu, Interview, November 10, 2018.

79. Branstetter, Interview, August 7, 2018.

80. McGregor and Molyneux, "Twitter's Influence on News Judgment."

81. Mark Deuze and Tamara Witschge, "Beyond Journalism: Theorizing the Transformation of Journalism," *Journalism* 19, no. 2 (2017): 165–181; Scott Reinardy, *Journalism's Lost Generation: The Un-doing of U.S. Newspaper Newsrooms* (New York: Routledge, 2016).

82. Mark Deuze and Leopoldina Fortunati, "Atypical Newswork, Atypical Media Management," in *Managing Media Work*, ed. Mark Deuze (Thousand Oaks, CA: SAGE, 2011), 111–120; Nicole S. Cohen, *Writers' Rights: Freelance Journalism in a Digital Age* (Montreal: McGill-Queen's University Press, 2016).

83. Of course, there is a right-leaning (and often outright fascistic) counterpart to the set of left-leaning digital-first outlets. However, during my time in the field, these

outlets were much less connected to the agendas of the legacy press and exerted a much smaller influence over the content of the legacy press than the more mainstream left-leaning outlets; see Bennett, *News*.

84. Branstetter, Interview, August 7, 2018.

85. Branstetter, Interview, August 7, 2018.

86. W. Russell Neuman et al., "The Dynamics of Public Attention: Agenda-Setting Theory Meets Big Data," *Journal of Communication* 64, no. 2 (2014): 193–214.

87. Billard, "Setting the Transgender Agenda."

88. See also Karpf, *Analytic Activism*.

89. Neal Caren, Kenneth T. Andrews, and Todd Lu, "Contemporary Social Movements in a Hybrid Media Environment," *Annual Review of Sociology* 46 (2020): 443–465. However, for a discussion of how algorithmic filtration on social media limits the ability of organizations to achieve mass visibility, see Etter and Albu, "Activists in the Dark."

90. Hermida and Thurman, "A Clash of Cultures"; Shannon C. McGregor, "Social Media as Public Opinion: How Journalists Use Social Media to Represent Public Opinion," *Journalism* 20, no. 8 (2019): 1070–1086; Steve Paulussen and Raymond A. Harder, "Social Media References in Newspapers: Facebook, Twitter, and YouTube as Sources in Newspaper Journalism," *Journalism Practice* 8, no. 5 (2014): 542–551.

91. Field Notes, June 6, 2018.

92. Branstetter, Interview, August 21, 2018.

93. Mary Emily O'Hara, "Trans Women Say the State Department Is Retroactively Revoking Their Passports," *them*, July 27, 2018, https://www.them.us/story/trans-women-state-department-passports.

94. Danni Askini (danniaskini), Twitter post, June 29, 2018, 4:08 p.m., https://twitter.com/danniaskini/status/1012835342183874560; Janus Rose (zenalbatross), Twitter post, July 25, 2018, 8:59 p.m., https://twitter.com/zenalbatross/status/10222399 16170911747.

95. NCTE, Twitter post, September 12, 2018, 11:47 p.m., https://twitter.com/transequal ity/status/1040084494823370753.

96. NCTE, Twitter post, September 13, 2018, 12:27 p.m., https://twitter.com/TransE quality/status/1040275698022330368.

97. Askini, Twitter post, June 29, 2018, 4:08 p.m., https://twitter.com/danniaskini/sta tus/1012835342183874560.

98. Rose, Twitter post, July 25, 2018, 8:59 p.m., https://twitter.com/zenalbatross/status/ 1022239916170911747.

99. Field Notes, July 27, 2018.

100. O'Hara, "Trans Women Say."

101. David Boddiger, "The State Department Is Retroactively Revoking Transgender Women's Passports, Report Says," *Splinter*, July 28, 2018, https://splinternews.com/ the-state-department-is-retroactively-revoking-transgen-1827946847;   Morgan Brinlee, "Trans Women Claim Trump's Admin Revoked Their Passports After They Changed Their Gender Marker," *Bustle*, July 28, 2018, https://www.bustle.com/p/

trans-women-claim-trumps-admin-revoked-their-passports-after-they-changed-their-gender-marker-report-9921036; Chelsea Steiner, "The State Department is Revoking Trans Women's' Passports as We March Ever Closer to The Handmaid's Tale," *The Mary Sue*, July 28, 2018, https://www.themarysue.com/state-department-trans-passports/; Michael Sykes, "Report: State Department Retroactively Revoking Passports from Transgender Women," *Axios*, July 28, 2018, https://www.axios.com/trans-women-passport-issue-state-department-trump-aa249a45-55aa-4923-8090-ad26ba220e98.html.

102. NCTE, Twitter post, July 28, 2018, 12:57 p.m., https://twitter.com/transequality/status/1023251181320253440.

103. Laurel Powell, Interview, August 28, 2018.

104. It was retweeted a mere 175 times and liked only 205 times.

105. NCTE, Twitter post, July 28, 2018, 12:57 p.m., https://twitter.com/transequality/status/1023251181320253440.

106. Field Notes, July 30, 2018.

107. Branstetter, Interview, August 7, 2018.

108. Branstetter, Interview, August 7, 2018.

109. Christian, Interview, September 6, 2018.

110. Branstetter, Interview, August 7, 2018.

111. Branstetter, Interview, August 7, 2018.

112. Branstetter, Interview, August 7, 2018.

113. Field Notes, July 30, 2018.

114. Field Notes, July 30, 2018.

115. Christian, Interview, September 6, 2018.

116. Branstetter, Interview, August 21, 2018.

117. Field Notes, July 30, 2018.

118. Ranjani Chakraborty, "How ID Laws Can Put Trans People in Danger," *Vox*, August 16, 2018, https://www.vox.com/videos/2018/8/16/17698442/id-laws-trans-people-danger-murder"; Ranjani Chakraborty, Lucas Waldron, and Ken Schwencke, "Video: For Trans People, It's Difficult and Costly to Update an ID. But It Can Also Be Dangerous Not To," *ProPublica*, August 16, 2018, https://www.propublica.org/article/for-trans-people-difficult-and-costly-to-update-an-id-but-it-can-also-be-dangerous-not-to.

119. Christian, Interview, September 6, 2018.

120. Field Notes, July 30, 2018.

121. Sarah Toce, "Advocates Say Fears About Trans People's Passports are Overblown," *LGBTQ Nation*, July 28, 2018, https://www.lgbtqnation.com/2018/07/state-department-retroactively-revoking-passports-trans-citizens/.

122. Field Notes, September 12, 2018.

123. Field Notes, September 12, 2018.

124. Field Notes, September 12, 2018.

125. Field Notes, September 12, 2018.

126. Field Notes, September 12, 2018.

127. Field Notes, September 12, 2018.

128. Field Notes, September 12, 2018.

129. Samantha Allen, "Trump State Department Just Made an Ominous Passport Change for Transgender Americans," *The Daily Beast*, September 13, 2018, https://www.thedailybeast.com/trump-state-department-just-made-an-ominous-passport-change-for-transgender-americans"; Katelyn Burns, "State Department Changes Passport Website Language for Transgender People," *Rewire News Group*, September 13, 2018, https://rewire.news/article/2018/09/13/state-department-changes-passport-website-language/; Lilly Dancyger, "For Trans People Seeking Passports, State Department Abruptly Changes Language," *Rolling Stone*, September 13, 2018, https://www.rollingstone.com/culture/culture-news/transgender-passport-sex-gender-state-department-723984; Ariel Sobel, "Is the Trump Administration Trying to Discourage Trans Travelers?" *The Advocate*, September 13, 2018, https://www.advocate.com/transgender/2018/9/13/trump-administration-trying-discourage-trans-travelers.

130. Monica Hunter-Hart, "Passport Language for Trans People Changed Overnight—Then Was Reversed After Criticism," *Bustle*, September 13, 2018, https://www.bustle.com/p/passport-language-for-trans-people-changed-overnight-then-was-reversed-after-criticism-11907452.

131. Field Notes, September 13, 2018.

132. Field Notes, September 13, 2018.

133. Field Notes, September 13, 2018.

134. Field Notes, September 13, 2018.

135. Field Notes, September 13, 2018.

136. NCTE, Twitter post, September 13, 2018, 12:27 p.m., https://twitter.com/transequality/status/1040275696793395208.

137. Allen, "Trump State Department"; Burns, "State Department Changes."

138. Hunter-Hart, "Passport Language."

139. John Paul Brammer, "Trans Advocates Worry Over the State Department's Language on Passport Policy," *them*, September 14, 2018, https://www.them.us/story/state-department-language-passport-policy"; NCTE, Facebook post, September 14, 2018, 11:19 a.m., https://www.facebook.com/TransEqualityNow/videos/2248985215330563/; NCTE, Twitter post, September 14, 2018, 4:07 p.m., https://twitter.com/TransEquality/status/1040693471395434496.

140. Chadwick, *The Hybrid Media System*; Hermida and Thurman, "A Clash of Cultures"; Klinger and Svensson, "Network Media Logic."

141. Barker-Plummer, "News as a Political Resource."

142. Carroll and Ratner, "Media Strategies."

143. Papacharissi and Oliveira, "Affective News."

144. Castells, *Networks of Outrage and Hope*.

145. Andrews and Caren, "Making the News"; Barker-Plummer, "Producing Public Voice"; Gandy, "Information in Health"; Rohlinger, *Abortion Politics*.

146. Papacharissi and Oliveira, "Affective News."

Chapter 4

1. Matthew Impelli, "Oklahoma City Black Man Shot and Killed by Police, Sparking Immediate Protests," *Newsweek*, December 11, 2020, https://www.newsweek.com/oklahoma-city-man-shot-killed-police-sparking-immediate-protests-1554245; Associated Press, "Man Fatally Shot by Oklahoma Police Threatened Postal Worker," *Associated Press*, December 15, 2020, https://apnews.com/article/shootings-police-oklahoma-city-oklahoma-assault-and-battery-dbafa53a7459fa71c40e4f08069a2ea9.

2. Territory OKC (territoryokc), Instagram post, December 12, 2020, https://www.instagram.com/p/CItp8qpF4VK/.

3. My concepts of placefulness and placelessness are related to but distinct from the concepts of place and placelessness first advanced by influential Canadian geographer Edward Relph in 1976; see Edward Relph, *Place and Placelessness* (London: Pion, 1976). For Relph, "place" constitutes an expression of that which is specific and local to a space and is given unity by shared meanings. "Placelessness," in contrast, describes the quality of some places that have had their distinctiveness eroded by modernity such that they lack clear identity. These placeless places are artificially standardized to a degree that they are indistinguishable from any other place of a similar kind. The city of Venice, for instance, has a quality of "place" because it is a space constructed with a specific and identifiable arrangement of geographic features that carry recognizable symbolic meanings and distinguish it from other places. In contrast, many gentrified neighborhoods have been criticized for their "inauthentic" and symbolically impotent geographies, such that a gentrified neighborhood in Washington, DC, is indistinguishable from one in Seattle; they are, in short, "placeless." My concepts of placefulness and placelessness, while specific to media, parallel Relph's concepts in that I view "placefulness" as a quality of media that are specific and local and that carry meanings with place-specific relevance, while I view "placelessness" as a quality of media that are made universal in their relevance and, as such, divorced from any local specificity. Moreover, my argument that digital media have rendered placeful media also placeless parallels Relph's argument that modernity has eroded the placeful qualities of place and made them placeless.

4. Here I use "imagined" not in the sense of artificial or fabricated, but rather in the sense that political historian Benedict Anderson used it to describe the fact that most citizens will never know, meet, or even hear of their fellow nationals and yet nonetheless live with the idea that they are bound in communion with them; see Benedict Anderson, *Imagined Communities: Reflections on the Origin and Spread of Nationalism* (New York: Verso, 1983). For further discussion of "imagined" identities in the specific context of news media, see Jacob L. Nelson, *Imagined Audiences: How Journalists Perceive and Pursue the Public* (New York: Oxford University Press, 2021).

5. Josh Greenberg, Tim May, and Charlene Elliott, "Homelessness and Media Activism in the Voluntary Sector: A Case Study," *The Philanthropist* 20, no. 2 (2006): 131–152; Gross, *Up from Invisibility*; William Hoynes, "Media Research and Media Activism," in *Rhyming Hope and History: Activists, Academics, and Social Movement Scholarship*, ed. David Croteau, William Hoynes, and Charlotte Ryan (Minneapolis: University of

Minnesota Press, 2005), 97–114; Montgomery, *Target, Prime Time*; Ryan, *Prime Time Activism*; cf. Kristen Schilt, "'AM/FM Activism': Taking National Media Tools to a Local Level," *Journal of Gay & Lesbian Social Services* 16, no. 3–4 (2004): 181–192.

6. On journalism studies' increasing focus on local news outlets, see, e.g., Kristy Hess and Lisa Waller, "Geo-Social Journalism: Reorienting the Study of Small Commercial Newspapers in a Digital Environment," *Journalism Practice* 8, no. 2 (2014): 121–136; Rasmus Kleis Nielsen, *Local Journalism: The Decline of Newspapers and the Rise of Digital Media* (New York: I.B. Tauris, 2015); Karin Wahl-Jorgensen, "The Challenge of Local News Provision," *Journalism* 20, no. 1 (2019): 163–166. On journalism studies' increasing focus on the role of place in the production and consumption of news, see, e.g., Rachel Davis Mersey, "Online News Users' Sense of Community: Is Geography Dead?" *Journalism Practice* 3, no. 3 (2009): 347–360; Chris Peters, "Spaces and Places of News Consumption," in *The SAGE Handbook of Digital Journalism*, ed. Tamara Witschge et al. (Thousand Oaks: SAGE, 2016), 354–369; Usher, "Putting 'Place' in the Center"; Usher, *News for the Rich*. On journalism studies' increasing focus on the role of identity and community membership in media consumption practices, see, representing various perspectives, Silvia Knobloch-Westerwick and Matthias R. Hastall, "Please Your Self: Social Identity Effects on Selective Exposure to News About in- and Out-Groups," *Journal of Communication* 60, no. 1 (2010): 515–535; Mirca Madianou, "Contested Communicative Spaces: Rethinking Identities, Boundaries and the Role of the Media among Turkish Speakers in Greece," *Journal of Ethnic and Migration Studies* 31, no. 3 (2005): 521–541; Chris Peters and Kim Christian Schrøder, "Beyond the Here and Now of News Audiences: A Process-Based Framework for Investigating News Repertoires," *Journal of Communication* 68, no. 6 (2018): 1079–1103; Sue Robinson, "The Active Citizen's Information Media Repertoire: An Exploration of Community News Habits During the Digital Age," *Mass Communication and Society* 17, no. 4 (2014): 509–530; Ryan Salzman, "News or Noticias: A Social Identity Approach to Understanding Latinos' Preferred Language for News Consumption in the United States," *Mass Communication and Society* 17, no. 1 (2014): 54–73; Andrea Wenzel, "Red State, Purple Town: Polarized Communities and Local Journalism in Rural and Small-Town Kentucky," *Journalism* 21, no. 4 (2018): 557–573.

7. See, e.g., Hau Ling Cheng, "Constructing a Transnational, Multilocal Sense of Belonging: An Analysis of *Ming Pao (West Canadian Edition)*," *Journal of Communication Inquiry* 29, no. 2 (2005): 141–159; Julie Freeman, "Differentiating Distance in Local and Hyperlocal News," *Journalism* 21, no. 4 (2020): 524–540; Kristy Hess, "Breaking Boundaries: Recasting the 'Local' Newspaper as 'Geo-social' News in a Digital Landscape," *Digital Journalism* 1, no. 1 (2013): 48–63; Henrik Örnebring, Eva Kingsepp, and Cecilia Möller, "Journalism in Small Towns," *Journalism* 21, no. 4 (2020): 447–452.

8. Cheng, "Constructing a Transnational."

9. Jock Lauterer, *Community Journalism: Relentlessly Local*, 3rd ed. (Chapel Hill: University of North Carolina Press, 2006), 1, emphasis added.

10. See, e.g., Wenzel, "Red State, Purple Town."

11. For example, Joshua Gamson, "Gay Media, Inc.: Media Structures, the New Gay Conglomerates, and Collective Sexual Identities," in *Cyberactivism: Online Activism in Theory and Practice*, ed. Martha McCaughey and Michael Ayers (New York: Routledge, 2003), 255–278; Miya Williams Fayne, "Advocacy Journalism in the 21st Century: Rethinking Entertainment in Digital Black Press Outlets," *Journalism* 24, no. 4 (2023): 328–345.

12. Hess, "Breaking Boundaries"; Hess and Waller, "Geo-Social Journalism."

13. On the importance of expressive norms to community media, see, e.g., Catherine Knight Steele, "Black Bloggers and Their Varied Publics: The Everyday Politics of Black Discourse Online," *Television & New Media* 19, no. 2 (2018): 112–127.

14. See Ball-Rokeach, Kim, and Matei, "Storytelling Neighborhood"; Yong-Chan Kim, Joo-Young Jung, and Sandra J. Ball-Rokeach, "'Geo-Ethnicity' and Neighborhood Engagement: A Communication Infrastructure Perspective," *Political Communication* 23, no. 4 (2006): 421–441.

15. Squires, "Rethinking the Black Public Sphere"; see also, e.g., Dennis K. K. Leung and Francis L. F. Lee, "Cultivating an Active Online Counterpublic: Examining Usage and Political Impact of Internet Alternative Media," *International Journal of Press/Politics* 19, no. 3 (2014): 340–359"; cf. Steele, "Black Bloggers."

16. For a stimulating discussion of this dynamic, see Andreas Hepp, Piet Simon, and Monika Sowinska, "Living Together in the Mediatized City: The Figurations of Young People's Urban Communities," in *Communicative Figurations: Transforming Communications in Times of Deep Mediatization*, ed. Andreas Hepp, Andreas Breiter, and Uwe Hasebrink (Cham: Palgrave Macmillan, 2017), 51–80.

17. On newsmakers' concepts of their audiences, see Nelson, *Imagined Audiences*.

18. See National Center for Transgender Equality, *Failing to Protect and Serve: Police Department Policies Towards Transgender People* (Washington, DC: National Center for Transgender Equality, 2019).

19. Field Notes, September 13, 2018.

20. Mateo De La Torre, Interview, August 28, 2018.

21. De La Torre, Interview, August 28, 2018; Field Notes, September 13, 2018.

22. On the financial threats to minority-serving media, see, e.g., Trish Bendix, "Does LGBT Media Have a Future?" *Buzzfeed News*, January 25, 2019, https://www.buzzfeednews.com/article/trishbendix/future-of-lgbt-media-out-advocate-autostraddle-into-grindr; Angela Ford, Kevin McFall, and Bob Dabney, *African American Media Today: Building the Future From the Past* (Washington, DC: Democracy Fund, 2019).

23. Raffi Freedman-Gurspan, Interview, October 12, 2018.

24. Such "storyteller" programs are not unique to NCTE or to the transgender movement. In fact, these programs are an increasingly prominent feature of social movement politics in the United States and elsewhere that have begun to attract the attention of social movement scholars. Thus far, scholars have focused their analyses of these programs on the limits of storytelling as a bridge to solidarity and on the neoliberal impulses that make storytelling attractive programs for nonprofit organizations and non-governmental organizations to pursue. While these critiques have been generative, my focus on these storytelling programs is less critical and aims less

to provide normative assessments of the value of these programs. Rather, my interest is in understanding the communicative logics that motivate these programs and how these programs reflect the strategic necessities of navigating the contemporary communication system. For the more critical perspectives I have described, see, for example, Sujatha Fernandes, *Curated Storytelling: The Uses and Misuses of Storytelling* (New York: Oxford University Press, 2017); Francesca Polletta, *Inventing the Ties That Bind: Imagined Relationships in Moral and Political Life* (Chicago: University of Chicago Press, 2020); Francesca Polletta et al., "Personal Storytelling in Professionalized Social Movements," *Mobilization* 26, no. 1 (2021): 65–86; Filippo Trevisan et al., "Mobilizing Personal Narratives: The Rise of Digital 'Story Banking' in U.S. Grassroots Advocacy," *Journal of Information Technology & Politics* 17, no. 2 (2020): 146–160.

25. Rebecca Kling, Interview, August 21, 2018; De La Torre, Interview, August 28, 2018.
26. Kling, Interview, August 21, 2018; DeShanna Neal, Interview, August 7, 2018.
27. Neal, Interview, August 7, 2018.
28. Neal, Interview, August 7, 2018.
29. For more about the reactivity of storyteller programs, see Trevisan et al., "Mobilizing Personal Narratives."
30. Freedman-Gurspan, Interview, October 12, 2018.
31. Kling, Interview, August 21, 2018.
32. Debi Jackson, Interview, August 16, 2018.
33. Importantly, this uneven distribution in trans people across the country is not a simple matter of urban/rural divide. Rather, trans people are unevenly distributed among the US states, in part because of which states transition-related care can more easily be accessed in. Within states, however, trans people are often distributed across urban *and* rural locales. For a breakdown of the geographic distribution of trans people in the United States, see Avery Rose Everhart, "Incomplete Data and Insufficient Methods: Transgender Population Health Research in the US," PhD diss., University of Southern California, 2022; Flores et al., *How Many Adults Identify as Transgender in the United States?* (Los Angeles: Williams Institute, 2016).
34. Kling, Interview, August 21, 2018.
35. Kling, Interview, August 21, 2018.
36. Jackson, Interview, August 16, 2018.
37. Kling, Interview, August 21, 2018.
38. Kling, Interview, August 21, 2018.
39. Leslie McMurray, Interview, November 30, 2018.
40. Jackson, Interview, August 16, 2018.
41. Jackson, Interview, August 16, 2018.
42. Gillian Branstetter, Interview, August 7, 2018.
43. Evans, "National Transgender Rights Group."
44. Branstetter, Interview, August 7, 2018.
45. Dave Noble, Interview, October 17, 2018. Of course, these kinds of stories are strategically beneficial for an identity-based movement attempting to seed public opinion with more sympathetic social attitudes. Other kinds of movements would not

prioritize these kinds of stories in their activism. Nonetheless, the strategic significance of local and community media remains relevant across movements—the types of stories they push for would simply be different.

46. Noble, Interview, October 17, 2018.

47. Kling, Interview, August 21, 2018.

48. Amanda Hinnant, María E. Len-Ríos, and Rachel Young, "Journalistic Use of Exemplars to Humanize Health News," *Journalism Studies* 14, no. 4 (2013): 539–554.

49. Debi Jackson, Interview, October 10, 2018.

50. See, for instance, R. Lucas Platero, "The Narratives of Transgender Rights Mobilization in Spain," *Sexualities* 14, no. 5 (2011): 597–614.

51. De La Torre, Interview, August 28, 2018.

52. Ray Gibson, Interview, December 1, 2018.

53. De La Torre, Interview, August 28, 2018.

54. See, for example, Billard "Writing in the Margins"; Robert M. Entman and Andrew Rojecki, *The Black Image in the White Mind: Media and Race in America* (Chicago: University of Chicago Press, 2001); Usher, *News for the Rich*.

55. Cathy Cohen's concept of "secondary marginalization" was first developed to explain how and why the needs of Black individuals who hold additional marginalized identities (sexual identities, gender identities, etc.) are not prioritized within mainstream Black politics; see Cathy Cohen, *The Boundaries of Blackness: AIDS and the Breakdown of Black Politics* (Chicago: University of Chicago Press, 1999). Here I borrow from, but slightly invert, Cohen's formulation to reference both how the concerns of trans people of color are left out of the mainstream politics of many communities of color *and* how the concerns of trans people of color are left out of the mainstream politics of trans communities.

56. Branstetter, Interview, August 7, 2018.

57. Kling, Interview, October 12, 2018.

58. See, for example, Doyle, *Making Out in the Mainstream*; Julian Kevon Glover, "Redefining Realness? On Janet Mock, Laverne Cox, TS Madison, and the Representation of Transgender Women of Color in Media," *Souls* 18, no. 2–4 (2016): 338–387; Gross, *Up from Invisibility*; Katherine Sender, "Gay Readers, Consumers, and a Dominant Gay Habitus: 25 Years of the *Advocate* Magazine," *Journal of Communication* 51, no. 1 (2001): 73–99.

59. See, for example, Dominique Adams-Santos, "'Something a Bit More Personal': Digital Storytelling and Intimacy Among Queer Black Women," *Sexualities* 23, no. 8 (2020): 1434–1456; Moya Bailey, *Misogynoir Transformed: Black Women's Digital Resistance* (New York: New York University Press, 2021); Sarah J. Jackson, "(Re) Imagining Intersectional Democracy from Black Feminism to Hashtag Activism," *Women's Studies in Communication* 39, no. 4 (2016): 375–379; Allissa V. Richardson, "Dismantling Respectability: The Rise of New Womanist Communication Models in the Era of Black Lives Matter," *Journal of Communication* 69, no. 2 (2019): 193–213.

60. See, for example, my discussion of the tensions between the LGB movement and the transgender movement over trans-exclusion from the Employment Non-Discrimination Act in Chapter 2.

61. Jackson, Interview, August 16, 2018; Jackson, Interview, October 10, 2018.

62. Jackson, Interview, October 10, 2018.

63. Neal, Interview, August 7, 2018.

64. For example, McMurray, Interview, November 30, 2018.

65. Jo Ivester, Interview, December 2, 2018.

66. Branstetter, Interview, August 21, 2018.

67. Kling, Interview, August 21, 2018.

68. As explained in Note 3 earlier in this chapter, I mean "imagined" in the sense intended by Anderson in his conception of "imagined communities"; see Anderson, *Imagined Communities*.

69. Verburg, "Sun Prairie Soldier."

70. Verburg, "Trump Ban."

71. De La Torre, Interview, August 28, 2018.

72. McMurray, Interview, November 30, 2018.

73. See for further exploration of the ways local media appeal to imagined, rather than geographic, relationships, see Hess, "Breaking Boundaries"; Hess and Waller, "Geo-Social Journalism."

74. Freedman-Gurspan, Interview, October 12, 2018.

75. Freedman-Gurspan, Interview, October 12, 2018.

76. The student and her mother have been pseudonymized out of respect for their choice to not publicize their identities around this controversy.

77. Field Notes, October 4, 2018.

78. Field Notes, October 4, 2018; Field Notes, October 26, 2018; Freedman-Gurspan, Interview, October 12, 2018.

79. Jeff Branscome, "Stafford Superintendent Apologizes to Transgender Student Amid National Outcry," *The Free Lance-Star*, October 9, 2018, https://www.fredericksb urg.com/news/local/stafford/stafford-superintendent-apologizes-to-transgender-student-amid-national-outcry/article_8d0f967a-2092-57c0-9328-33a68a084c15. html; RVA Staff, "Stafford County School Board Responds to Transgender Student Singled Out During Active Shooter Drill," *RVA*, October 10, 2018, https://rvamag. com/news/stafford-country-school-board-responds-to-transgender-student-signa led-out-during-active-shooter-drill.html.

80. Tanya Chen, "A Transgender Student Was Allegedly Blocked from Sheltering in Both Boys and Girls Bathrooms During a Safety Drill," *Buzzfeed News*, October 9, 2018, https://www.buzzfeednews.com/article/tanyachen/transgender-student-ban ned-boys-girls-drill-virginia; Tim Fitzsimons, "Virginia School Allegedly Barred Trans Student from Active-Shooter Drill," *NBC News*, October 9, 2018, https:// www.nbcnews.com/feature/nbc-out/virginia-school-allegedly-barred-trans-stud ent-active-shooter-drill-n918216; Drew Schwartz, "Trans Student Blocked from Both Locker Rooms During School Safety Drill," *Vice*, October 8, 2018, https:// www.vice.com/en_us/article/7x3dqd/trans-student-not-allowed-in-locker-rooms-school-safety-drill-virginia-vgtrn"; Hannah Smothers, "Middle School Allegedly Excluded Trans Student from Participating in Active Shooter Drill," *Cosmopolitan*,

October 10, 2018, https://www.cosmopolitan.com/lifestyle/a23709601/virginia-middle-school-excludes-trans-student-shooter-drill/.

81. Field Notes, October 10, 2018.

82. Noble, Interview, October 17, 2018.

83. Noble, Interview, October 17, 2018.

84. See, for example, Nicolas M. Anspach, "The New Personal Influence: How Our Facebook Friends Influence the News We Read," *Political Communication* 34, no. 4 (2017): 590–606; Annika Bergström and Maria Jervelycke Belfrage, "News in Social Media: Incidental Consumption and the Role of Opinion Leaders," *Digital Journalism* 6, no. 5 (2018): 583–598; Johannes Kaiser, Tobias R. Keller, and Katharina Kleinen-von Königslöw, "Incidental News Exposure on Facebook as a Social Experience: The Influence of Recommender and Media Cues on News Selection," *Communication Research* 48, no. 1 (2021): 77–99; Anna Sophie Kümpel, "The Issue Takes It All? Incidental News Exposure and News Engagement on Facebook," *Digital Journalism* 7, no. 2 (2019): 165–186; Thorson and Wells, "Curated Flows."

85. Noble, Interview, October 17, 2018.

86. See, for example, Leysia Palen et al., "Twitter-Based Information Distribution during the 2009 Red River Valley Flood Threat," *Bulletin of the American Society for Information Science and Technology* 36, no. 5 (2010): 13–17.

87. Jamie K. Taylor et al., "Content and Complexity in Policy Reinvention and Diffusion: Gay and Transgender-Inclusive Laws against Discrimination," *State Politics & Policy Quarterly* 12, no. 1 (2012): 75–98.

88. Branstetter, Interview, August 7, 2018.

89. Branstetter, Interview, August 7, 2018.

90. Branstetter, Interview, August 7, 2018.

91. Field Notes, October 3, 2018.

92. Field Notes, October 3, 2018.

93. Field Notes, October 3, 2018.

94. Field Notes, October 3, 2018.

95. Field Notes, October 3, 2018.

96. Caitlin Emma, "DeVos Investigates Whether School Transgender Bathroom Policy Led to Sexual Assault," *Politico*, October 3, 2018, https://www.politico.com/story/2018/10/03/devos-investigates-transgender-bathroom-policy-assault-827018.

97. Field Notes, October 3, 2018.

98. Field Notes, October 3, 2018.

99. Field Notes, October 3, 2018; Gabriel Owens, "Parents' Coalition Speaks Against Decatur Schools Transgender Policies During Meeting," *Decaturish*, September 15, 2017, https://decaturish.com/2017/09/parents-coalition-speaks-against-decatur-schools-transgender-policies-during-meeting/; Dan Whisenhunt, "Information is Scarce About Parents Opposed to City Schools of Decatur's Transgender Policy," *Decaturish*, October 9, 2017, https://decaturish.com/2017/10/information-is-scarce-about-parents-opposed-to-city-schools-of-decaturs-transgender-policy.

100. In their complaint, ADF incorrectly claimed that this memo put the policy in place. They further claimed no notice had been given to the parents outside of a Facebook

post, arguing that parents deserved a chance to be heard before the policy was implemented.

101. Owens, "Parents' Coalition Speaks."
102. Whisenhunt, "Information is Scarce."
103. Field Notes, October 3, 2018.
104. Field Notes, October 3, 2018.
105. Field Notes, October 3, 2018.
106. Field Notes, October 3, 2018.
107. Field Notes, October 3, 2018.
108. Field Notes, October 3, 2018.
109. Joining the call were the transgender rights lawyer in Lambda Legal's Atlanta office, a staff member from the American Civil Liberties Union (ACLU), a staff member from the LGBTQ K-12 education advocacy organization GLSEN, a staff member from the Southern Poverty Law Center (SPLC), and a staff member at the LGBTQ right organization Freedom for All Americans.
110. For example, Natisha Lance, "Mom Alleges Daughter Assaulted by Transgender Student in Elementary School Bathroom," *11alive*, October 3, 2018, https://www.11alive.com/article/news/local/decatur/mom-alleges-daughter-assaulted-by-transgender-student-in-elementary-school-bathroom/85-600627949; see also Tim Darnell, "Oakhurst Student Claims Sexual Assault by 'Gender-Fluid' Boy," *The Decatur Patch*, October 4, 2018, https://patch.com/georgia/decatur/oakhurst-student-claims-sexual-assault-gender-fluid-boy.
111. Field Notes, October 3, 2018.
112. Field Notes, October 3, 2018.
113. Field Notes, October 3, 2018.
114. Field Notes, October 4, 2018.
115. Benjamin Wermund, "LGBTQ Advocates Worry About Politics in DeVos' New Civil Rights Probe," *Politico*, October 4, 2018, https://www.politico.com/newsletters/morning-education/2018/10/04/lgbtq-advocates-worry-about-politics-in-devos-new-civil-rights-probe-362006.
116. Field Notes, October 4, 2018.
117. Field Notes, October 4, 2018.
118. Field Notes, October 4, 2018.
119. Dan Whisenhunt, "Education Department Investigating ClaimTransgender Oakhurst Elementary Student Committed Assault," *Decaturish*, October 3, 2018, https://decaturish.com/2018/10/u-s-department-of-education-investigating-claim-transgender-oakhurst-elementary-student-committed-assault.
120. Moriah Balingit, "After Alleged Sexual Assault, Officials Open Investigation of Transgender Bathroom Policy," *Washington Post*, October 9, 2018, https://www.washingtonpost.com/local/education/after-alleged-sexual-assault-officials-open-investigation-of-transgender-bathroom-policy/2018/10/09/431e7024-c7fd-11e8-9b1c-a90f1daae309_story.html.
121. Field Notes, October 10, 2018.
122. Field Notes, October 10, 2018.

123. Field Notes, October 10, 2018.
124. Tanasia Kenney, "Mother's Lawsuit Takes Aim at School's Gender-Neutral Bathroom Policy After She Claims Daughter Was Molested by 'Gender Fluid Student,'" *Atlanta Black Star*, October 5, 2018, https://atlantablackstar.com/2018/10/05/mothers-laws uit-takes-aim-at-schools-gender-neutral-bathroom-policy-after-she-claims-daugh ter-was-molested-by-gender-fluid-student/.
125. Charlie James Cote, "Dear *Decaturish*—Responding to Allegations About Transgender Students," *Decaturish*, October 18, 2018, https://decaturish.com/2018/10/dear-dec aturish-responding-to-allegations-about-transgender-students/.

Chapter 5

1. Somewhat amusingly to me later, NCTE's eventual offices on the third floor of the Verizon building put them directly next to Ogilvy on 19th Street. In fact, NCTE's windows looked directly into Ogilvy's, which were mere feet away across a narrow alley.
2. For example, Roderick J. Brodie, Maureen Benson-Rea, and Christopher J. Medlin, "Branding as a Dynamic Capability: Strategic Advantage from Integrating Meanings with Identification," *Marketing Theory* 17, no. 2 (2017): 183–199; Mary Jo Hatch and Majken Schultz, "Toward a Theory of Brand Co-creation with Implications for Brand Governance," *Journal of Brand Management* 17, no. 8 (2010): 590–604; Pitt et al., "The Penguin's Window: Corporate Brands from an Open Source Perspective," *Journal of the Academy of Marketing Science* 34, no. 2 (2006): 115–127.
3. Thomas J Billard, "Citizen Typography and Political Brands in the 2016 US Presidential Election Campaign," *Marketing Theory* 18, no. 3 (2018): 421–431; Thomas J Billard, "Fonts of Potential: Areas for Typographic Research in Political Communication," *International Journal of Communication* 10 (2016): 4570–4592; Thomas J Billard and Rachel E. Moran, "Networked Political Brands: Consumption, Community, and Political Expression in Contemporary Brand Culture," *Media, Culture & Society* 42, no. 4 (2020): 588–604; Rachel E. Moran and Thomas J Billard, "Imagining Resistance to Trump through the Networked Branding of the National Park Service," in *Popular Culture and the Civic Imagination: Case Studies of Creative Social Change*, ed. Henry Jenkins, Gabriel Peters-Lazaro, and Sangita Shresthova (New York: New York University Press, 2020), 231–240.
4. Jo Ivester, Interview, December 2, 2018.
5. Ivester, Interview, December 2, 2018.
6. Ivester, Interview, December 2, 2018.
7. Ivester, Interview, December 2, 2018.
8. Ivester, Interview, December 2, 2018.
9. Ivester, Interview, December 2, 2018.
10. Ivester, Interview, December 2, 2018.
11. Storytelling has always been a fundamental feature of social movement communication. It is often through narratives (and not just "framing") that movement

actors develop shared identities, explain the complexities of systemic problems, recruit participants for their strategic actions, raise consciousness among the public, persuade powerholders to adopt new policies, and influence the norms of media representation; see Sharon Nepstad, "Creating Transnational Solidarity: The Use of Narrative in the U.S.–Central America Peace Movement," *Mobilization* 6, no. 1 (2001): 21–36; Francesca Polletta, "Contending Stories: Narrative in Social Movements," *Qualitative Sociology* 21, no. 4 (1998): 419–446; Francesca Polletta, *It Was Like a Fever: Storytelling in Protest and Politics* (Chicago: University of Chicago Press, 2006); Francesca Polletta et al., "The Sociology of Storytelling," *Annual Review of Sociology* 37 (2011): 109–130; Joseph E. Davis, "Narrative and Social Movements: The Power of Stories," in *Stories of Change: Narrative and Social Movements*, ed. Joseph E. Davis (Albany: State University of New York Press, 2002), 3–22. Over time, social movement organizations have sought to systematize storytelling as a form of strategic communication through storytelling programs analogous to VTE and FTE; see Sujatha Fernandes, *Curated Storytelling: The Uses and Misuses of Storytelling* (New York: Oxford University Press, 2017); Francesca Polletta, *Inventing the Ties That Bind: Imagined Relationships in Moral and Political Life* (Chicago: University of Chicago Press, 2020); Francesca Polletta et al., "Personal Storytelling in Professionalized Social Movements," *Mobilization* 26, no. 1 (2021): 65–86; Trevisan et al., "Mobilizing Personal Narratives." As such, the novelty of my argument is not that programs like VTE and FTE exist and that they are used to affect change both nationally and locally within communities. Rather, the novelty of my argument lies in my focus on how NCTE's storytelling programs fit into a broader system of change-making that consciously seeks to saturate the media system with the voices of trans people and their families, and to do so by deploying storytelling in contexts generally considered outside the purview of social movement organization activity.

12. Rasmus Kleis Nielsen, *Ground Wars: Personalized Communication in Political Campaigns* (Princeton, NJ: Princeton University Press, 2012), 7 (emphasis original).

13. Nielsen, *Ground Wars*, 7, 9.

14. Rachel Gonzales, Interview, December 4, 2018.

15. Gonzales, Interview, December 4, 2018.

16. Leslie McMurray, Interview, November 30, 2018.

17. Gonzales, Interview, December 4, 2018.

18. Paula Sophia Schonauer, Interview, December 22, 2018.

19. Schonauer, Interview, December 22, 2018.

20. McMurray, Interview, November 30, 2018.

21. McMurray, Interview, November 30, 2018.

22. Rebecca Kling, Interview, August 21, 2018; Nicola van Kuilenburg, Interview, December 5, 2018.

23. McMurray, Interview, November 30, 2018.

24. McMurray, Interview, November 30, 2018.

25. Gonzales, Interview, November 30, 2018.

26. Kling, Interview, August 21, 2018.

27. Kling, Interview, October 12, 2018.

28. Jackson, Interview, August 16, 2018.

29. For more scholarship on the uses of storyteller programs across different movement, see, for example, Fernandes, *Curated Storytelling*; Polletta, *Inventing the Ties*; Polletta et al., "Personal Storytelling"; Trevisan et al., "Mobilizing Personal Narratives."

30. Field Notes, September 17, 2018.

31. Chris Massie and Andrew Kaczynksi, "Trump Judicial Nominee Said Transgender Children Are Part of 'Satan's Plan,' Defended 'Conversion Therapy,' " *CNN*, September 20, 2017, https://www.cnn.com/2017/09/20/politics/kfile-jeff-mateer-lgbt-remarks/index.html.

32. Sarah Watson, Interview, December 4, 2018.

33. McMurray, Interview, November 30, 2018.

34. Watson, Interview, December 4, 2018.

35. van Kuilenburg, Interview, December 5, 2018.

36. Watson, Interview, December 4, 2018.

37. McMurray, Interview, November 30, 2018.

38. Benjamin Kennedy, Interview, December 3, 2018.

39. See, for example, Florence Ashley, "Gatekeeping Hormone Replacement Therapy for Transgender Patients is Dehumanising," *Journal of Medical Ethics* 45, no. 7 (2019): 480–482; Jae A. Puckett et al., "Barriers to Gender-Affirming Care for Transgender and Gender Nonconforming Individuals," *Sexuality Research and Social Policy* 15, no. 1 (2018): 48–59.

40. Kennedy, Interview, December 3, 2018.

41. Gonzales, Interview, December 4, 2018.

42. Gonzales, Interview, December 4, 2018.

43. Gonzales, Interview, December 4, 2018.

44. Gonzales, Interview, December 4, 2018.

45. For the original concept of "opinion leaders" in communication research, see Eilhu Katz and Paul F. Lazarsfeld, *Personal Influence: The Part Played by People in the Flow of Mass Communications* (Glencoe, IL: Free Press, 1955). For more recent articulations of how opinion leadership occurs in the contemporary media environment, see Elihu Katz, "Back to the Street: When Media and Opinion Leave Home," *Mass Communication and Society* 17, no. 4 (2014): 454–463; Elihu Katz, "His Master's Voice," *International Journal of Communication* 16 (2022): 608–615; Stephan Winter and German Neubaum, "Examining Characteristics of Opinion Leaders in Social Media: A Motivational Approach," *Social Media + Society* 2, no. 3 (2016).

46. Kennedy, Interview, December 3, 2018.

47. Kennedy, Interview, December 3, 2018.

48. Kennedy, Interview, December 3, 2018.

49. Kennedy, Interview, December 3, 2018.

50. Jackson, Interview, October 10, 2018.

51. See, for example, Jackson, Bailey, and Foucault Welles, *#HashtagActivism*; Micó and Casero-Ripollés, "Political Activism Online"; Filippo Trevisan, *Disability Rights Advocacy Online: Voice, Empowerment and Global Connectivity* (New York: Routledge,

2017); cf. Broad et al., "Understanding Communication Ecologies to Bridge Communication Research and Community Action," *Journal of Applied Communication Research* 41, no. 4 (2013): 325–345; Ognyanova et al., "Online Participation in a Community Context: Civic Engagement and Connections to Local Communication Resources," *International Journal of Communication* 7 (2013): 2433–2456.

52. Watson, Interview, December 4, 2018.

53. Transgender Allies, "Parents of Transgender Children Ask Trump Administration to Reverse Course on Gender Memo," *Teen Vogue*, October 25, 2018, https://www. teenvogue.com/story/parents-transgender-children-ask-trump-administration-reve rse-course-on-gender-memo.

54. Jackson, Interview, August 16, 2018.

55. Specifically, these incidents involved distant family members, parents of classmates, and other community members alleging that the parents were *making* their children transgender as a form of abuse.

56. Field Notes, October 3, 2018; Field Notes, October 10, 2018; DeShanna Neal, Interview, December 9, 2018.

57. See, for example, Anna Sophie Kümpel, "Social Media Information Environments and Their Implications for the Uses and Effects of News: The PINGS Framework," *Communication Theory* 32, no. 2 (2022): 223–242; Eun-Ju Lee, "That's Not the Way It Is: How User-Generated Comments on the News Affect Perceived Media Bias," *Journal of Computer-Mediated Communication* 18, no. 1 (2012): 32–45; Eun-Ju Lee and Yoon Jae Jang, "What Do Others' Reactions to News on Internet Portal Sites Tell Us? Effects of Presentation Format and Readers' Need for Cognition on Reality Perception," *Communication Research* 37, no. 6 (2010): 825–846; Eun-Ju Lee and Edson C. Tandoc, Jr., "When News Meets the Audience: How Audience Feedback Online Affects News Production and Consumption," *Human Communication Research* 43, no. 4 (2017): 436–449; Florian Toepfl and Eunike Piwoni, "Public Spheres in Interaction: Comment Sections of News Websites as Counterpublic Spaces," *Journal of Communication* 65, no. 3 (2015): 465–488; T. Franklin Waddell, "What Does the Crowd Think? How Online Comments and Popularity Metrics Affect News Credibility and Issue Importance," *New Media & Society* 20, no. 8 (2018): 3068–3083.

58. Jackson, Interview, August 16, 2018.

59. Jackson, Interview, August 16, 2018.

60. Neal, Interview, December 9, 2018.

61. Neal, Interview, December 9, 2018.

62. Gonzales, Interview, November 30, 2018.

63. Ivester, Interview, December 2, 2018.

64. Ivester, Interview, December 2, 2018.

65. Laurel Powell, Interview, August 10, 2018.

66. Powell, Interview, August 10, 2018.

67. Powell, Interview, August 10, 2018.

68. Watson, Interview, December 4, 2018.

69. Neal, Interview, December 9, 2018.

70. For my full analysis, see Thomas J Billard, "Deciding What's (Sharable) News: Social Movement Organizations as Curating Actors in the Political Information System," *Communication Monographs* 89, no. 3 (2022): 354–375. On "curating actors," see Thorson and Wells, "Curated Flows."

71. Thorson and Wells, "Curated Flows," 310.

72. See, for example, Jackson, Bailey, and Foucault Welles, *#HashtagActivism*.

73. See, for example, Bennett and Segerberg, "The Logic of Connective Action"; Aaron Franklin Brantly, "From Cyberspace to Independence Square: Understanding the Impact of Social Media on Physical Protest Mobilization During Ukraine's Euromaidan Revolution," *Journal of Information Technology & Politics* 16, no. 4 (2019): 360–378; Castells, *Networks of Outrage and Hope*; Earl and Kimport, *Digitally Enabled Social Change*; Tufekci, *Twitter and Tear Gas*.

74. See, for example, Candi Carter Olson, "#BringBackOurGirls: Digital Communities Supporting Real-World Change and Influencing Mainstream Media Agendas," *Feminist Media Studies* 16, no. 5 (2016): 772–787; Deen Freelon, Charlton McIlwain, and Meredith Clark, "Quantifying the Power and Consequences of Social Media Protest," *New Media & Society* 20, no. 3 (2018): 990–1011; Maximillian Hänska, "Networked Communication and the Arab Spring: Linking Broadcast and Social Media," *New Media & Society* 18, no. 1 (2016): 99–116; Kate Hunt and Mike Gruszczynski, "The Influence of New and Traditional Media Coverage on Public Attention to Social Movements: The Case of the Dakota Access Pipeline Protests," *Information, Communication & Society* 24, no. 7 (2021): 1024–1040.

75. The concept of "news events" more broadly owes its genesis to Daniel Dayan and Elihu Katz's concept of "media events," or instances of mediated communication that command, if not demand, the attention of the mass public and that invite individuals to participate in social discussion about that communication; see Daniel Dayan and Elihu Katz, *Media Events: The Live Broadcasting of History* (Cambridge, MA: Harvard University Press, 1992). News events, by extension, are instances of communication *mediated by news institutions* that command widespread attention and invite large-scale social discussion about the incident being reported on. Digital media have particularly transformed how such news events are discussed and circulated by the public; see, for example, Jacob Ørmen, "Googling the News: Opportunities and Challenges in Studying News Events through Google Search," *Digital Journalism* 4, no. 1 (2016): 107–124. Importantly, person-to-person communication is a key driver of the spread of news events beyond news media's original audiences; see Bradley S. Greenberg, "Person-to-Person Communication in the Diffusion of News Events," *Journalism Quarterly* 41, no. 4 (1964): 489–494; see also Bree McEwan, Christopher J. Carpenter, and Jill E. Hopke, "Mediated Skewed Diffusion of Issues Information: A Theory," *Social Media + Society* 4, no. 3 (2018).

76. Green, Benner, and Pear, "'Transgender' Could Be."

77. Green, Benner, and Pear, "'Transgender' Could Be."

78. On "profile picture activism" and HRC's red equal sign logo, see, among others, Rhonda Gibson, *Same-Sex Marriage and Social Media: How Online Networks Accelerated the Marriage Equality Movement* (New York: Routledge, 2018); Joel

Penney, *The Citizen Marketer: Promoting Political Opinion in the Social Media Age* (New York: Oxford University Press, 2017); Brady Robards and Bob Buttigieg, "Marriage Equality, Facebook Profile Pictures, and Civic Participation," in *Civic Media: Technology, Design, Practice*, ed. Eric Gordon and Paul Mihailidis (Cambridge, MA: MIT Press, 2016), 131–137.

79. Field Notes, October 21, 2018.

80. Field Notes, October 21, 2018.

81. Field Notes, October 21, 2018.

82. Field Notes, October 21, 2018.

83. Field Notes, October 21, 2018.

84. Field Notes, October 21, 2018.

85. National Center for Transgender Equality (TransEquality), Twitter Post, October 21, 2018, 9:18 a.m., https://twitter.com/TransEquality/status/1054029067031400450.

86. Field Notes, October 21, 2018.

87. Field Notes, October 21, 2018.

88. See, for example, Luc Athayde-Rizzaro (LucRizarro), Twitter post, October 21, 2018, 7:01 p.m., https://twitter.com/lucrizzaro/status/1054145600877404166; Gillian Branstetter (GBBranstetter), Twitter post, October 21, 2018, 9:51 p.m., https://twitter.com/GBBranstetter/status/1054188348049367041; Debi Jackson (the_debijackson), Twitter post, October 21, 2018, 3:42 p.m., https://twitter.com/the_debijackson/status/1054095661497507841; Mara Keisling (MaraKesiling), Twitter post, October 21, 2018, 3:24 p.m., https://twitter.com/MaraKeisling/status/1054090988535328768; Rebecca Kling (RebeccaKling), Twitter post, October 21, 2018, 5:07 p.m., https://twitter.com/RebeccaKling/status/1054116868812877824; Jay Wu (jhtripleu), Twitter post, October 21, 2018, 1:59 p.m., https://twitter.com/jhtripleu/status/1054069797393235969.

89. National Center for Transgender Equality (TransEquality), Twitter post, October 21, 2018, 1:40 p.m., https://twitter.com/TransEquality/status/1054064920566874113; National Center for Transgender Equality (TransEquality), Twitter post, October 21, 2018, 2:41 p.m., https://twitter.com/TransEquality/status/1054080325654069248.

90. The Leadership Conference (civilrightsorg), Twitter post, October 21, 2018, 3:19 p.m., https://twitter.com/civilrightsorg/status/1054089827673690113.

91. ACLU, Twitter post, October 21, 2018, 3:52 p.m., https://twitter.com/ACLU/status/1054098176607698946; GLAAD, Twitter post, October 21, 2018, 10:30 a.m., https://twitter.com/glaad/status/1054062455570268165; Lambda Legal (LambdaLegal), Twitter post, October 21, 2018, 2:31 p.m., https://twitter.com/LambdaLegal/status/1054077824833908737; LGBTQ Progress (LGBTQProgress), Twitter post, October 21, 2018, 3:11 p.m., https://twitter.com/LGBTProgress/status/105408767 8092869633; Netroots Nation (Netroots_Nation), Twitter post, October 21, 2018, 2:12 p.m., https://twitter.com/Netroots_Nation/status/1054072966047260675; Planned Parenthood Action (PPact), Twitter post, October 21, 2018, 11:55 a.m., https://twitter.com/PPact/status/1054038409952587776.

92. Field Notes, October 21, 2018; Emily Birnbaum, "LGBTQ Groups to Rally in Response to NYT Report on Trump's Gender Policy Proposal," *The Hill*, October 21,

2018, https://thehill.com/homenews/administration/412455-lgbtq-groups-annou
nce-rallies-in-response-to-nyt-report-on-trumps; Mary Papenfus, "Activists Blast
White House Plan To Eradicate Transgender From Gender Definition," *Huffpost*,
October 21, 2018, https://www.huffpost.com/entry/angry-reactions-against-
trump-administration-plan-to-sharply-limit-gender-definition_n_5bccf42be4b0d
38b5879741f.

93. Sarah Mervosh and Christine Hauser, "At Rallies and Online, Transgender People
Say They #WontBeErased," *New York Times*, October 22, 2018, https://www.nyti
mes.com/2018/10/22/us/transgender-reaction-rally.html.

94. Field Notes, October 22, 2018.

95. Field Notes, October 22, 2018.

96. Field Notes, October 22, 2018.

97. Field Notes, October 22, 2018.

98. For example, American Psychological Association (APA), Twitter post, October 22,
2018, 3:53 p.m., https://twitter.com/APA/status/1054460847756599296; NAESV
(endsxlviolence), Twitter post, October 22, 2018, 2:02 p.m., https://twitter.com/
endsxlviolence/status/1054432875817435136; NASP (nasponline), Twitter post,
October 22, 2018, 2:51 p.m., https://twitter.com/nasponline/status/105444506787
4852870; NNDEV, Twitter post, October 22, 2018, 12:26 p.m., https://twitter.com/
nnedv/status/1054408590440779777.

99. Field Notes, October 23, 2018.

100. Field Notes, October 23, 2018.

101. Field Notes, October 23, 2018.

102. Field Notes, October 23, 2018.

103. Field Notes, October 23, 2018.

104. Field Notes, October 23, 2018.

105. Field Notes, October 23, 2018.

106. Field Notes, October 23, 2018.

107. Field Notes, October 23, 2018.

108. Field Notes, October 23, 2018.

109. Field Notes, October 23, 2018.

110. Field Notes, October 23, 2018.

111. Field Notes, October 23, 2018.

112. Field Notes, October 23, 2018.

113. Amber Tamblyn (ambertamblyn), Twitter post, October 23, 2018, 5:35 p.m., https://
twitter.com/ambertamblyn/status/1054848921997053952.

114. Elizabeth Tulloch (BitsieTulloch), Twitter post, October 23, 2018, 3:04 p.m., https://
twitter.com/BitsieTulloch/status/1054856114628689920; Gigi Gorgeous Getty
(TheGigiGorgeous), Twitter post, October 23, 2018, 9:04 p.m., https://twitter.com/
TheGigiGorgeous/status/1054901286150135808.

115. National Center for Transgender Equality (TransEquality), Twitter post, October 23,
2018, 7:45 p.m., https://twitter.com/TransEquality/status/1054881530483535872;
National Center for Transgender Equality (TransEquality), Twitter post, October 23,
2018, 8:30 p.m., https://twitter.com/TransEquality/status/1054892763064471554.

116. Transgender Allies, "Parents of Transgender Children."

117. Jen Richard (SmartassJen), Twitter post, October 25, 2018, 12:52 p.m., https://twit ter.com/SmartAssJen/status/1055502321180794880.

118. Tara Strong (tarastrong), Twitter post, October 25, 2018, 2:31 p.m., https://twit ter.com/tarastrong/status/1055527191222484993; Sara Ramirez (SaraRamirez), Twitter post, October 25, 2018, 11:39 a.m., https://twitter.com/SaraRamirez/status/ 1055483975857188865.

119. Tegan and Sara (teganandsara), Twitter post, October 26, 2018, 6:55 p.m., https://twit ter.com/teganandsara/status/1055956055199371264; Piper Perabo (PiperPerabo), Twitter post, October 26, 2018, 5:53 p.m., https://twitter.com/PiperPerabo/status/ 1055940568520503299.

120. For example, Jackson, Bailey, and Foucault Welles, *#HashtagActivism*; Meraz and Papacharissi, "Networked Gatekeeping"; Micó and Casero-Ripollés, "Political Activism Online"; Tufekci, *Twitter and Tear Gas*.

Chapter 6

1. Ingrid Ege Apaydın (happygoingrid), Twitter post, March 12, 2019, 2:56 p.m., https://twitter.com/happygoingrid/status/1105543066348212225.

2. Katelyn Burns (transscribe), Twitter post, March 12, 2019, 3:06 p.m., https://twitter. com/transscribe/status/1105545740473024512.

3. TJ Billard (thomasjbillard), Twitter post, March 12, 2019, 3:43 p.m., https://twitter. com/ThomasJBillard/status/1105552699393601536.

4. Tracey E. Gilchrist, "College Scam Movie About Felicity Huffman Should Star a Trans Woman, Says Twitter," *The Advocate*, March 12, 2019, https://www.advocate. com/transgender/2019/3/12/college-scam-movie-about-felicity-huffman-should- star-trans-woman-says-twitter.

5. Although this time, thankfully, in the form of a leaked policy *intention*, not an actual policy change.

6. For example, Barker-Plummer, "News as a Political Resource"; Barker-Plummer, "Media and Social Movements"; Barker-Plummer, "Producing Public Voice"; Doyle, *Making Out in the Mainstream*; Gamson and Wolfsfeld, "Movements and Media"; Gross, *Up from Invisibility*; Lopez, *Asian American Media Activism*; Montgomery, "Gay Activists"; Montgomery, *Target, Prime Time*; Ryan, *Prime Time Activism*.

7. For example, Doyle, *Making Out in the Mainstream*; Gross, *Up from Invisibility*.

8. See, for example, Benkler, *The Wealth of Networks*; Friedland, Hove, and Rojas, "The Networked Public Sphere"; Reese and Shoemaker, "Media Sociology."

9. For example, Julian Ausserhofer and Axel Maireder, "National Politics on Twitter: Structures and Topics of a Networked Public Sphere," *Information, Communication & Society* 16, no. 3 (2013): 291–314; Bruns and Highfield, "Is Habermas on Twitter"; Jackson and Foucault Welles, "#Ferguson is Everywhere."

10. For scholarship in the former debate, see, for example, Peter Dahlgren, "The Internet, Public Spheres, and Political Communication: Dispersion and Deliberation,"

Political Communication 22, no. 2 (2005): 147–162; Friedland, Hove, and Rojas, "The Networked Public Sphere"; Hindman, *The Internet Trap*; Jackson, "(Re) Imagining Intersectional Democracy." For scholarship in the latter debate, see, for example, Rodney Benson, "Shaping the Public Sphere: Habermas and Beyond," *The American Sociologist* 40, no. 3 (2009): 175–197; Matt Carlson, "Establishing the Boundaries of Journalism's Public Mandate," in *Rethinking Journalism Again: Societal Role and Public Relevance in a Digital Age*, ed. Chris Peters and Marcel Broersma (New York: Routledge, 2017), 49–63; Castells, "Communication, Power and Counter-power"; Papacharissi and Oliveira, "Affective News"; Reese and Shoemaker, "Media Sociology"; Nikki Usher and Matt Carlson, "The Midlife Crisis of the Network Society," *Media and Communication* 6, no. 4 (2018): 107–110.

11. Chadwick, *The Hybrid Media System*.

12. For example, Bennett and Segerberg, "The Logic of Connective Action"; Castells, *Networks of Outrage and Hope*; Costanza-Chock, *Out of the Shadows*; Earl and Kimport, *Digitally Enabled Social Change*; Jackson, Bailey, and Foucault Welles, *#HashtagActivism*; Shirky, "The Political Power"; Tufekci, *Twitter and Tear Gas*. The term "repertoire of contention" was coined by historian and political sociologist Charles Tilly to describe the "whole set of means [a collective] has for making claims of different types" on individuals and institutions with societal power; see Charles Tilly, *The Contentious French* (Cambridge, MA: Harvard University Press, 1986), 2.

13. I am not alone in this endeavor. For important convergent perspectives, see, for example, Caren, Andrews, and Lu, "Contemporary Social Movements"; David Karpf, *The MoveOn Effect: The Unexpected Transformation of American Political Advocacy* (New York: Oxford University Press, 2012); David Karpf, "What Social Movement Studies and Political Communication Can Learn from One Another," *Information, Communication & Society* 22, no. 5 (2019): 747–753; Wells, *The Civic Organization*.

14. As sociologist of technology Zeynep Tufekci has shown, the individuals most capable for attracting attention within ostensibly decentralized movements are those with large pre-existing platforms—what we might colloquially call "influencers." Beyond those influencers, few people succeed in attracting attention at an individual level; attention is gained in the aggregate only once a critical mass of individual participants are involved; see Zeynep Tufekci, " 'Not This One': Social Movements, the Attention Economy, and Microcelebrity Activism," *American Behavioral Scientist* 57, no. 7 (2013): 848–870. See also Sandra González-Bailón, Javier Borge-Holthoefer, and Yamir Moreno, "Broadcasters and Hidden Influentials in Online Protest Diffusion," *American Behavioral Scientist* 57, no. 7 (2013): 943–965.

15. See Stinchcombe, "Social Structure and Organizations"; see also Marquis and Tilcsik, "Imprinting."

16. For more on media as a resource for social movements, see Barker-Plummer, "Producing Public Voice." For the concept of social movement "resources," see John McCarthy and Mayer Zald, "Resource Mobilization and Social Movements: A Partial Theory," *American Journal of Sociology* 82, no. 6 (1977): 1212–1241.

17. For more on the cost that media-centric work has for wider movement activity, see Sobieraj, *Soundbitten*.

18. See Fernandes, *Curated Storytelling*; Polletta, *Inventing the Ties*; Polletta et al., "Personal Storytelling"; Trevisan et al., "Mobilizing Personal Narratives."

19. For example, Thomas J Billard, "'Gender Critical' Discourse as Disinformation: Unpacking TERF Strategies of Political Communication," *Women's Studies in Communication* 46, no. 2 (2023): 235–243.

Appendix 1

1. See Billard, "Out of the Tower"; Billard and Waisbord, "The Promethean Imperative."

2. Michael Burawoy, "The Extended Case Method," in *Ethnography Unbound: Power and Resistance in the Modern Metropolis*, ed. Michael Burawoy et al. (Berkeley: University of California Press, 1991), 281. See also Michael Burawoy, "The Extended Case Method," *Sociological Theory* 16, no. 1 (1998): 4–33; Michael Burawoy, *The Extended Case Method: Four Countries, Four Decades, Four Great Transformations, and One Theoretical Tradition* (Berkeley: University of California Press, 2009).

3. Burawoy, *The Extended Case Method*, xv.

4. See, for example, Nina Eliasoph and Paul Lichterman, "We Begin with Our Favorite Theory': Reconstructing the Extended Case Method," *Sociological Theory* 17, no. 2 (1999): 228–234; Lichterman, "Seeing Structure Happen: Theory-Driven Participant Observation," in *Methods of Social Movement Research*, ed. Bert Klandermans and Suzanne Staggenborg (Minneapolis: University of Minnesota Press, 2002), 118–145; see also Iddo Tavory and Stefan Timmermans, "Two Cases of Ethnography: Grounded Theory and the Extended Case Method," *Ethnography* 10, no. 3 (2009): 243–263.

5. Burawoy, "The Extended Case Method," *Sociological Theory*; Burawoy, *The Extended Case Method*.

6. Burawoy, "The Extended Case Method," *Sociological Theory*, 15.

7. Burawoy, "The Extended Case Method," *Sociological Theory*, 15.

8. See Michael Burawoy, "Reconstructing Social Theories," in *Ethnography Unbound: Power and Resistance in the Modern Metropolis*, ed. Michael Burawoy et al. (Berkeley: University of California Press, 1991), 8–27; see also Eliasoph and Lichterman, "We Begin."

9. At the time I participated in the program, COMPASS was jointly sponsored by the Annenberg School for Communication and Journalism at the University of Southern California, the Annenberg School for Communication at the University of Pennsylvania, the Moody College of Communication at the University of Texas at Austin, the School of Communication and Information at Rutgers University, the Department of Communication Studies at the University of Michigan, and the Donald P. Bellisario College of Communications at the Pennsylvania State University, and jointly run by Mark Lloyd of USC and Victor Pickard of UPenn. As of 2018, the program has been run by the Media, Inequality & Change Center, which is a collaboration between the UPenn Annenberg School and the Rutgers School of Communication and Information.

10. For more information on the Trans Equality Archive, as the project came to be called, see Thomas J Billard, "Preserving Transgender History in its Own Right: A Case Study of the Trans Equality Archive," *Bulletin of Applied Transgender Studies* 2, no. 1–2 (2023): 119–127.

11. Quoted in Burawoy et al., "Public Sociologies: A Symposium from Boston College," *Social Problems* 51, no. 1 (2004): 103–130.

12. Michale Burawoy, "Public Sociologies: Contradictions, Dilemmas, and Possibilities," *Social Forces* 82, no. 4 (2004): 1607.

13. See, for an introduction, Burawoy, "Public Sociologies"; Michael Burawoy, "The Public Sociology Wars," in *Handbook of Public Sociology*, ed. Vincent Jeffries (Lanham, MD: Rowman & Littlefield, 2009), 449–473; Michael Burawoy, "Sociology as a Vocation," *Contemporary Sociology* 45, no. 4 (2016): 379–393.

14. Burawoy, "Public Sociologies," 1607.

15. Burawoy, "Public Sociologies," 1608; Burawoy, "Sociology as a Vocation," 390.

16. Burawoy, "Sociology as a Vocation," 390.

17. See Billard, "Out of the Tower"; Billard and Waisbord, "The Promethean Imperative." On participatory action research, see, for example, Budd L. Hall, "From Margins to Center? The Development and Purpose of Participatory Research," *The American Sociologist* 23, no. 4 (1992): 15–28; Lynnell Simonson and Virginia Bushaw, "Participatory Action Research: Easier Said Than Done," *The American Sociologist* 24, no. 1 (1993): 27–37; Randy Stoecker, "Are Academics Irrelevant? Roles for Scholars in Participatory Research," *American Behavioral Scientist* 42, no. 5 (1999): 840–854; Yoland Wadsworth, "'Gouldner's Child?' Some Reflections on Sociology and Participatory Action Research," *Journal of Sociology* 41, no. 3 (2005): 267–284; William F. Whyte, "Advancing Scientific Knowledge Through Participatory Action Research," *Sociological Forum* 4, no. 3 (1989): 367–385.

18. This phrasing borrows heavily from a number of sources: Billard, "Out of the Tower," 3518; Michael Burawoy, "The Critical Turn to Public Sociology," *Critical Sociology* 31, no. 3 (2005): 319; Michael Burawoy, "For Public Sociology," *American Sociological Review* 70, no. 1 (2005): 24; Silvio Waisbord, *The Communication Manifesto* (Medford, MA: Polity, 2020).

19. See Josh Seim, "Participant Observation, Observant Participation, and Hybrid Ethnography," *Sociological Methods & Research*, published ahead of print, February 10, 2021.

20. Tensions over just needing another body recurred in my second round of field-work as well, particularly when I would work rallies or press events, or when I was deployed for field organizing in the Yes on 3 campaign in Massachusetts over election week 2018.

21. Thomas J Billard and Brian L. MacAuley, "'It's a Bird! It's a Plane! It's a Transgender Superhero!': Transgender Characters in Marvel, DC, and Image Comics," in *Heroes, Heroines, and Everything in Between: Challenging Gender and Sexuality Stereotypes in Children's Entertainment Media*, ed. CarrieLynn D. Reinhard and Christopher J. Olson (Lanham, MD: Lexington Books, 2017), 233–252.

22. Billard, "Setting the Transgender Agenda."

23. Billard, "Writing in the Margins."
24. Angèle Christin, *Metrics at Work: Journalism and the Contested Meaning of Algorithms* (Princeton, NJ: Princeton University Press, 2020).
25. R. Stuart Giger and David Ribes, "Trace Ethnography: Following Coordination through Documentary Practices," in *Proceedings of the 44th Hawaii International Conference on System Sciences* (Los Alamitos, CA: IEEE Computer Society Press, 2011).
26. Richard Swedberg, *The Art of Social Theory* (Princeton, NJ: Princeton University Press, 2014).
27. See Robert M. Emerson, Rachel I. Fretz, and Linda L. Shaw, *Writing Ethnographic Fieldnotes* (Chicago: University of Chicago Press, 2011).
28. See Lichterman, "Seeing Structure Happen." See also Juliet Corbin and Anselm Strauss, *Basics of Qualitative Research: Techniques and Procedures for Developing Grounded Theory* (Thousand Oaks, CA: SAGE, 2008).
29. Eliasoph and Lichterman, "We Begin."
30. Eliasoph and Lichterman, "We Begin," 228.
31. Nina Eliasoph and Paul Lichterman, "Culture in Interaction," *American Journal of Sociology* 108, no. 4 (2003): 735.
32. See Michael Burawoy, "Introduction," in *Ethnography Unbound: Power and Resistance in the Modern Metropolis*, ed. Michael Burawoy et al. (Berkeley: University of California Press, 1991), 1–7; Burawoy, "The Extended Case Method," *Ethnography Unbound*.
33. Eliasoph and Lichterman, "Culture in Interaction."
34. Eliasoph and Lichterman, "Culture in Interaction."

References

Interviews by Author

Positions listed for NCTE staff reflect those held at the time I left the field. For a breakdown of all positions held by staff interviewees over my full time in the field, see Table 2.1.

Branstetter, Gillian. Media Relations Manager, Communications (Comms), National Center for Transgender Equality (NCTE). August 7, 2018.

Branstetter, Gillian. Media Relations Manager, Communications (Comms), National Center for Transgender Equality (NCTE). August 21, 2018.

Cartwright, Donna. Founding board member, NCTE. November 27, 2018.

Christian, Arli. State Policy Director, Policy, NCTE. September 6, 2018.

Davis, Masen. Former board member, NCTE. December 21, 2018.

De La Torre, Mateo. Racial and Economic Justice Policy Advocate, Policy, NCTE. August 28, 2018.

Freedman-Gurspan, Raffi. Director of External Relations, Outreach & Education (O&E), NCTE. October 12, 2018.

Gibson, Ray. Voices for Transgender Equality (VTE) program member. December 1, 2018.

Gonzales, Rachel. Families for Transgender Equality (FTE) program member. November 30, 2018.

Gonzales, Rachel. Families for Transgender Equality (FTE) program member. December 4, 2018.

Ivester, Jo. FTE program member. December 2, 2018.

Jackson, Debi. Family Organizer, O&E, NCTE. August 16, 2018.

Jackson, Debi. Family Organizer, O&E, NCTE. October 10, 2018.

Keisling, Mara. Executive Director, NCTE. December 5, 2018.

Kennedy, Benjamin. VTE program member. December 3, 2018.

Kling, Rebecca. Education Program Director, O&E, NCTE. August 21, 2018.

Kling, Rebecca. Education Program Director, O&E, NCTE. October 12, 2018.

Kuilenburg, Nicola van. FTE program member. December 5, 2018.

LaCasse, Chloé. VTE program member. December 5, 2018.

McMurray, Leslie. VTE program member. November 30, 2018.

Minter, Shannon. Cofounder, Transgender Law & Policy Institute. December 6, 2018.

Mottet, Lisa. Deputy Executive Director, NCTE. November 28, 2018.

Mottet, Lisa. Deputy Executive Director, NCTE. December 12, 2018.

Neal, DeShanna. Family Organizer, O&E, NCTE. August 7, 2018.

Neal, DeShanna. Family Organizer, O&E, NCTE. December 9, 2018.

Noble, Dave. Interim Communications Director, Comms, NCTE. October 17, 2018.

Powell, Laurel. Digital Campaigns Manager, Comms, NCTE. August 10, 2018.

Powell, Laurel. Digital Campaigns Manager, Comms, NCTE. August 28, 2018.

Raghavan, Gautam. Former Associate Director of President Barack Obama's White House Office of Public Engagement. August 27, 2018.

Sanchez, Diego Miguel. Former board member, NCTE. December 19, 2018.

Schonauer, Paula Sophia. VTE program member. December 22, 2018.

Villano, Vincent Paolo. Former Communications Manager, Comms, NCTE. November 20, 2018.

Watson, Sarah. FTE program member. December 4, 2018.

White, Stephanie. Former Managing Director, NCTE. September 12, 2018.

Wu, Jay. Director of Communications, Comms, NCTE. August 22, 2018.

Wu, Jay. Director of Communications, Comms, NCTE. November 10, 2018.

Newspaper, Magazine, and Other Popular Publication Articles

Allen, Samantha. "Trump State Department Just Made an Ominous Passport Change for Transgender Americans." *The Daily Beast*, September 13, 2018. https://www.thedailybe ast.com/trump-state-department-just-made-an-ominous-passport-change-for-tran sgender-americans.

Associated Press. "Man Fatally Shot by Oklahoma Police Threatened Postal Worker." *Associated Press*, December 15, 2020. https://apnews.com/article/shootings-police-oklahoma-city-oklahoma-assault-and-battery-dbafa53a7459fa71c40e4f08069a2ea9.

Balingit, Moriah. "After Alleged Sexual Assault, Officials Open Investigation of Transgender Bathroom Policy." *Washington Post*, October 9, 2018. https://www.was hingtonpost.com/local/education/after-alleged-sexual-assault-officials-open-invest igation-of-transgender-bathroom-policy/2018/10/09/431e7024-c7fd-11e8-9b1c-a90 f1daae309_story.html.

Bendix, Trish. "Does LGBT Media Have a Future?" *Buzzfeed News*, January 25, 2019. https://www.buzzfeednews.com/article/trishbendix/future-of-lgbt-media-out-advoc ate-autostraddle-into-grindr.

Birnbaum, Emily. "LGBTQ Groups to Rally in Response to NYT Report on Trump's Gender Policy Proposal." *The Hill*, October 21, 2018. https://thehill.com/homenews/ administration/412455-lgbtq-groups-announce-rallies-in-response-to-nyt-report-on-trumps.

Birnbaum, Emily. "Transgender Rights Group Unfurls Massive Flag in Front of Lincoln Memorial." *The Hill*, October 29, 2018. https://thehill.com/business-a-lobbying/413 706-transgender-rights-group-unfurls-massive-flag-in-front-of-lincoln.

Boddiger, David. "The State Department Is Retroactively Revoking Transgender Women's Passports, Report Says." *Splinter*, July 28, 2018. https://splinternews.com/the-state-dep artment-is-retroactively-revoking-transgen-1827946847.

Boddiger, David. "The State Department Is Retroactively Revoking Transgender Women's Passports, Report Says." *MSN*, July 28, 2018. https://www.msn.com/en-us/news/us/ the-state-department-is-retroactively-revoking-transgender-women%E2%80%99s-passports-report-says/ar-BBLbhRs.

Brammer, John Paul. "Trans Advocates Worry Over the State Department's Language on Passport Policy." *them*, September 14, 2018. https://www.them.us/story/state-departm ent-language-passport-policy.

Branscome, Jeff. "Stafford Superintendent Apologizes to Transgender Student Amid National Outcry." *The Free Lance-Star*, October 9, 2018. https://www.fredericksburg.

com/news/local/stafford/stafford-superintendent-apologizes-to-transgender-stud
ent-amid-national-outcry/article_8d0f967a-2092-57c0-9328-33a68a084c15.html.

Brinlee, Morgan. "Trans Women Claim Trump's Admin Revoked Their Passports After
They Changed Their Gender Marker." *Bustle*, July 28, 2018. https://www.bustle.com/
p/trans-women-claim-trumps-admin-revoked-their-passports-after-they-changed-
their-gender-marker-report-9921036.

Bugg, Sean. "Trans Mission: Mara Keisling and the Politics of ENDA." *Metro Weekly*,
August 19, 2004.

Burns, Katelyn. "State Department Changes Passport Website Language for Transgender
People." *Rewire News Group*, September 13, 2018. https://rewire.news/article/2018/09/
13/state-department-changes-passport-website-language/.

Chakraborty, Ranjani. "How ID Laws Can Put Trans People in Danger." *Vox*, August 16,
2018. https://www.vox.com/videos/2018/8/16/17698442/id-laws-trans-people-dan
ger-murder.

Chakraborty, Ranjani, Lucas Waldron, and Ken Schwencke. "Video: For Trans People, It's
Difficult and Costly to Update an ID. But It Can Also Be Dangerous Not To." *ProPublica*,
August 16, 2018. https://www.propublica.org/article/for-trans-people-difficult-and-
costly-to-update-an-id-but-it-can-also-be-dangerous-not-to.

Chen, Tanya. "A Transgender Student Was Allegedly Blocked from Sheltering in Both
Boys and Girls Bathrooms During a Safety Drill." *Buzzfeed News*, October 9, 2018.
https://www.buzzfeednews.com/article/tanyachen/transgender-student-banned-
boys-girls-drill-virginia.

Concerned Transgender Community Leaders. "Over 400 Trans Community Leaders
Stand with Former NCTE Staff." *Out*, December 12, 2019. https://www.out.com/activ
ism/2019/12/11/over-400-trans-community-leaders-stand-former-ncte-staff.

Cote, Charlie James. "Dear *Decaturish*—Responding to Allegations About Transgender
Students." *Decaturish*, October 18, 2018. https://decaturish.com/2018/10/dear-decatur
ish-responding-to-allegations-about-transgender-students/.

Dancyger, Lilly. "For Trans People Seeking Passports, State Department Abruptly
Changes Language." *Rolling Stone*, September 13, 2018. https://www.rollingstone.com/
culture/culture-news/transgender-passport-sex-gender-state-department-723984/.

Darnell, Tim. "Oakhurst Student Claims Sexual Assault by 'Gender-Fluid' Boy." *The
Decatur Patch*, October 4, 2018. https://patch.com/georgia/decatur/oakhurst-student-
claims-sexual-assault-gender-fluid-boy.

Emma, Caitlin. "DeVos Investigates Whether School Transgender Bathroom Policy Led
to Sexual Assault." *Politico*, October 3, 2018. https://www.politico.com/story/2018/10/
03/devos-investigates-transgender-bathroom-policy-assault-827018.

Evans, Gordon. "Director of National Transgender Rights Group Says 'The Law Is On
Our Side.'" *WMUK*, May 30, 2018. https://www.wmuk.org/post/wsw-director-natio
nal-transgender-rights-group-says-law-our-side.

Fitzsimons, Tim. "Virginia School Allegedly Barred Trans Student from Active-Shooter
Drill." *NBC News*, October 9, 2018. https://www.nbcnews.com/feature/nbc-out/virgi
nia-school-allegedly-barred-trans-student-active-shooter-drill-n918216.

Former Staff of NCTE. "This Is Why We Left the National Center for Trans Equality."
Out, November 15, 2019. https://www.out.com/transgender/2019/11/15/why-we-left-
americas-largest-trans-advocacy-organization.

Gilchrist, Tracy E. "College Scam Movie About Felicity Huffman Should Star a Trans
Woman, Says Twitter." *The Advocate*, March 12, 2019. https://www.advocate.com/tran

sgender/2019/3/12/college-scam-movie-about-felicity-huffman-should-star-trans-woman-says-twitter.

Green, Erica L., Katie Benner, and Robert Pear. "'Transgender' Could be Defined Out of Existence Under Trump Administration." *New York Times*, October 21, 2018. https://www.nytimes.com/2018/10/21/us/politics/transgender-trump-administration-sex-definition.html.

Hunter-Hart, Monica. "Passport Language for Trans People Changed Overnight—Then Was Reversed After Criticism." *Bustle*, September 13, 2018. https://www.bustle.com/p/passport-language-for-trans-people-changed-overnight-then-was-reversed-after-criticism-11907452.

Impelli, Matthew. "Oklahoma City Black Man Shot and Killed by Police, Sparking Immediate Protests." *Newsweek*, December 11, 2020. https://www.newsweek.com/oklahoma-city-man-shot-killed-police-sparking-immediate-protests-1554245.

Johnson, Chris. "Nat'l Center for Trans Equality Regroups After Mass Staff Departures." *Washington Blade*, December 11, 2019. https://www.washingtonblade.com/2019/12/11/natl-center-for-trans-equality-regroups-after-mass-staff-departures/.

Kahn, Mattie. "A Trans Air Force Veteran Responds to Trump's Ban." *Elle*, July 26, 2017. http://www.elle.com/culture/career-politics/news/a46960/trans-veteran-trump-military-ban-responds/.

Kenney, Tanasia. "Mother's Lawsuit Takes Aim at School's Gender-Neutral Bathroom Policy After She Claims Daughter Was Molested by 'Gender Fluid Student.'" *Atlanta Black Star*, October 5, 2018. https://atlantablackstar.com/2018/10/05/mothers-lawsuit-takes-aim-at-schools-gender-neutral-bathroom-policy-after-she-claims-daughter-was-molested-by-gender-fluid-student/.

Lance, Natisha. "Mom Alleges Daughter Assaulted by Transgender Student in Elementary School Bathroom." *11alive*, October 3, 2018. https://www.11alive.com/article/news/local/decatur/mom-alleges-daughter-assaulted-by-transgender-student-in-elementary-school-bathroom/85-600627949.

Massie, Chris, and Andrew Kaczynksi. "Trump Judicial Nominee Said Transgender Children Are Part of 'Satan's Plan,' Defended 'Conversion Therapy.'" *CNN*, September 20, 2017. https://www.cnn.com/2017/09/20/politics/kfile-jeff-mateer-lgbt-remarks/index.html.

Mervosh, Sarah, and Christine Hauser. "At Rallies and Online, Transgender People Say They #WontBeErased." *New York Times*, October 22, 2018. https://www.nytimes.com/2018/10/22/us/transgender-reaction-rally.html.

O'Hara, Mary Emily. "Trans Women Say the State Department Is Retroactively Revoking Their Passports." *them*, July 27, 2018. https://www.them.us/story/trans-women-state-department-passports.

Owens, Gabriel. "Parents' Coalition Speaks Against Decatur Schools Transgender Policies During Meeting." *Decaturish*, September 15, 2017. https://decaturish.com/2017/09/parents-coalition-speaks-against-decatur-schools-transgender-policies-during-meeting/.

Papenfus, Mary. "Activists Blast White House Plan To Eradicate Transgender From Gender Definition." *Huffpost*, October 21, 2018. https://www.huffpost.com/entry/angry-reactions-against-trump-administration-plan-to-sharply-limit-gender-definition_n_5bccf42be4b0d38b5879741f.

RVA Staff. "Stafford County School Board Responds to Transgender Student Singled Out During Active Shooter Drill." *RVA*, October 10, 2018. https://rvamag.com/news/staff

ord-country-school-board-responds-to-transgender-student-signaled-out-during-active-shooter-drill.html.

Schwartz, Drew. "Trans Student Blocked from Both Locker Rooms During School Safety Drill." *Vice*, October 8, 2018. https://www.vice.com/en_us/article/7x3dqd/trans-stud ent-not-allowed-in-locker-rooms-school-safety-drill-virginia-vgtrn.

Smothers, Hannah. "Middle School Allegedly Excluded Trans Student from Participating in Active Shooter Drill." *Cosmopolitan*, October 10, 2018. https://www.cosmopolitan. com/lifestyle/a23709601/virginia-middle-school-excludes-trans-student-shooter-drill/.

Sobel, Ariel. "Is the Trump Administration Trying to Discourage Trans Travelers?" *The Advocate*, September 13, 2018. https://www.advocate.com/transgender/2018/9/13/trump-administration-trying-discourage-trans-travelers.

Sosin, Kate. "Harper Jean Tobin to Leave NCTE as Fallout Grows." *NewNowNext*, December 20, 2019. http://www.newnownext.com/harper-jean-tobin-leaving-natio nal-center-for-trans-equality/12/2019/.

Sosin, Kate. "National Center for Trans Equality Staff Walks Out Over Union Woes, Racism." *NewNowNext*, August 20, 2019. http://www.newnownext.com/national-cen ter-for-trans-equality-walkout/08/2019/.

Sosin, Kate. "NCTE's Mara Keisling Talks Next Steps After Calls for Her to Step Down." *NewNowNext*, December 13, 2019. http://www.newnownext.com/mara-keisling-natio nal-center-for-trans-equality-racism-union-busting-allegations/12/2019/.

Steiner, Chelsea. "The State Department is Revoking Trans Women's' Passports as We March Ever Closer to The Handmaid's Tale." *The Mary Sue*, July 28, 2018. https://www. themarysue.com/state-department-trans-passports/.

Steinmetz, Katy. "The Transgender Tipping Point." *TIME*, May 29, 2014. https://time. com/135480/transgender-tipping-point/.

Sykes, Michael. "Report: State Department Retroactively Revoking Passports from Transgender Women." *Axios*, July 28, 2018. https://www.axios.com/trans-women-passport-issue-state-department-trump-aa249a45-55aa-4923-8090-ad26ba220 e98.html.

Toce, Sarah. "Advocates Say Fears About Trans People's Passports are Overblown." *LGBTQ Nation*, July 28, 2018. https://www.lgbtqnation.com/2018/07/state-department-retroa ctively-revoking-passports-trans-citizens/.

Transgender Allies. "Parents of Transgender Children Ask Trump Administration to Reverse Course on Gender Memo." *Teen Vogue*, October 25, 2018. https://www.teenvo gue.com/story/parents-transgender-children-ask-trump-administration-reverse-cou rse-on-gender-memo.

Trotta, Daniel. "Staff Exodus Hits Top U.S. Transgender Group on Eve of 2020 Election Campaign." *Reuters*, November 15, 2019. https://www.reuters.com/article/us-usa-lgbt-transgender-idUSKBN1XP2FI.

Urquhart, Evan. "Facing Bullies and Court Battles, Transgender Kids Head Back to School." *Slate*, August 24, 2018. https://slate.com/human-interest/2018/08/facing-bull ies-and-court-battles-transgender-kids-head-back-to-school.html.

Verburg, Steven. "Sun Prairie Soldier Fears Trump Transgender Ban Will Force Her from Army." *Wisconsin State Journal*, July 27, 2017. http://host.madison.com/wsj/news/ local/govt-and-politics/sun-prairie-soldier-fears-trump-transgender-ban-will-force-her/article_2f543bac-bac0-57fa-82c2-896a8dd2b143.html.

Verburg, Steven. "Trump Ban on Transgender Military Service Hits Home for Some in Wisconsin." *Wisconsin State Journal*, July 27, 2017. http://host.madison.com/wsj/news/local/govt-and-politics/trump-ban-on-transgender-military-service-hits-home-for-some/article_7d47e877-0d54-57f1-99d8-0ed2d4443b86.html.

Villarreal, Daniel. "Most of the Staffers at One of the Nation's Biggest Trans Organization Just Quit." *LGBTQ Nation*, November 15, 2019. https://www.lgbtqnation.com/2019/11/workers-countrys-biggest-trans-organization-just-quit/.

Wermund, Benjamin. "LGBTQ Advocates Worry About Politics in DeVos' New Civil Rights Probe." *Politico*, October 4, 2018. https://www.politico.com/newsletters/morning-education/2018/10/04/lgbtq-advocates-worry-about-politics-in-devos-new-civil-rights-probe-362006.

Whisenhunt, Dan. "Education Department Investigating Claim Transgender Oakhurst Elementary Student Committed Assault." *Decaturish*, October 3, 2018. https://decaturish.com/2018/10/u-s-department-of-education-investigating-claim-transgender-oakhurst-elementary-student-committed-assault/.

Whisenhunt, Dan. "Information is Scarce About Parents Opposed to City Schools of Decatur's Transgender Policy." *Decaturish*, October 9, 2017. https://decaturish.com/2017/10/information-is-scarce-about-parents-opposed-to-city-schools-of-decaturs-transgender-policy/.

Bibliography

Abbott, Carl. *Political Terrain: Washington, DC, from Tidewater Town to Global Metropolis.* Chapel Hill: University of North Carolina Press, 1999.

Adams-Santos, Dominique. "'Something a Bit More Personal': Digital Storytelling and Intimacy Among Queer Black Women." *Sexualities* 23, no. 8 (2020): 1434–1456.

Amenta, Edwin, and Neal Caren. *Rough Draft of History: A Century of US Social Movements in the News.* Princeton, NJ: Princeton University Press, 2022.

Amenta, Edwin, Thomas Allan Elliott, Nichole Shortt, Amber C. Tierney, Didem Türkoğlu, and Burrel Vann, Jr. "Making Good News: What Explains the Quality of Coverage of the Civil Rights Movement." *Mobilization* 24, no. 1 (2019): 19–37.

Anderson, Benedict. *Imagined Communities: Reflections on the Origin and Spread of Nationalism.* New York: Verso, 1983.

Andrews, Kenneth, and Neal Caren. "Making the News: Movement Organizations, Media Attention, and the Public Agenda." *American Sociological Review* 75, no. 6 (2010): 841–866.

Anspach, Nicolas M. "The New Personal Influence: How Our Facebook Friends Influence the News We Read." *Political Communication* 34, no. 4 (2017): 590–606.

Ashley, Florence. "Gatekeeping Hormone Replacement Therapy for Transgender Patients is Dehumanising." *Journal of Medical Ethics* 45, no. 7 (2019): 480–482.

Ausserhofer, Julian, and Axel Maireder. "National Politics on Twitter: Structures and Topics of a Networked Public Sphere." *Information, Communication & Society* 16, no. 3 (2013): 291–314.

Bail, Christopher A. "The Fringe Effect: Civil Society Organizations and the Evolution of Media Discourse about Islam since the September 11th Attacks." *American Sociological Review* 77, no. 6 (2012): 855–879.

Bailey, Moya. *Misogynoir Transformed: Black Women's Digital Resistance*. New York: New York University Press, 2021.

Ball-Rokeach, Sandra J. "The Legitimation of Violence." In *Collective Violence*, edited by James F. Short, Jr. and Marvin Wolfgang, 100–111. Chicago: Aldine, 1971.

Ball-Rokeach, Sandra J., Yong-Chan Kim, and Sorin Matei. "Storytelling Neighborhood: Paths to Belonging in Diverse Urban Environments." *Communication Research* 28, no. 4 (2001): 392–428.

Barker-Plummer, Bernadette. "The Dialogic of Media and Social Movements." *Peace Review* 8, no. 1 (1996): 27–33.

Barker-Plummer, Bernadette. "News as a Political Resource: Media Strategies and Political Identity in the U.S. Women's Movement, 1966–1975." *Critical Studies in Mass Communication* 12, no. 3 (1995): 306–324.

Barker-Plummer, Bernadette. "Producing Public Voice: Resource Mobilization and Media Access in the National Organization for Women." *Journalism & Mass Communication Quarterly* 79, no. 1 (2002): 188–205.

Bassichis, Morgan, Alexander Lee, and Dean Spade. "Building an Abolitionist Trans and Queer Movement with Everything We've Got." In *Captive Genders: Trans Embodiment and the Prison Industrial Complex*, edited by Eric A. Stanley and Nat Smith, 15–40. Oakland, CA: AK Press, 2011.

Benford, Robert. "Frame Disputes within the Nuclear Disarmament Movement." *Social Forces* 71, no. 3 (1993): 677–701.

Benford, Robert, and David Snow. "Framing Processes and Social Movements: An Overview and Assessment." *Annual Review of Sociology* 26 (2000): 611–639.

Benkler, Yochai. *The Wealth of Networks: How Social Production Transforms Markets and Freedom*. New Haven, CT: Yale University Press, 2006.

Bennett, W. Lance. *News: The Politics of Illusion*. 10th ed. Chicago: University of Chicago Press, 2016.

Bennett, W. Lance, and Shanto Iyengar. "A New Era of Minimal Effects? The Changing Foundations of Political Communication." *Journal of Communication* 58, no. 4 (2008): 707–731.

Bennett, W. Lance, and Alexandra Segerberg. "The Logic of Connective Action: Digital Media and Personalization of Contentious Politics." *Information, Communication & Society* 15, no. 5 (2012): 739–768.

Bennett, W. Lance, Alexandra Segerberg, and Yunkang Yang. "The Strength of Peripheral Networks: Negotiating Attention and Meaning in Complex Media Ecologies." *Journal of Communication* 68, no. 4 (2018): 659–684.

Benson, Rodney. "Shaping the Public Sphere: Habermas and Beyond." *The American Sociologist* 40, no. 3 (2009): 175–197.

Bergström, Annika, and Maria Jervelycke Belfrage. "News in Social Media: Incidental Consumption and the Role of Opinion Leaders." *Digital Journalism* 6, no. 5 (2018): 583–598.

Berkowitz, Dan, and Douglas B. Adams. "Information Subsidy and Agenda-Building in Local Television News." *Journalism Quarterly* 67, no. 4 (1990): 723–731.

Billard, Thomas J. "Citizen Typography and Political Brands in the 2016 US Presidential Election Campaign." *Marketing Theory* 18, no. 3 (2018): 421–431.

Billard, Thomas J. "Deciding What's (Sharable) News: Social Movement Organizations as Curating Actors in the Political Information System." *Communication Monographs* 89, no. 3 (2022): 354–375.

Billard, Thomas J. "Fonts of Potential: Areas for Typographic Research in Political Communication." *International Journal of Communication* 10 (2016): 4570–4592.

Billard, Thomas J. "'Gender Critical' Discourse as Disinformation: Unpacking TERF Strategies of Political Communication." *Women's Studies in Communication* 46, no. 2 (2023): 235–243.

Billard, Thomas J. "Hybrid Social Movements: An Historical Perspective on Social Movement Hybridization in the Case of the US Transgender Movement." Unpublished manuscript, Northwestern University, 2023.

Billard, Thomas J. "Movement–Media Relations in the Hybrid Media System: A Case Study from the U.S. Transgender Rights Movement." *The International Journal of Press/Politics* 26, no. 2 (2021): 341–361.

Billard, Thomas J. "The Origins and Development of the National Transgender Rights Movement in the United States of America." *Journal of Social History*, forthcoming.

Billard, Thomas J. "Out of the Tower and Into the Field: Fieldwork as Public Scholarship in the Face of Social Injustice." *International Journal of Communication* 13 (2019): 3512–3528.

Billard, Thomas J. "Preserving Transgender History in its Own Right: A Case Study of the Trans Equality Archive." *Bulletin of Applied Transgender Studies* 2, no. 1–2 (2023): 119–127.

Billard, Thomas J. "Setting the Transgender Agenda: Intermedia Agenda-Setting in the Digital News Environment." *Politics, Groups, and Identities* 7, no. 1 (2019): 165–176.

Billard, Thomas J. "Together We Rise: The Role of Communication and Community Connectedness in Transgender Citizens' Civic Engagement in the United States." *Mass Communication and Society* 25, no. 3 (2022): 335–360.

Billard, Thomas J. "Writing in the Margins: Mainstream News Media Representations of Transgenderism." *International Journal of Communication* 10 (2016): 4193–4218.

Billard, Thomas J, and Brian L. MacAuley. "'It's a Bird! It's a Plane! It's a Transgender Superhero!': Transgender Characters in Marvel, DC, and Image Comics." In *Heroes, Heroines, and Everything in Between: Challenging Gender and Sexuality Stereotypes in Children's Entertainment Media*, edited by CarrieLynn D. Reinhard and Christopher J. Olson, 233–252. Lanham, MD: Lexington Books, 2017.

Billard, Thomas J, and Larry Gross. "LGBTQ Politics in Media and Culture." In *The Oxford Research Encyclopedia of Politics*, edited by William R. Thompson. New York: Oxford University Press, 2020.

Billard, Thomas J, and Rachel E. Moran. "Networked Political Brands: Consumption, Community, and Political Expression in Contemporary Brand Culture." *Media, Culture & Society* 42, no. 4 (2020): 588–604.

Billard, Thomas J, and Silvio Waisbord. "The Promethean Imperative: An Introduction to Public Scholarship in Communication Studies." In *Public Scholarship in Communication Studies*, edited by Thomas J Billard and Silvio Waisbord. Urbana-Champaign: University of Illinois Press, 2024.

Billard, Thomas J, Avery R. Everhart, and Erique Zhang. "Whither Trans Studies? On Fields, Post-Disciplines, and the Need for an Applied Transgender Studies." *Bulletin of Applied Transgender Studies* 1, no. 1–2 (2022): 1–18.

Boczkowski, Pablo J., and Zizi Papacharissi, eds. *Trump and the Media*. Cambridge, MA: MIT Press, 2018.

Boorstin, Daniel J. *The Image: A Guide to Pseudo-Events in America*. New York: Vintage Books, 1992.

Boumans, Jelle. "Subsidizing the News? Organizational Press Releases' Influence on News Media's Agenda and Content." *Journalism Studies* 19, no. 15 (2018): 2264–2282.

Box-Steffensmeier, Janet M., and Dino P. Christenson. "The Evolution and Formation of Amicus Curiae Networks." *Social Networks* 36 (2014): 82–96.

Brantly, Aaron Franklin. "From Cyberspace to Independence Square: Understanding the Impact of Social Media on Physical Protest Mobilization During Ukraine's Euromaidan Revolution." *Journal of Information Technology & Politics* 16, no. 4 (2019): 360–378.

Broad, Garrett M., Sandra J. Ball-Rokeach, Katherine Ognyanova, Benjamin Stokes, Tania Picasso, and George Villanueva. "Understanding Communication Ecologies to Bridge Communication Research and Community Action." *Journal of Applied Communication Research* 41, no. 4 (2013): 325–345.

Brodie, Roderick J., Maureen Benson-Rea, and Christopher J. Medlin. "Branding as a Dynamic Capability: Strategic Advantage from Integrating Meanings with Identification." *Marketing Theory* 17, no. 2 (2017): 183–199.

Bruns, Axel, and Tim Highfield. "Is Habermas on Twitter? Social Media and the Public Sphere." In *Routledge Companion to Social Media and Politics*, edited by Axel Bruns, Gunn Enli, Eli Skogerbo, Anders Olof Larsson, and Christian Christensen, 56–73. New York: Routledge, 2015.

Bunce, Mel, Kate Wright, and Martin Scott. "'Our Newsroom in the Cloud': Slack, Virtual Newsrooms and Journalistic Practice." *New Media & Society* 20, no. 9 (2017): 3381–3399.

Burawoy, Michael. "The Critical Turn to Public Sociology." *Critical Sociology* 31, no. 3 (2005): 313–326.

Burawoy, Michael. "The Extended Case Method." In *Ethnography Unbound: Power and Resistance in the Modern Metropolis*, edited by Michael Burawoy, Alice Burton, Ann Arnett Ferguson, Kathryn J. Fox, Joshua Gamson, Nadine Gartrell et al., 271–287. Berkeley: University of California Press, 1991.

Burawoy, Michael. "The Extended Case Method." *Sociological Theory* 16, no. 1 (1998): 4–33.

Burawoy, Michael. *The Extended Case Method: Four Countries, Four Decades, Four Great Transformations, and One Theoretical Tradition*. Berkeley: University of California Press, 2009.

Burawoy, Michael. "For Public Sociology." *American Sociological Review* 70, no. 1 (2005): 4–28.

Burawoy, Michael. "Introduction." In *Ethnography Unbound: Power and Resistance in the Modern Metropolis*, edited by Michael Burawoy, Alice Burton, Ann Arnett Ferguson, Kathryn J. Fox, Joshua Gamson, Nadine Gartrell et al., 1–7. Berkeley: University of California Press, 1991.

Burawoy, Michael. "Public Sociologies: Contradictions, Dilemmas, and Possibilities." *Social Forces* 82, no. 4 (2004): 1603–1618.

Burawoy, Michael. "The Public Sociology Wars." In *Handbook of Public Sociology*, edited by Vincent Jeffries, 449–473. Lanham, MD: Rowman & Littlefield, 2009.

Burawoy, Michael. "Reconstructing Social Theories." In *Ethnography Unbound: Power and Resistance in the Modern Metropolis*, edited by Michael Burawoy, Alice Burton, Ann Arnett Ferguson, Kathryn J. Fox, Joshua Gamson, Nadine Gartrell et al., 8–27. Berkeley: University of California Press, 1991.

Burawoy, Michael. "Sociology as a Vocation." *Contemporary Sociology* 45, no. 4 (2016): 379–393.

Burawoy, Michael, William Gamson, Charlotte Ryan, Stephen Pfohl, Diane Vaughan, Charles Derber et al.. "Public Sociologies: A Symposium from Boston College." *Social Problems* 51, no. 1 (2004): 103–130.

Calhoun, Craig. "Introduction." In *Habermas and the Public Sphere*, edited by Craig Calhoun, 1–48. Cambridge, MA: MIT Press, 1992.

Caple, Helen. "News Values and Newsworthiness." In *The Oxford Research Encyclopedia of Communication*, edited by Jon Nussbaum. New York: Oxford University Press, 2018.

Capuzza, Jamie C., and Leland G. Spencer. "Regressing, Progressing, or Transgressing on the Small Screen? Transgender Characters on U.S. Scripted Television Series." *Communication Studies* 65, no. 2 (2018): 214–230.

Caren, Neal, Kenneth T. Andrews, and Todd Lu. "Contemporary Social Movements in a Hybrid Media Environment." *Annual Review of Sociology* 46 (2020): 443–465.

Carlson, Matt. "Establishing the Boundaries of Journalism's Public Mandate." In *Rethinking Journalism Again: Societal Role and Public Relevance in a Digital Age*, edited by Chris Peters and Marcel Broersma, 49–63. New York: Routledge, 2017.

Carlson, Matt. "Journalistic Epistemology and Digital News Circulation: Infrastructure, Circulation Practices, and Epistemic Contests." *New Media & Society* 22, no. 2 (2020): 206–246.

Carroll, William, and R. S. Ratner. "Media Strategies and Political Projects: A Comparative Study of Social Movements." *Canadian Journal of Sociology* 24, no. 1 (1999): 1–34.

Carter Olson, Candi. "#BringBackOurGirls: Digital Communities Supporting Real-World Change and Influencing Mainstream Media Agendas." *Feminist Media Studies* 16, no. 5 (2016): 772–787.

Castells, Manuel. "Communication, Power and Counter-power in the Network Society." *International Journal of Communication* 1 (2007): 238–266.

Castells, Manuel. *Networks of Outrage and Hope: Social Movements in the Internet Age*. Medford, MA: Polity, 2015.

Chadwick, Andrew. *The Hybrid Media System: Politics and Power*. 2nd ed. New York: Oxford University Press, 2017.

Chadwick, Andrew. "The Political Information Cycle in a Hybrid News System: The British Prime Minister and the 'Bullygate' Affair." *The International Journal of Press/Politics* 16, no. 1 (2011): 3–29.

Cheng, Hau Ling. "Constructing a Transnational, Multilocal Sense of Belonging: An Analysis of *Ming Pao (West Canadian Edition)*." *Journal of Communication Inquiry* 29, no. 2 (2005): 141–159.

Christin, Angèle. *Metrics at Work: Journalism and the Contested Meaning of Algorithms*. Princeton, NJ: Princeton University Press, 2020.

Cohen, Cathy. *The Boundaries of Blackness: AIDS and the Breakdown of Black Politics*. Chicago: University of Chicago Press, 1999.

Cohen, Nicole S. *Writers' Rights: Freelance Journalism in a Digital Age*. Montreal: McGill-Queen's University Press, 2016.

Corbin, Juliet, and Anselm Strauss. *Basics of Qualitative Research: Techniques and Procedures for Developing Grounded Theory*. Thousand Oaks, CA: SAGE, 2008.

Costanza-Chock, Sasha. *Out of the Shadows, Into the Streets: Transmedia Organizing and the Immigrant Rights Movement*. Cambridge, MA: MIT Press, 2014.

Couldry, Nick, and Andreas Hepp. "Conceptualizing Mediatization: Contexts, Traditions, Arguments." *Communication Theory* 23, no. 3 (2013): 191–202.

Currid-Halkett, Elizabeth. *Starstruck: The Business of Celebrity*. New York: Faber and Faber, 2010.

Curtis, Russell L., and Louis A. Zurcher. "Stable Resources of Protest Movements: The Multi-Organizational Field." *Social Forces* 52, no. 1 (1973): 53–61.

Dahlberg, Lincoln. "The Habermasian Public Sphere: Taking Difference Seriously?" *Theory and Society* 34, no. 2 (2005): 111–136.

Dahlgren, Peter. "The Internet, Public Spheres, and Political Communication: Dispersion and Deliberation." *Political Communication* 22, no. 2 (2005): 147–162.

Davis, Joseph E. "Narrative and Social Movements: The Power of Stories." In *Stories of Change: Narrative and Social Movements*, edited by Joseph E. Davis, 3–22. Albany: State University of New York Press, 2002.

Dayan, Daniel, and Elihu Katz. *Media Events: The Live Broadcasting of History*. Cambridge, MA: Harvard University Press, 1992.

Deuze, Mark, and Leopoldina Fortunati. "Atypical Newswork, Atypical Media Management." In *Managing Media Work*, edited by Mark Deuze, 111–120. Thousand Oaks, CA: SAGE, 2011.

Deuze, Mark, and Tamara Witschge. "Beyond Journalism: Theorizing the Transformation of Journalism." *Journalism* 19, no. 2 (2017): 165–181.

Djerf-Pierre, Monika. "The Crowding-Out Effect: Issue Dynamics and Attention to Environmental Issues in Television News Reporting Over 30 Years." *Journalism Studies* 13, no. 4 (2012): 499–516.

Doyle, Vincent. *Making Out in the Mainstream: GLAAD and the Politics of Respectability*. Montreal: McGill-Queen's University Press, 2016.

Earl, Jennifer, and Katrina Kimport. *Digitally Enabled Social Change: Activism in the Internet Age*. Cambridge, MA: MIT Press, 2011.

Edelman, Elijah Adiv. *Trans Vitalities: Mapping Ethnographies of Trans Social and Political Coalitions*. New York: Routledge, 2020.

Eggleston, W. Neil, and Amanda Elbogen. "The Trump Administration and the Breakdown of Intra-Executive Legal Process." *Yale Law Journal Forum* 127 (2018): 825–847.

Eliasoph, Nina, and Paul Lichterman. "Culture in Interaction." *American Journal of Sociology* 108, no. 4 (2003): 735–794.

Eliasoph, Nina, and Paul Lichterman. "'We Begin with Our Favorite Theory': Reconstructing the Extended Case Method." *Sociological Theory* 17, no. 2 (1999): 228–234.

Emerson, Robert M., Rachel I. Fretz, and Linda L. Shaw. *Writing Ethnographic Fieldnotes*. Chicago: University of Chicago Press, 2011.

Entman, Robert M. *Democracy Without Citizens: Media and the Decay of American Politics*. New York: Oxford University Press, 1989.

Entman, Robert M., and Andrew Rojecki. *The Black Image in the White Mind: Media and Race in America*. Chicago: University of Chicago Press, 2001.

Etter, Michael, and Oana Brindusa Albu. "Activists in the Dark: Social Media Algorithms and Collective Action in Two Social Movement Organizations." *Organization* 28, no. 1 (2021): 68–91.

Everhart, Avery Rose. "Incomplete Data and Insufficient Methods: Transgender Population Health Research in the US." PhD diss., University of Southern California, 2022.

Fei, Rosemary E., and Eric K. Gorovitz. "Practitioner Perspectives on Using 501(c)(4) Organizations for Charitable Lobbying." *NYU Journal of Legislation & Public Policy* 21 (2018): 535–582.

Fernandes, Sujatha. *Curated Stories: The Uses and Misuses of Storytelling*. New York: Oxford University Press, 2017.

Ferrara, Emilio, and Zeyao Yang. "Measuring Emotional Contagion in Social Media." *PLOS ONE* 10 (2015): e0142390.

Flores, Andrew R., Jody L. Herman, Gary J. Gates, and Taylor N. T. Brown. *How Many Adults Identify as Transgender in the United States?* Los Angeles: Williams Institute, 2016.

Ford, Angela, Kevin McFall, and Bob Dabney. *African American Media Today: Building the Future From the Past*. Washington, DC: Democracy Fund, 2019.

Forde, Susan, and Jane Johnston. "The News Triumvirate: Public Relations, Wire Agencies and Online Copy." *Journalism Studies* 14, no. 1 (2013): 113–129.

Foust, Christina R., and Kate Drazner Hoyt. "Social Movement 2.0: Integrating and Assessing Scholarship on Social Media and Movement." *Review of Communication* 18, no. 1 (2018): 37–55.

Fraser, Nancy. "Rethinking the Public Sphere: A Contribution to the Critique of Actually Existing Democracy." *Social Text* 25/26 (1990): 56–80.

Freelon, Deen, Charlton McIlwain, and Meredith Clark. "Quantifying the Power and Consequences of Social Media Protest." *New Media & Society* 20, no. 3 (2018): 990–1011.

Freeman, Julie. "Differentiating Distance in Local and Hyperlocal News." *Journalism* 21, no. 4 (2020): 524–540.

Freudenburg, William R. "Sociology in Legis-Land: An Ethnographic Report on Congressional Culture." *The Sociological Quarterly* 27, no. 3 (1986): 313–326.

Friedland, Lewis, Thomas Hove, and Hernando Rojas. "The Networked Public Sphere." *Javnost—The Public* 13, no. 4 (2006): 5–26.

Gamson, Joshua. "Gay Media, Inc.: Media Structures, the New Gay Conglomerates, and Collective Sexual Identities." In *Cyberactivism: Online Activism in Theory and Practice*, edited by Martha McCaughey and Michael Ayers, 255–278. New York: Routledge, 2003.

Gamson, William. "Constructing Social Protest." In *Social Movements and Culture*, edited by Hank Johnston and Bert Klandermans, 85–106. Minneapolis: University of Minnesota Press, 1995.

Gamson, William R., and Gadi Wolfsfeld. "Movements and Media as Interacting Systems." *Annals of the American Academy of Political and Social Science* 528 (1993): 114–125.

Gandy, Oscar. "Information in Health: Subsidized News." *Media, Culture & Society* 2, no. 2 (1980): 103–115.

Gans, Herbert J. *Deciding What's News: A Study of CBS Evening News, NBC Nightly News, Newsweek, and Time*. New York: Vintage, 1979.

Geiger, R. Stuart, and David Ribes. "Trace Ethnography: Following Coordination through Documentary Practices." In *Proceedings of the 44th Hawaii International Conference on System Sciences*. Los Alamitos, CA: IEEE Computer Society Press, 2011.

Gibson, Rhonda. *Same-Sex Marriage and Social Media: How Online Networks Accelerated the Marriage Equality Movement*. New York: Routledge, 2018.

Gitlin, Todd. *The Whole World Is Watching: Mass Media in the Making & Unmaking of the New Left*. Berkeley: University of California Press, 1980.

Glover, Julian Kevon. "Redefining Realness? On Janet Mock, Laverne Cox, TS Madison, and the Representation of Transgender Women of Color in Media." *Souls* 18, no. 2–4 (2016): 338–387.

González-Bailón, Sandra, Javier Borge-Holthoefer, and Yamir Moreno. "Broadcasters and Hidden Influentials in Online Protest Diffusion." *American Behavioral Scientist* 57, no. 7 (2013): 943–965.

Grant, Jaime M., Lisa A. Mottet, Justin Tanis, Jack Harrison, Jody L. Herman, and Mara Keisling. *Injustice at Every Turn: A Report of the National Transgender Discrimination Survey*. Washington, DC: National Center for Transgender Equality and National Gay and Lesbian Task Force, 2011.

Greenberg, Bradley S. "Person-to-Person Communication in the Diffusion of News Events." *Journalism Quarterly* 41, no. 4 (1964): 489–494.

Greenberg, Josh, Tim May, and Charlene Elliott. "Homelessness and Media Activism in the Voluntary Sector: A Case Study." *The Philanthropist* 20, no. 2 (2006): 131–152.

Gross, Larry. "Out of the Mainstream: Sexual Minorities and the Mass Media." *Journal of Homosexuality* 21, no. 1–2 (1991): 19–46.

Gross, Larry. *Up from Invisibility: Lesbians, Gay Men, and the Media in America*. New York: Columbia University Press, 2001.

Guggenheim, Lauren, Mo Jang, Soo Young Bae, and Russell Neuman. "The Dynamics of Issue Frame Competition in Traditional and Social Media." *Annals of the American Academy of Political and Social Science* 659 (2015): 207–224.

Haak, Bregtje van der, Michael Parks, and Manuel Castells. "The Future of Journalism: Networked Journalism." *International Journal of Communication* 6 (2012): 2923–2938.

Habermas, Jürgen. "The Public Sphere: An Encyclopedia Article." *New German Critique* 3 (1974): 49–55.

Habermas, Jürgen. *The Structural Transformation of the Public Sphere: An Inquiry into a Category of Bourgeois Society*. Cambridge, MA: MIT Press, 1991.

Hall, Budd L. "From Margins to Center? The Development and Purpose of Participatory Research." *The American Sociologist* 23, no. 4 (1992): 15–28.

Hall, Stuart. "Media Power: The Double Bind." *Journal of Communication* 24, no. 4 (1974): 19–26.

Hallin, Daniel C. *The Uncensored War: The Media and Vietnam*. Berkeley: University of California Press, 1989.

Hallin, Daniel C., Claudio Mellado, and Paolo Mancini. "The Concept of Hybridity in Journalism Studies." *The International Journal of Press/Politics* 28, no. 1 (2023): 219–237.

Hänska, Maximillian. "Networked Communication and the Arab Spring: Linking Broadcast and Social Media." *New Media & Society* 18, no. 1 (2016): 99–116.

Hasell, Ariel. "Shared Emotion: The Social Amplification of Partisan News on Twitter." *Digital Journalism* 9, no. 8 (2021): 1085–1102.

Hatch, Mary Jo, and Majken Schultz. "Toward a Theory of Brand Co-creation with Implications for Brand Governance." *Journal of Brand Management* 17, no. 8 (2010): 590–604.

Hayes, Kathryn, and Henry Silke. "The Networked Freelancer? Digital Labour and Freelance Journalism in the Age of Social Media." *Digital Journalism* 6, no. 8 (2018): 1018–1028.

Hepp, Andreas, Stig Hjarvard, and Knut Lundby. "Mediatization: Theorizing the Interplay Between Media, Culture and Society." *Media, Culture & Society* 37, no. 2 (2015): 314–324.

Hepp, Andreas, Piet Simon, and Monika Sowinska. "Living Together in the Mediatized City: The Figurations of Young People's Urban Communities." In *Communicative Figurations: Transforming Communications in Times of Deep Mediatization*, edited by Andreas Hepp, Andreas Breiter, and Uwe Hasebrink, 51–80. Cham: Palgrave Macmillan, 2017.

Herman, Edward, and Noam Chomsky. *Manufacturing Consent: The Political Economy of the Mass Media*. New York: Pantheon Books, 1988.

Hermida, Alfred. "Twittering the News: The Emergence of Ambient Journalism." *Journalism Practice* 4, no. 3 (2010): 297–308.

Hermida, Alfred, and Neil Thurman. "A Clash of Cultures: The Integration of User-Generated Content within Professional Journalistic Frameworks at British Newspaper Websites." *Journalism Practice* 2, no. 3 (2008): 343–356.

Hess, Kristy. "Breaking Boundaries: Recasting the 'Local' Newspaper as 'Geo-social' News in a Digital Landscape." *Digital Journalism* 1, no. 1 (2013): 48–63.

Hess, Kristy, and Lisa Waller. "Geo-Social Journalism: Reorienting the Study of Small Commercial Newspapers in a Digital Environment." *Journalism Practice* 8, no. 2 (2014): 121–136.

Hindman, Matthew. *The Internet Trap: How the Digital Economy Builds Monopolies and Undermines Democracy*. Princeton, NJ: Princeton University Press, 2018.

Hinnant, Amanda, María E. Len-Ríos, and Rachel Young. "Journalistic Use of Exemplars to Humanize Health News." *Journalism Studies* 14, no. 4 (2013): 539–554.

Holton, Avery E. "Intrapreneurial Informants: An Emergent Role of Freelance Journalists." *Journalism Practice* 10, no. 7 (2016): 917–927.

Hoonaard, Will C. van den. "Is Anonymity an Artifact in Ethnographic Research?" *Journal of Academic Ethics* 1, no. 2 (2003): 141–151.

Hoynes, William. "Media Research and Media Activism." In *Rhyming Hope and History: Activists, Academics, and Social Movement Scholarship*, edited by David Croteau, William Hoynes, and Charlotte Ryan, 97–114. Minneapolis: University of Minnesota Press, 2005.

Hunt, Kate, and Mike Gruszczynski. "The Influence of New and Traditional Media Coverage on Public Attention to Social Movements: The Case of the Dakota Access Pipeline Protests." *Information, Communication & Society* 24, no. 7 (2021): 1024–1040.

Hyra, Derek, and Sabiyha Prince, eds. *Capital Dilemma: Growth and Inequality in Washington, DC*. New York: Routledge, 2016.

Ibarra, Herminia, and Mark Lee Hunter. "How Leaders Create and Use Networks." *Harvard Business Review* 85 (2007): 40–47.

Irving, Dan. "Against the Grain: Teaching Transgender Human Rights." *Sexualities* 16, no. 3–4 (2013): 319–335.

Irving, Dan. "Transgender Politics." In *The Wiley Blackwell Encyclopedia of Gender and Sexuality Studies*, edited by Nancy A. Naples. Hoboken, NJ: John Wiley & Sons, 2016.

Isaac, Larry W., Jonathan S. Coley, Quan D. Mai, and Anna W. Jacobs. "Striking News: Discursive Power of the Press as Capitalist Resource in Gilded Age Strikes." *American Journal of Sociology* 127, no. 5 (2022): 1602–1663.

Jackson, Daniel, and Kevin Moloney. "Inside Churnalism: PR, Journalism and Power Relationships in Flux." *Journalism Studies* 17, no. 6 (2016): 763–780.

Jackson, Sarah J. "(Re)Imagining Intersectional Democracy from Black Feminism to Hashtag Activism." *Women's Studies in Communication* 39, no. 4 (2016): 375–379.

Jackson, Sarah J., Moya Bailey, and Brooke Foucault Welles. *#HashtagActivism: Networks of Race and Gender Justice*. Cambridge, MA: MIT Press, 2020.

Jackson, Sarah J., and Brooke Foucault Welles. "#Ferguson is Everywhere: Initiators in Emerging Counterpublic Networks." *Information, Communication & Society* 19, no. 3 (2016): 397–418.

Jungherr, Andreas. "The Logic of Political Coverage on Twitter: Temporal Dynamics and Content." *Journal of Communication* 64, no. 2 (2014): 239–259.

Jungherr, Andreas, Oliver Posegga, and Jisun An. "Discursive Power in Contemporary Media Systems: A Comparative Framework." *The International Journal of Press/Politics* 24, no. 4 (2019): 404–425.

Kaiser, Johannes, Tobias R. Keller, and Katharina Kleinen-von Königslöw. "Incidental News Exposure on Facebook as a Social Experience: The Influence of Recommender and Media Cues on News Selection." *Communication Research* 48, no. 1 (2021): 77–99.

Karpf, David. *Analytic Activism: Digital Listening and the New Political Strategy*. New York: Oxford University Press, 2016.

Karpf, David. "Digital Politics after Trump." *Annals of the International Communication Association* 41, no. 2 (2017): 198–207.

Karpf, David. *The MoveOn Effect: The Unexpected Transformation of American Political Advocacy*. New York: Oxford University Press, 2012.

Karpf, David. "What Social Movement Studies and Political Communication Can Learn from One Another." *Information, Communication & Society* 22, no. 5 (2019): 747–753.

Katz, Elihu. "Back to the Street: When Media and Opinion Leave Home." *Mass Communication and Society* 17, no. 4 (2014): 454–463.

Katz, Elihu. "His Master's Voice." *International Journal of Communication* 16 (2022): 608–615.

Katz, Elihu, and Paul F. Lazarsfeld. *Personal Influence: The Part Played by People in the Flow of Mass Communications*. Glencoe, IL: Free Press, 1955.

Kaye, Jeff, and Stephen Quinn. *Funding Journalism in the Digital Age: Business Models, Strategies, Issues and Trends*. New York: Peter Lang, 2010.

Kim, Yong-Chan, and Sandra J. Ball-Rokeach. "Civic Engagement from a Communication Infrastructure Perspective." *Communication Theory* 16, no. 2 (2006): 173–197.

Kim, Yong-Chan, Joo-Young Jung, and Sandra J. Ball-Rokeach. "'Geo-Ethnicity' and Neighborhood Engagement: A Communication Infrastructure Perspective." *Political Communication* 23, no. 4 (2006): 421–441.

Klandermans, Bert. "The Social Construction of Protest and Multiorganizational Fields." In *Frontiers in Social Movement Theory*, edited by Aldon D. Morris and Carol McClurg Mueller, 77–103. New Haven: Yale University Press, 1992.

Klinger, Ulrike, and Jakob Svensson. "The Emergence of Network Media Logic in Political Communication: A Theoretical Approach." *New Media & Society* 17, no. 8 (2015): 1241–1257.

Knobloch-Westerwick, Silvia, and Matthias R. Hastall. "Please Your Self: Social Identity Effects on Selective Exposure to News About in- and Out-Groups." *Journal of Communication* 60, no. 1 (2010): 515–535.

Kreiss, Daniel. *Taking Our Country Back: The Crafting of Networked Politics from Howard Dean to Barack Obama*. New York: Oxford University Press, 2012.

Krieken, Kobie van, and José Sanders. "What Is Narrative Journalism? A Systematic Review and an Empirical Agenda." *Journalism* 22, no. 6 (2021): 1393–1412.

Kümpel, Anna Sophie. "The Issue Takes It All? Incidental News Exposure and News Engagement on Facebook." *Digital Journalism* 7, no. 2 (2019): 165–186.

Kümpel, Anna Sophie. "Social Media Information Environments and Their Implications for the Uses and Effects of News: The PINGS Framework." *Communication Theory* 32, no. 2 (2022): 223–242.

Lang, Kurt, and Gladys Engel Lang. "Mass Society, Mass Culture, and Mass Communication: The Meaning of Mass." *International Journal of Communication* 3 (2009): 998–1024.

LaPira, Timothy M., and Herschel F. Thomas III. "Revolving Door Lobbyists and Interest Representation." *Interest Groups & Advocacy* 3, no. 1 (2014): 4–29.

Lauterer, Jock. *Community Journalism: Relentlessly Local*. 3rd ed. Chapel Hill: University of North Carolina Press, 2006.

Lee, Eun-Ju. "That's Not the Way It Is: How User-Generated Comments on the News Affect Perceived Media Bias." *Journal of Computer-Mediated Communication* 18, no. 1 (2012): 32–45.

Lee, Eun-Ju, and Yoon Jae Jang. "What Do Others' Reactions to News on Internet Portal Sites Tell Us? Effects of Presentation Format and Readers' Need for Cognition on Reality Perception." *Communication Research* 37, no. 6 (2010): 825–846.

Lee, Eun-Ju, and Edson C. Tandoc, Jr. "When News Meets the Audience: How Audience Feedback Online Affects News Production and Consumption." *Human Communication Research* 43, no. 4 (2017): 436–449.

Lee, Francis LF. "Social Media, Political Information Cycle, and the Evolution of News." *Communication and the Public* 3, no. 1 (2018): 67–76.

Lichterman, Paul. "Seeing Structure Happen: Theory-Driven Participant Observation." In *Methods of Social Movement Research*, edited by Bert Klandermans and Suzanne Staggenborg, 118–145. Minneapolis: University of Minnesota Press, 2002.

Lopez, Lori Kido. *Asian American Media Activism: Fighting for Cultural Citizenship*. New York: New York University Press, 2016.

Leung, Dennis K. K., and Francis L. F. Lee. "Cultivating an Active Online Counterpublic: Examining Usage and Political Impact of Internet Alternative Media." *The International Journal of Press/Politics* 19, no. 3 (2014): 340–359.

Madianou, Mirca. "Contested Communicative Spaces: Rethinking Identities, Boundaries and the Role of the Media among Turkish Speakers in Greece." *Journal of Ethnic and Migration Studies* 31, no. 3 (2005): 521–541.

Mananzala, Rickke, and Dean Spade. "The Nonprofit Industrial Complex and Trans Resistance." *Sexuality Research & Social Policy* 5, no. 1 (2008): 53–71.

Marquis, Christopher, and András Tilcsik. "Imprinting: Toward a Multilevel Theory." *Academy of Management Annals* 7, no. 1 (2013): 193–243.

Marres, Noortje. "Issues Spark a Public into Being: A Key but Often Forgotten Point of the Lippmann-Dewey Debate." In *Making Things Public: Atmospheres of Democracy*, edited by Bruno Latour and Peter Weibel, 208–217. Cambridge, MA: MIT Press, 2005.

Mathisen, Birgit Røe. "Entrepreneurs and Idealists: Freelance Journalists at the Intersection of Autonomy and Constraints." *Journalism Practice* 13, no. 8 (2019): 1003–1007.

Mazur, Allan. "Putting Radon on the Public Risk Agenda." *Science, Technology and Human Values* 12, no. 3/4 (1987): 86–93.

McAdam, Doug, Sidney Tarrow, and Charles Tilly. *Dynamics of Contention*. New York: Cambridge University Press, 2001.

McCarthy, John, and Mayer Zald. "Resource Mobilization and Social Movements: A Partial Theory." *American Journal of Sociology* 82, no. 6 (1977): 1212–1241.

McCombs, Maxwell, and Amy Reynolds. "How the News Shapes our Civic Agenda." In *Media Effects: Advances in Theory and Research*, edited by Jennings Bryant and Mary Beth Oliver, 1–16. New York: Routledge, 2009.

McCrain, Joshua. "Revolving Door Lobbyists and the Value of Congressional Staff Connections." *Journal of Politics* 80, no. 4 (2018): 1369–1383.

McEwan, Bree, Christopher J. Carpenter, and Jill E. Hopke. "Mediated Skewed Diffusion of Issues Information: A Theory." *Social Media + Society* 4, no. 3 (2018).

McGregor, Shannon C. "Social Media as Public Opinion: How Journalists Use Social Media to Represent Public Opinion." *Journalism* 20, no. 8 (2019): 1070–1086.

McGregor, Shannon C., and Logan Molyneux. "Twitter's Influence on News Judgment: An Experiment Among Journalists." *Journalism* 21, no. 5 (2020): 597–613.

Meerwijk, Esther L., and Jae Sevelius. "Transgender Population Size in the United States: A Meta-Regression of Population-Based Probability Samples." *American Journal of Public Health* 107, no. 2 (2017): 216.

Meraz, Sharon, and Zizi Papacharissi. "Networked Gatekeeping and Networked Framing on #Egypt." *The International Journal of Press/Politics* 18, no. 2 (2013): 138–166.

Mersey, Rachel Davis. "Online News Users' Sense of Community: Is Geography Dead?" *Journalism Practice* 3, no. 3 (2009): 347–360.

Micó, Josep-Lluís, and Andreu Casero-Ripollés. "Political Activism Online: Organization and Media Relations in the Case of 15M in Spain." *Information, Communication, & Society* 17, no. 7 (2014): 858–871.

Montgomery, Kathryn C. "Gay Activists and the Networks." *Journal of Communication* 31, no. 3 (1981): 49–57.

Montgomery, Kathryn C. *Target, Prime Time: Advocacy Groups and the Struggle over Entertainment Television*. New York: Oxford University Press, 1989.

Moran, Rachel E. "Subscribing to Transparency: Trust-Building Within Virtual Newsrooms on Slack." *Journalism Practice* 15, no. 10 (2021): 1580–1596.

Moran, Rachel E., and Thomas J Billard. "Imagining Resistance to Trump through the Networked Branding of the National Park Service." In *Popular Culture and the Civic Imagination: Case Studies of Creative Social Change*, edited by Henry Jenkins, Gabriel Peters-Lazaro, and Sangita Shresthova, 231–240. New York: New York University Press, 2020.

Murib, Zein. "Transgender: Examining an Emerging Political Identity Using Three Political Processes." *Politics, Groups, and Identities* 3, no. 3 (2015): 381–397.

Napoli, Philip M. *Audience Evolution: New Technologies and the Transformation of Media Audiences*. New York: Columbia University Press, 2011.

National Center for Transgender Equality. *2018 Annual Report*. Washington, DC: National Center for Transgender Equality, 2019.

National Center for Transgender Equality. *Failing to Protect and Serve: Police Department Policies Towards Transgender People*. Washington, DC: National Center for Transgender Equality, 2019.

Nelson, Jacob L. *Imagined Audiences: How Journalists Perceive and Pursue the Public*. New York: Oxford University Press, 2021.

Nepstad, Sharon. "Creating Transnational Solidarity: The Use of Narrative in the U.S.–Central America Peace Movement." *Mobilization* 6, no. 1 (2001): 21–36.

Neuman, W. Russell, Lauren Guggenheim, Mo Jang, and Soo Young Bae. "The Dynamics of Public Attention: Agenda-Setting Theory Meets Big Data." *Journal of Communication* 64, no. 2 (2014): 193–214.

Nielsen, Rasmus Kleis. *Ground Wars: Personalized Communication in Political Campaigns.* Princeton, NJ: Princeton University Press, 2012.

Nielsen, Rasmus Kleis, ed. *Local Journalism: The Decline of Newspapers and the Rise of Digital Media.* New York: I.B. Tauris, 2015.

Nimmo, Dan, and James E. Combs. *The Political Pundits.* New York: Praeger, 1992.

Nonprofit Professional Employees Union (NPEU). "Nonprofit Professional Employees Union Files Unfair Labor Practice Against National Center for Transgender Equality Leadership For Retaliation Against Staff Organizing." *Nonprofit Professional Employees Union,* November 15, 2019. https://npeu.org/news/2019/11/15/nonprofit-professio nal-employees-union-files-unfair-labor-practice-against-national-center-for-tran sgender-equality-leadership-for-retaliation-against-staff-organizing.

Nownes, Anthony. *Organizing for Transgender Rights: Collective Action, Group Development, and the Rise of a New Social Movement.* Albany: State University of New York Press, 2019.

Ognyanova, Katherine, Nien-Tsu Nancy Chen, Sandra J. Ball-Rokeach, Zheng An, Minhee Son, Michael Parks, and Daniela Gerson. "Online Participation in a Community Context: Civic Engagement and Connections to Local Communication Resources." *International Journal of Communication* 7 (2013): 2433–2456.

Ørmen, Jacob. "Googling the News: Opportunities and Challenges in Studying News Events through Google Search." *Digital Journalism* 4, no. 1 (2016): 107–124.

Örnebring, Henrik, Eva Kingsepp, and Cecilia Möller. "Journalism in Small Towns." *Journalism* 21, no. 4 (2020): 447–452.

Palen, Leysia, Kate Starbird, Sarah Vieweg, and Amanda Hughes. "Twitter-Based Information Distribution during the 2009 Red River Valley Flood Threat." *Bulletin of the American Society for Information Science and Technology* 36, no. 5 (2010): 13–17.

Papacharissi, Zizi, and Maria de Fatima Oliveira. "Affective News and Networked Publics: The Rhythms of News Storytelling on #Egypt." *Journal of Communication* 62, no. 2 (2012): 266–282.

Park, Pauline. "GenderPAC, the Transgender Rights Movement and the Perils of a Post-Identity Politics Paradigm." *Georgetown Journal of Gender and the Law* 4 (2003): 747–766.

Paulussen, Steve, and Raymond A. Harder. "Social Media References in Newspapers: Facebook, Twitter, and YouTube as Sources in Newspaper Journalism." *Journalism Practice* 8, no. 5 (2014): 542–551.

Penney, Joel. *The Citizen Marketer: Promoting Political Opinion in the Social Media Age.* New York: Oxford University Press, 2017.

Peters, Chris. "Spaces and Places of News Consumption." In *The SAGE Handbook of Digital Journalism,* edited by Tamara Witschge, C. W. Anderson, David Domingo, and Alfred Hermida, 354–369. Thousand Oaks: SAGE, 2016.

Peters, Chris, and Kim Christian Schrøder. "Beyond the Here and Now of News Audiences: A Process-Based Framework for Investigating News Repertoires." *Journal of Communication* 68, no. 6 (2018): 1079–1103.

Pitt, Leyland F., Richard T. Watson, Pierre Berthon, Donald Wynn, and George Zinkhan. "The Penguin's Window: Corporate Brands from an Open Source Perspective." *Journal of the Academy of Marketing Science* 34, no. 2 (2006): 115–127.

Platero, R. Lucas. "The Narratives of Transgender Rights Mobilization in Spain." *Sexualities* 14, no. 5 (2011): 597–614.

Polletta, Francesca. "Contending Stories: Narrative in Social Movements." *Qualitative Sociology* 21, no. 4 (1998): 419–446.

Polletta, Francesca. *Inventing the Ties That Bind: Imagined Relationships in Moral and Political Life*. Chicago: University of Chicago Press, 2020.

Polletta, Francesca. *It Was Like a Fever: Storytelling in Protest and Politics*. Chicago: University of Chicago Press, 2006.

Polletta, Francesca, Pang Ching Bobby Chen, Beth Gharrity Gardner, and Alice Motes. "The Sociology of Storytelling." *Annual Review of Sociology* 37 (2011): 109–130.

Polletta, Francesca, Tania DoCarmo, Kelly Marie Ward, and Jessica Callahan. "Personal Storytelling in Professionalized Social Movements." *Mobilization* 26, no. 1 (2021): 65–86.

Powers, Matthew. *NGOs as Newsmakers: The Changing Landscape of International News*. New York: Columbia University Press, 2018.

Puckett, Jae A., Peter Cleary, Kinton Rossman, Brian Mustanski, and Michael E. Newcomb. "Barriers to Gender-Affirming Care for Transgender and Gender Nonconforming Individuals." *Sexuality Research and Social Policy* 15, no. 1 (2018): 48–59.

Ray, Victor. "A Theory of Racialized Organizations." *American Sociological Review* 84, no. 1 (2019): 26–53.

Reese, Stephen D., and Pamela J. Shoemaker. "A Media Sociology for the Networked Public Sphere: The Hierarchy of Influences Model." *Mass Communication and Society* 19, no. 4 (2015): 389–410.

Reinardy, Scott. *Journalism's Lost Generation: The Un-doing of U.S. Newspaper Newsrooms*. New York: Routledge, 2016.

Relph, Edward. *Place and Placelessness*. London: Pion, 1976.

Richardson, Allissa V. "Dismantling Respectability: The Rise of New Womanist Communication Models in the Era of Black Lives Matter." *Journal of Communication* 69, no. 2 (2019): 193–213.

Rider, G. Nic, Barbara J. McMorris, Amy L. Gower, Eli Coleman, and Marla E. Eisenberg. "Health and Care Utilization of Transgender and Gender Nonconforming Youth: A Population-Based Study." *Pediatrics* 141 (2018): e20171683.

Robards, Brady, and Bob Buttigieg. "Marriage Equality, Facebook Profile Pictures, and Civic Participation." In *Civic Media: Technology, Design, Practice*, edited by Eric Gordon and Paul Mihailidis, 131–137. Cambridge, MA: MIT Press, 2016.

Robinson, Sue. "The Active Citizen's Information Media Repertoire: An Exploration of Community News Habits During the Digital Age." *Mass Communication and Society* 17, no. 4 (2014): 509–530.

Rohlinger, Deana. *Abortion Politics, Mass Media, and Social Movements in America*. New York: Cambridge University Press, 2014.

Romzek, Barbara S., and Jennifer A. Utter. "Career Dynamics of Congressional Legislative Staff: Preliminary Profile and Research Questions." *Journal of Public Administration Research and Theory* 6, no. 3 (1996): 415–442.

Rossini, Patrícia, Jennifer Stromer-Galley, Erica Anita Baptista, and Vanessa Veiga de Oliveira. "Dysfunctional Information Sharing on WhatsApp and Facebook: The Role of Political Talk, Cross-cutting Exposure and Social Corrections." *New Media & Society* 23, no. 8 (2021): 2430–2451.

Ryan, Charlotte. *Prime Time Activism: Media Strategies for Grassroots Organizing.* Boston: South End Press, 1991.

Ryan, Charlotte. "It Takes a Movement to Raise an Issue: Media Lessons from the 1997 U.P.S. Strike." *Critical Sociology* 30, no. 2 (2004): 483–511.

Ryan, Charlotte, Kevin Carragee, and Cassie Schwerner. "Media, Movements, and the Quest for Social Justice." *Journal of Applied Communication Research* 26, no. 2 (1998): 165–181.

Salzman, Ryan. "News or Noticias: A Social Identity Approach to Understanding Latinos' Preferred Language for News Consumption in the United States." *Mass Communication and Society* 17, no. 1 (2014): 54–73.

Scheper-Hughes, Nancy. "Ire in Ireland." *Ethnography* 1, no. 1 (2000): 117–140.

Schilt, Kristen. "'AM/FM Activism': Taking National Media Tools to a Local Level." *Journal of Gay & Lesbian Social Services* 16, no. 3–4 (2004): 181–192.

Seim, Josh. "Participant Observation, Observant Participation, and Hybrid Ethnography." *Sociological Methods & Research*, published ahead of print, February 10, 2021.

Sender, Katherine. "Gay Readers, Consumers, and a Dominant Gay Habitus: 25 Years of the *Advocate* Magazine." *Journal of Communication* 51, no. 1 (2001): 73–99.

Shirky, Clay. "The Political Power of Social Media: Technology, the Public Sphere, and Political Change." *Foreign Affairs* 90, no. 1 (2011): 28–41.

Shoemaker, Pamela J. "The Perceived Legitimacy of Deviant Political Groups: Two Experiments on Media Effects." *Communication Research* 9, no. 2 (1982): 249–286.

Simonson, Lynnell, and Virginia Bushaw. "Participatory Action Research: Easier Said Than Done." *The American Sociologist* 24, no. 1 (1993): 27–37.

Sobieraj, Sarah. *Soundbitten: The Perils of Media-Centered Political Activism.* New York: New York University Press, 2011.

Spade, Dean. *Normal Life: Administrative Violence, Critical Trans Politics, and the Limits of Law.* Durham, NC: Duke University Press, 2015.

Squires, Catherine R. "Rethinking the Black Public Sphere: An Alternative Vocabulary for Multiple Public Sphere." *Communication Theory* 12, no. 4 (2002): 446–468.

Steele, Catherine Knight. "Black Bloggers and Their Varied Publics: The Everyday Politics of Black Discourse Online." *Television & New Media* 19, no. 2 (2018): 112–127.

Stein, Arlene. "Sex, Truths, and Audiotape: Anonymity and the Ethics of Exposure in Public Ethnography." *Journal of Contemporary Ethnography* 39, no. 5 (2010): 554–568.

Stinchcombe, Arthur L. "Social Structure and Organizations." In *Handbook of Organizations*, edited by James G. March, 142–193. Chicago: Rand McNally, 1965.

Stoecker, Randy. "Are Academics Irrelevant? Roles for Scholars in Participatory Research." *American Behavioral Scientist* 42, no. 5 (1999): 840–854.

Strömbäck, Jesper. "Four Phases of Mediatization: An Analysis of the Mediatization of Politics." *The International Journal of Press/Politics* 13, no. 3 (2008): 228–246.

Stryker, Susan. *Transgender History: The Roots of Today's Revolution.* New York: Seal Press, 2017.

Swedberg, Richard. *The Art of Social Theory.* Princeton, NJ: Princeton University Press, 2014.

Tavory, Iddo, and Stefan Timmermans. "Two Cases of Ethnography: Grounded Theory and the Extended Case Method." *Ethnography* 10, no. 3 (2009): 243–263.

Taylor, Jami K., Daniel C. Lewis, and Donald P. Haider-Markel. *The Remarkable Rise of Transgender Rights*. Ann Arbor: University of Michigan Press, 2018.

Taylor, Jami K., Daniel C. Lewis, Matthew L. Jacobsmeier, and Brian DiSarro. "Content and Complexity in Policy Reinvention and Diffusion: Gay and Transgender-Inclusive Laws against Discrimination." *State Politics & Policy Quarterly* 12, no. 1 (2012): 75–98.

Tellis, Gerard J., Deborah J. MacInnis, Seshadri Tirunillai, and Yanwei Zhang. "What Drives Virality (Sharing) of Online Digital Content? The Critical Role of Information, Emotion, and Brand Prominence." *Journal of Marketing* 83, no. 4 (2019): 1–20.

Thorson, Kjerstin, and Chris Wells. "Curated Flows: A Framework for Mapping Media Exposure in the Digital Age." *Communication Theory* 26, no. 3 (2016): 309–328.

Tilly, Charles. *The Contentious French*. Cambridge, MA: Harvard University Press, 1986.

Tilly, Charles. "Social Movements and National Politics." In *State-Making and Social Movements: Essays in History and Theory*, edited by Charles Bright and Susan Harding, 297–317. Ann Arbor: University of Michigan Press, 1984.

Toepfl, Florian, and Eunike Piwoni. "Public Spheres in Interaction: Comment Sections of News Websites as Counterpublic Spaces." *Journal of Communication* 65, no. 3 (2015): 465–488.

Trevisan, Filippo. *Disability Rights Advocacy Online: Voice, Empowerment and Global Connectivity*. New York: Routledge, 2017.

Trevisan, Filippo, Bryan Bello, Michael Vaughan, and Ariadne Vromen. "Mobilizing Personal Narratives: The Rise of Digital 'Story Banking' in U.S. Grassroots Advocacy." *Journal of Information Technology & Politics* 17, no. 2 (2020): 146–160.

Tufekci, Zeynep. "'Not This One': Social Movements, the Attention Economy, and Microcelebrity Activism." *American Behavioral Scientist* 57, no. 7 (2013): 848–870.

Tufekci, Zeynep. *Twitter and Tear Gas: The Power and Fragility of Networked Protest*. New Haven, CT: Yale University Press, 2017.

Usher, Nikki. *Making News at The New York Times*. Ann Arbor: University of Michigan Press, 2014.

Usher, Nikki. *News for the Rich, White, and Blue: How Place and Power Distort American Journalism*. New York: Columbia University Press, 2021.

Usher, Nikki. "Putting 'Place' in the Center of Journalism Research: A Way Forward to Understand Challenges to Trust and Knowledge in News." *Journalism & Communication Monographs* 21, no. 2 (2019): 84–146.

Usher, Nikki, and Matt Carlson. "The Midlife Crisis of the Network Society." *Media and Communication* 6, no. 4 (2018): 107–110.

Usher, Nikki, and Yee Man Margaret Ng. "Sharing Knowledge and 'Microbubbles': Epistemic Communities and Insularity in US Political Journalism." *Social Media + Society* 6, no. 2 (2020).

Vonbun, Ramona, Katharina Kleinen-von Königslöw, and Klaus Schoenbach. "Intermedia Agenda-Setting in a Multimedia News Environment." *Journalism* 17, no. 8 (2016): 1054–1073.

Waddell, T. Franklin. "What Does the Crowd Think? How Online Comments and Popularity Metrics Affect News Credibility and Issue Importance." *New Media & Society* 20, no. 8 (2018): 3068–3083.

Wadsworth, Yoland. "'Gouldner's Child?' Some Reflections on Sociology and Participatory Action Research." *Journal of Sociology* 41, no. 3 (2005): 267–284.

Wahl-Jorgensen, Karin. "The Challenge of Local News Provision." *Journalism* 20, no. 1 (2019): 163–166.

Waisbord, Silvio. *The Communication Manifesto*. Medford, MA: Polity, 2020.

Warner, Michael. "Publics and Counterpublics." *Public Culture* 14, no. 1 (2002): 49–90.

Wells, Chris. *The Civic Organization and the Digital Citizen Communicating Engagement in a Networked Age*. New York: Oxford University Press, 2015.

Wells, Chris, Dhavan Shah, Josephine Lukito, Ayellet Pelled, Jon C. W. Pevehouse, and JungHwan Yang. "Trump, Twitter, and News Media Responsiveness: A Media Systems Approach." *New Media & Society* 22, no. 4 (2020): 659–682.

Wenzel, Andrea. "Red State, Purple Town: Polarized Communities and Local Journalism in Rural and Small-Town Kentucky." *Journalism* 21, no. 4 (2018): 557–573.

Whyte, William F. "Advancing Scientific Knowledge Through Participatory Action Research." *Sociological Forum* 4, no. 3 (1989): 367–385.

Williams Fayne, Miya. "Advocacy Journalism in the 21st Century: Rethinking Entertainment in Digital Black Press Outlets." *Journalism* 24, no. 4 (2023): 328–345.

Winter, Stephan, and German Neubaum. "Examining Characteristics of Opinion Leaders in Social Media: A Motivational Approach." *Social Media + Society* 2, no. 3 (2016).

Witschge, Tamara, C. W. Anderson, David Domingo, and Alfred Hermida. "Dealing With the Mess (We Made): Unraveling Hybridity, Normativity, and Complexity in Journalism Studies." *Journalism* 20, no. 5 (2019): 651–659.

Wolfe, Michelle. "Putting on the Brakes or Pressing on the Gas? Media Attention and the Speed of Policymaking." *Policy Studies Journal* 40, no. 1 (2012): 109–126.

Yanovitzky, Itzhak. "Effects of News Coverage on Policy Attention and Actions: A Closer Look into the Media–Policy Connection." *Communication Research* 29, no 4. (2002): 422–451.

Youmans, William Lafi. *An Unlikely Audience: Al Jazeera's Struggle in America*. New York: Oxford University Press, 2017.

Young, Iris Marion. "De-centering Deliberative Democracy." *Kettering Review* 24, no. 3 (2006): 43–53.

Young, Lindsay Erin, and Paul M. Leonardi. "Social Issue Emergence on the Web: A Dual Structurational Model." *Journal of Computer-Mediated Communication* 17, no. 2 (2012): 231–246.

Index

For the benefit of digital users, indexed terms that span two pages (e.g., 52–53) may, on occasion, appear on only one of those pages.
Figures are indicated by *f* following the page number

Printed in the USA/Agawam, MA
October 3, 2023

852510.022